Celebrity

LIES!

By the same author:

The Films of Jane Fonda

Hispanic Hollywood

Leading Ladies (UK)

Hollywood Babble On

Hollywood Lesbians

Bette Davis Speaks

Hollywood Gays

Sing Out! (formerly *The Vinyl Closet*)

Hollywood & Whine

Celebrity Feuds!

In or Out

The Lavender Screen (updated edition)

Celluloid Gaze (formerly *Conversations With My Elders*)

Celebrity LIES!

Boze Hadleigh

Fort Lee, New Jersey

Published by Barricade Books Inc.
185 Bridge Plaza North
Suite 308-A
Fort Lee, NJ 07024

www.barricadebooks.com

Library of Congress Cataloging-in-Publication Data
Catalog information is available upon request from the Library of Congress.

ISBN 1-56980-245-9

Manufactured in the United States of America
First Printing

Contents

To Ronnie:

—27 Years—

and in memory of our Rusty

Introduction

Animals don't do it, but humans occasionally do. Lie. Fib. Prevaricate. Tell whoppers. Especially in show business, which is all about image, fantasy, selective presentation, and the struggle for fame...*and* fortune, maybe the greatest motivator for lying there ever was.

It still often comes as a surprise that actors act. Offscreen, as well. No coincidence that in ancient Greece, the birthplace of theatrical drama, the word for *actor* was the same as for *hypocrite*. Life in show biz—as well as in such "performance" fields as sports and politics— tends to be all about public relations, which basically means telling the general public what it wants to hear, truth be damned.

Shakespeare recognized that all the world's a stage. Everybody's a player, and at one time or another who hasn't told an untruth? F. Scott Fitzgerald once wrote, "I am one of the few honest people that I have ever known." But not about himself, that is, for it wouldn't likely be true about him in light of his Hollywood associations and his alcoholism. Not to mention the fact that he lived with gossip columnist Sheilah Graham, for by nature a columnist's output is semi-fictional. Liz Smith has admitted that if she were concerned with strict veracity she'd "have to question 80% of the marriages" she reports about.

The point of this first-on-the-topic collection of quotes is not to label any or every quoted individual "a liar," since nobody in or out of show business is immune. Everyone has fibbed and been fibbed about. Including this author/editor. Before appearing on "Larry King Live" I twice asked the on-set producer in Los Angeles whether King would ask me a question that I preferred not to answer in public yet (due partly to a future inheritance). She twice reassured me that Larry wouldn't ask it.

Sure enough, via remote from Atlanta, it was one of his first questions. I was inwardly shocked and annoyed, but managed to respond not with a lie but with a partial truth. Which of course is thus a partial *untruth*, therefore a little white lie (enough of those, you can frost a cake), and technically a lie.

Conversely, having been interviewed almost half as often as I've interviewed, I know how frequently one gets misquoted in periodicals, particularly newspapers, which have such a short lead time. (Books afford one the true luxury of ample research time.) However, sometimes it's not just a misquote but a complete reversal of reality.

In 1996 Liz Smith's column declared that I'd made a romantic proposal to the late, great Bette Davis and been turned down! In truth, as my book *Bette Davis Speaks* noted, the star had offered me a job, which I turned down. How such an egregious error was made, I didn't ask, though I did point it out to the columnist and her assistants. (By the way, the column included no mention of my new book, which made the item—completely out of context—seem even more bizarre!)

But enough about me. Truth is said to be relative. Bette Midler has confessed, "I never know how much of what I say is true." Some people believe the truth isn't just what we say, it's how we feel when we say it. Cary Grant, who had a few skeletons in his closet—yes, closet— cleverly commented, "I pretended to be somebody I wanted to be until finally I became that person. Or he became me." Many or most celebrities eventually reach the place where a particular lie or formula has been repeated so often, it feels right and real.

Many a successful actor in time becomes an act, and the image becomes reality, more or less. A celebrity's success and acceptance become excuse enough for fiction. One Reagan-era politician, confronted with a falsehood, said on TV, "That's not a lie, it's a terminological inexactitude." Of course the media love doublespeak—almost as much as politicians, especially those trying to cloak bigotry and power-grabs in moderate's clothing. Another politician was fond of quoting, "When all else fails, tell the truth." Reality as a last resort.

And *My Favorite Martian's* Uncle Martin, an alien trying to pass for an earthling, advised, "Always tell the truth. It's the world's best lie." Reality as a cover-up. Which is akin to Oscar Wilde's dictum that nothing looks so innocent as an indiscretion. Think about it—most any two women except ex-couple Ellen and Anne, holding hands…would you suspect? Well, you wouldn't have fifteen years ago.

★　　★　　★

Since literacy and fact-checking have declined in the media, the line between a lie and an error has blurred. American Movie Classics referred to the title personage in *Mary, Queen of Scots* as "the queen of England" in a promo (the more promos, the more chance for screwups). The A&E cable network, whose Biography series often ignores or reworks the sexuality of non-heterosexual subjects, described Sandra Dee as TV's Gidget although she only played that role on the big screen (Sally Field was the small-screen Gidget, or "girl midget").

Other "errors" are more calculated, whether it's presenting religious myth and dogma as fact—everywhere from *TV Guide*'s programming descriptions to political speeches—or that ongoing habit of books, plays, TV and movies ignoring or reworking minority sexuality and religion (color is harder to change). One example: A TV movie about anchorwoman Jessica Savitch that left out her being Jewish and also the documented bisexuality of herself and her husband, both deceased and therefore not legal threats to a television entity which is nonetheless still intrinsically homophobic and anti-Semitic.

As Hitler, who rose to power via propaganda, pointed out, the public will more readily accept a big lie than a small one. And the longer a lie is allowed to flourish, the more it becomes accepted as truth. For instance, calling equal rights "special rights" when applied to a group unpopular with one political party. Or something less pernicious, like the widespread misuse of the adjective "platonic," from the Greek philosopher Plato. Long ago, "platonic" was a code word for "the love that dare not speak its name." More recently, it has come to mean the absence of sex, a definition far from its original meaning.

When are lies not full-fledged lies? When they're good manners. If your overweight aunt asks how she looks in tight pants and you know she won't be dissuaded from their use, is it better to say they look awful on her—or she looks awful in them—or merely to answer, "Fine, fine"? Is it that much more of a lie to say, "You look great in those"?

When does a lie count for more than truth? When a court of law, which usually demands evidence, automatically upholds the legal claim of a publicly indignant, privately afraid and generally greedy star who has been correctly described as gay or bisexual. Justice is far from blind. And truth is not necessarily more popular than fiction. Look at so much of religion. Look at the elderly female fans of the stereotypically flamboyant Liberace, whom they blindly insisted was not gay.

As with good manners, the need for dignity or drama may engender a fabrication. When renowned Mexican revolutionary Pancho Villa was shot and lay dying in less than heroic circumstances, he told the one literally nearest him, "Don't let it end like this. Tell them I said something." Something special, memorable. Worthy of the legend. One wonders how many reported "last words" are true?

Contradiction also borders on lying. Humans are creatures of contradiction, for life isn't "either/or," but rather, "and/yet." Hypocrisy, contradiction's sibling, is part of the human condition, nothing to be encouraged, yet something very few are entirely free of. Caroline Kennedy, who grew up knowing what it's like to have family privacy invaded, was snuck into Graceland after Elvis Presley's death. She was an aspiring and ambitious young journalist. The people there assumed she'd come as a Kennedy and possibly a fan. Only. Inevitably, she wrote about the people and goings-on inside Graceland, and about Elvis himself.

The resultant article was rejected by the *New York Daily News* but picked up by *Rolling Stone*. Most of the Presley family were outraged, but Caroline never apologized for the piece. Elvis' father Vernon announced after reading it, "She not only insulted the memory of Elvis, she insulted her own family name." Caroline Kennedy later wrote a book about people's right to privacy. Hypocrisy and contradiction? Certainly. But it may be that every word she wrote about Graceland and Presley was true, if contrary to the gospel according to Elvis' followers. Every major celebrity has an image, more or less true, which that figure's fans or worshippers insist is truth, regardless. And Kennedy's book may have been entirely heartfelt and sincere, perhaps a valuable contribution. Truth, hypocrisy and contradiction all depend to some degree on context.

And on the subject of Elvis...shortly after his death the *National Enquirer* sent its religion reporter—bet you didn't know they had one—to the church where the singer was lying in peace. The reporter was disguised as a priest so he could obtain entry and get photographs on the sly. Upon exiting the church, the fake priest was approached by Geraldo Rivera and asked for an interview. The man admonished Geraldo for invading the mourning family's privacy! Obviously the reporter was lying for the benefit of his disguise, but was his admonishment genuine and emotional or was he parroting what he thought a real priest would say to a pushy TV reporter? Lie upon lie, or "just" one?

Of course it's not only journalists who prevaricate, it's often celebrities too. Not just about themselves, which is commonplace, but about each other. For whatever motive. The actor who played the eldest "Brady Bunch" son hid the fact that "Dad" was gay in real life. Tom Arnold, who became famous as "Mr. Roseanne," was discovered to be selling items about her to the tabloids. His motives? Money *and* publicity (for the items typically included dish on him too). Michael Jackson, who would publicly complain about or deny tabloid items about himself, regularly and secretly leaked myth-building "reports" to the media, and later sold photos of his alleged newborn son. And Peter Lawford, one-time MGM star and JFK's former brother-in-law, sold material on his dear friend Elizabeth Taylor to the tabs while she was staying at the Betty Ford Clinic and unaware of such betrayal. Small wonder (see later in this book) that Lawford's children wouldn't pay for his funeral or for his remains to stay at Westwood Memorial Cemetery, where lies Marilyn Monroe (another actress to whom he was a less than an ideal friend).

Many of the quotes in this book could have fit into more than one chapter. There is invariably some overlap. And not all the quotes are out and out lies. Some were statements contradicted by subsequent facts or comments. In some cases an individual simply spoke too soon. And too often, as with lesbian comedienne Ellen DeGeneres and bisexual actress Anne Heche. Their three-and-a-half-year relationship wasn't short by Hollywood standards, and outlasted Heche's reported two-year relationship with non-lesbian comedian Steve Martin. But though clearly in love—Ellen more clearly—they spoke like a long-time couple looking forward to their silver or golden anniversary. Sometimes perspective seems to undo a truth, but most of the quotations included here were lies then and are lies now.

This is not my first quotes book, but over the years as I've gathered quotations those which stuck out most were often celebrities' lies. Some funny, some sad or rather pathetic, some hilarious or mean-spirited (or both), some informative, some important, some trivial, and many appalling, especially when from the mouths of politicians and therefore affecting our lives much more than the opinions of entertainers.

The concept of *Celebrity Lies!* was mine, if not the terrific title. Yet if you think about it, what else would one call this book? *Counter-Factual Celebrity Quotes? Utterances of the Rich and Factually Challenged? Thespic and Poetic License-Plus?* The hardest part of putting it together wasn't what to use or even how to arrange it, but what to leave out. Besides, up till last night I kept finding great new celebrity lies. The supply is endless! Subjects are past and present celebs, some in sports and politics but mostly show-biz personalities doing what comes naturally. Show business is not a reality business, it's an image business. So while most people fib or bend the truth at times, in the illusion-based world of entertainment a lie or a front or a good story— or better yet a *great* story—is all but *de rigueur*!

Let the lies begin….

Image vs. Reality

"Making up presidential quotes is not lying. When you're a press secretary, you develop a bond of understanding with the President so that you think like the President. I knew those quotes were the way he felt."— Larry Speakes, press secretary to President Ronald Reagan.

★   ★   ★

"You can't have a star like that doin' stuff like that, spendin' their time…once they get to a certain point, they don't have time for none of that.…If his fans were dumb enough to believe Elvis sat there and autographed each and every photograph, then I don't have sympathy for anyone so gullible."—"Colonel" Tom Parker, Elvis Presley's manager. P.S. Was "Colonel" Sanders of Kentucky Fried Chicken a colonel either? (In the South, it's often an honorific title.)

★   ★   ★

"In my position, I'm able to help a great many people, hopefully."— Prince Charles.

But at the millennium eve party at the country estate of the prince, one of the world's richest men, it was a case of help yourself. As in BYOB. The magazine *Beverly Hills (213)* reported, "He is known to have several vast cellars crammed to the rafters with the finest wines and vintage champagnes." However, he thought it might be "rather droll and a jolly good wheeze" to make it a bring-your-own-bottle party. "More like just plain cheap. The only wine Charles drank, of course, was very expensive and his own. He, indeed, left his guests to drink the rougher stuff."

★   ★   ★

**"I love the fans. They touch my heart....They can always
reach out and touch me."— Diana Ross.**

But in 1999 an airport body-search made the diva see red. Columnist
Liz Smith commented, "Touch her in the morning, as the song goes, but
not at Heathrow." (One report alleged that Ross, who seems to get along
better with men than with women, had slapped a female flight attendant
some years before. In her memoirs, "Miss Ross" did allow that she has
few female friends.)

**"I like all people...I want to make people aware that
the sea is wonderful, that there is more chance to be killed by
lightning than by a shark...lightning, it strikes the earth about
6,000 times each minute."— Jacques Cousteau.**

Cousteau was a great oceanographer, but perhaps not so great a human
being. A random letter of his, written in the 1930s and auctioned posthumously, was blatantly anti-Semitic, grousing that during the Depression,
jobs were hard to come by in France because Jewish people had taken "our"
jobs. (Perhaps he evolved over the decades, and perhaps not.)

**"My hair is central to me and my image and who I am,
what I feel. It's just there...it's so strange to be asked
about hair length."— Candice Bergen.**

But after the death of her husband, French director Louis Malle, Bergen
chopped off her trademark long hair, later admitting, "The one thing I
really like about being older is getting rid of my hair. It was like walking
around with two people at the same time."

**"Yeah, it's my own. I like it piled up—I like
everything up....Yeah, the color's natural."— Mae West, blonde
sex symbol of the 1930s, interviewed in the 1970s.**

Her natural hair color was brown, as pre-Hollywood photos show. And
the style she wore in her seventies and eighties, a modified beehive over
a shoulder-length blonde coif, was a wig. When West made her last film,
Sextette, she was in her mid-eighties and had to be fed all her lines via a

radio transmitter concealed in the fluffy wig. One day, on the set, she reportedly picked up signals from LAX, and the "lines" she was repeating were instructions from an air traffic controller.

★ ★ ★

"It's amazing, to be a movie star…like, the glamour and everything."— Matt Damon.
But by 1999, after the release of *The Talented Mr. Ripley*, Damon complained, "I have been living out of duffel bags for years and it is very hard to do. This is a lifestyle I didn't anticipate living. I get up in the dark, get dressed, and then go to the set and put on a costume. Over and over and over." (But for a hell of a lot of money.)

★ ★ ★

"I cannot imagine any other life (than acting)….I look forward to doing wonderful roles as older women, including, but not only, mothers and grandmothers….Acting can be a wonderful way to entertain and sometimes even inspire people."
— Jane Fonda, two-time Oscar-winner.
But with her third marriage, to media mogul Ted Turner, she gave up her acting career—just like her character in *Rollover*, one of her final films. Plus Jane said she'd grown tired of "saying other people's words" as an actor. (During her Fonda-Turner phase, she said relatively few words, including her own.)

★ ★ ★

"I'm quite happy working in England…the Hollywood route's not for me."— Dudley Moore, in the 1960s.
But he did a standout supporting role in a popular Goldie Hawn movie (*Foul Play*, 1978), then starred in the surprise hit *10* the following year. Suddenly, he was no longer best known as the comedy partner of Peter Cook. But Moore's 1981 hit *Arthur* was followed by a string of Hollywood flops as well as personal and marital woes, culminating in his being fired by director Barbra Streisand after one day of incompetent work on *The Mirror Has Two Faces* (1996), later found to be due to the onset of an incurable brain disease.

★ ★ ★

15

"I'm kind of shy...sort of a loner."—Winona Ryder.
Maybe, but not where men are concerned. By age twenty-seven, the diminutive star had reportedly been romantically involved with Christian Slater, Daniel Day-Lewis, Eric Clapton, Jakob Dylan and David Duchovny—bearing in mind that many "romantic" press reports are fictional, especially when concerning costars. She's also been engaged to Johnny Depp and Soul Asylum rocker Dave Pirner and maintained a long, by Hollywood standards (over a year), relationship with Matt Damon.

P.S. The short-haired Ryder (née Horowitz) was mistaken at age twelve for a gay boy and beaten up by three bullies. "I had to have six stitches in my head after they slammed me into a school locker."

"I feel so accepted by my peers."— Amy Irving, after her Oscar nomination for *Yentl*, in which she played Barbra Streisand's wife.
In Hollywood, an actress is only as hot as her last film or her current husband. A month after she broke up with director Steven Spielberg, Irving found she wasn't invited to the same parties, the offers stopped coming in, the phone ceased ringing. Even a lunch with friends became unlikely. Years later she admitted, "I became like a leper in Hollywood. No one wanted to talk to me....I (had been) an appendage to a very wealthy man."

Fact: Hollywood is very male-driven. Before she wed Spielberg, she was pregnant by him, and the double-standard fuddyduddies who ran the Academy Awards weren't going to allow her to be a presenter on the show. Until Spielberg stepped in and said if Irving didn't appear on the show, he wouldn't either.

"Why should I work so hard? I've made it. I can take it easy... I don't need to work this hard."—Judy Garland, in the mid-1950s.
A dozen years later, she informed the press, "Once I was worth millions, but today I haven't got a dime. Once I had everybody at my feet, today only the name counts—the money is all gone. Altogether I must have earned around $8 million in my life, a million of that before I was eighteen. All I have to show for it is a debt of something like a million; I really don't know where it's all gone." She died soon after, twelve days after her forty-seventh birthday.

"I can't just let it all out, like the Hollywood stars regularly do....I'm very private, I think we [four] all are."—Beatle Paul McCartney, in the 1960s, on giving tell-all interviews.

But by the late '90s the widower (married thirty years) and ex-Beatle had become more extroverted: "I just let it all out—with friends and non-friends. When people came to the door, I told them the most intimate details, and now I am able to get on with my life." Telling all, he feels, helped him get over wife Linda's death.

★   ★   ★

"I don't throw tantrums....Sometimes they just want to write that I have this terrible temper."—supermodel Naomi Campbell.

The British beauty can seem demure or demonic, depending on her mood. She has alienated a number of designers and producers, both as a model and an actress. Designer Todd Oldham has declared, "I won't use her. We have a no-assholes clause." In early 2000, columnist Arlene Walsh reported that Campbell "desperately" wanted to marry her Italian millionaire beau Flavio Briatore, who "told her if she couldn't learn to contain her temper, the romance was over."

★   ★   ★

"I will be getting a divorce and marrying Christina and we will plan to live happily ever after."
— former James Bond Roger Moore.

But the best-laid plans of mice and Moore....After decades of marriage and children, Roger's Italian wife Luisa continued to deny him a divorce. She and his longtime companion Christina Tholstrup had once been friends. Then in late 1999 Tholstrup was knocked down by a drunken chauffeur. By 2000 she had recovered and Moore married her.

★   ★   ★

"I'm a good father."—Woody Allen.

The filmmaker became inappropriately intimate with longtime companion Mia Farrow's adopted daughter Soon-Yi, whom he eventually wed. Via Farrow, he'd become a father late in life. She got custody of their son, Seamus Farrow, now 11 and a prodigy who is attending college.

In 2000, *Beverly Hills (213)* noted, "He wants to take a full course load like the rest of the students, but his mom and the school are against it. They say he is too young and immature to take that on. The blond brain tells his classmates he wants nothing to do with his famous father."

"I think a little more mature woman is a better deal."
— Jack Nicholson, born 1937, at the time of his lengthy
relationship with Angelica Huston, born 1951.

But by 2000 Nicholson's ongoing relationship was with actress Lara Flynn Boyle, thirty-three years his junior, thus widening his age gap. It's been said that when a man chooses a much younger woman the youth he is seeking is not so much hers as his own.

"Matthew [McConaughey] is a doll....We will always be
friends, anyway."—Sandra Bullock.

Initially, Bullock said she and the blond actor were "just friends." Then they were reportedly engaged, but nothing happened further. By Christmas of 1999, when pals Matt Damon and Ben Affleck threw a party together, Sandra and Matthew were no longer romantically linked. Nor friendly. An insider revealed, "Their relationship must not have ended on a good note because they avoided each other all night. Sandra even showed her catty side by coaxing her girlfriend into making faces at Matthew all night."

(Hollywood parties are often more interesting for the people there who used to be together than for those who show up together.)

"I do all my own stunts. Unlike most of the
movie stars today, I am also a man. No other is in as good a
condition as me....My health is almost superhuman.
I will always be in excellent condition."—Jean-Paul Belmondo,
in 1964 (born 1933).

But at age sixty-six, Belmondo, performing on TV in Brest, France, collapsed from a mild heart attack.

★ ★ ★

"I think if an actor is not particularly well-informed, she does better to be quiet than to persistently look foolish."
—Glenda Jackson, in *Today*. Jackson is a former thespian, a Member of Parliament, and a candidate in the first-ever elections for mayor of London. (It was recently reported that Glenda declined the continuing role of M in the James Bond movies, so not to sully her political aspirations.)

★　　★　　★

" …but it's better if a child has a father who is not too old [so] they can grow up together."
— French star Sophie Marceau, in the early '90s.
By 1999 Marceau, thirty-three, star of the Bond movie *The World Is Not Enough*, had had a baby son by Polish director Andrzej Zulawsi, fifty-seven.

★　　★　　★

" …my wife Cher."— Sonny Bono, throughout the 1960s.
In 1964 Sonny and Cher supposedly got married. But not legally, for the previously matrimonied Bono was shy of further legal commitment. For their careers' sake, they had to seem married, which they contractually became in 1969, just in time for daughter Chastity's birth.

★　　★　　★

"Cher and me, it's partners—all the way down the line."
— Sonny Bono.
The couple's company was called Cher Enterprises but was anything but equal. The contract gave Cher no rights, no money, and no right to any work that the company didn't allow. Cher eventually discovered, "According to my contract, I was an employee of Cher Enterprises. Sonny owned 95% of the company, and Irwin, our lawyer (great lawyer!), owned the other 5%....I couldn't draw a check on the account unless it was signed by Sonny or Irwin. To make things worse, I was

signed exclusively to C.E. for two more years. I couldn't go out and do performances, or records, or TV, or anything on my own to make money."

When Cher asked that a new contract be drawn up, "one where we would split everything 50-50," Bono refused, and threatened a lawsuit.

"Barbara [Walters] and I have an understanding…marriage is not everything. I don't know if she's in love with me, [but] I do feel she's the most special woman in my life."
— Roy Cohn, ultra-right-wing attorney (eventually disbarred) and aide to communist-hunter Joseph McCarthy.

Cohn was a closeted, self-hating gay man, and "dated" Barbara Walters as a cover. An enemy to the gay community and to anyone left of Attila the Hun, he died—despite his denials—of AIDS.

"No, it's ours. They should never have it."
— John Wayne, on the Panama Canal; but eventually he supported President Carter's plan to cede it gradually to Panama.

"Two things I doubt you're ever going to see me do [on the screen]: do a nude scene or play a homosexual."
— Michael Caine, 1978.

In 1982 he played gay opposite Christopher Reeve in *Deathtrap*. Fortunately, he's refrained from acting naked.

"Who can tell? I might remarry someday."— Rock Hudson.
But the secretly gay star did not remarry—a female—and his one contractual marriage was by all accounts arranged. All accounts except Rock's manager Henry Willson, who arranged the sham wedding, and Willson's secretary, who participated as bride. Reportedly, the very first phone calls Hudson and wife made after the ceremony were not to family or friends, but to Hedda and Louella, Tinseltown's reigning gossip columnists, so they could go to work and give the public the wrong idea.

"Sandy and I, we're pals...for the long haul."
— Madonna, in 1989, on Sandra Bernhard.

The comedienne/singer, who prefers the label "bisexual" to "lesbian," felt the same. She wrote, "I dream about Madonna more than anyone I know or don't know; somehow she is indelibly written into my subconscious." Until 1992, when the blonde dropped Sandy and stole her openly lesbian girlfriend, Ingrid Casares, who remains pals with Madonna to this day. Bernhard remains Madonna's most frequently quoted non-fan.

★ ★ ★

"We're very lucky to have Bea [Arthur] in *Mame*....
She'll bring a lot to this movie."— Lucille Ball, during filming
of her screen swan song, *Mame* (1974).

Arthur, winner of a Tony award as Vera Charles in the Broadway *Mame*, brought out the sense of competition in Lucy, who'd already fired the much younger Madeline Kahn (details later in the book). When the then-myriad fan magazines began hinting that Ball (whom Johnny Carson once called Lucille Testicle) might also fire Arthur, Lucy threatened a round of lawsuits. The fanzines gave in meekly, and the star continued praising her supporting actress.

Male lead Robert Preston much later confessed, "Lucy is most definitely a queen bee...no other female's allowed to sparkle in her hive."

★ ★ ★

"Vivian [Vance] and I were the dearest friends...she is irreplaceable to me."— Lucille Ball, in 1986, during her final sitcom.

Ball and Vance eventually became friends, though not as close as Lucy led the press to believe. To Viv, Lucy was first the star—as opposed to second banana—and her employer. Nor did Vance forget Ball's chilliness during the first seasons of *I Love Lucy*. During her second pregnancy, Lucy's dressing room was situated right next to the *Lucy* set. Vivian's was on another soundstage. Before one scene which required that Lucy and Ethel enter together, Vance had to rush back to her dressing room, change costume, run *back* to the set, and as a breathless Vivian arrived, Ball informed her, "You almost missed your cue. You're late."

Viv inhaled and snapped, "I'd tell you to go fuck yourself if Desi hadn't already taken care of that!"

21

P.S. Ball had forbidden Vance the use of false eyelashes on *I Love Lucy*; only queen bee Lucy could look glamorous on the show. Vivian took to using them anyway—by then, "Lucy and Ethel" were as integral to the sitcom as "Lucy and Ricky."

**"Dave [Letterman] and I are good friends….
In this competitive business [comedy], it's real important
to have durable friends."—Jay Leno.**
But Letterman, more overtly competitive than Leno, never forgave Jay for inheriting *The Tonight Show*, the showcase that Dave had long craved. And while Jay casually says he watches Dave's show two or three times a week, Letterman claims he's never seen Leno's show.

**"Everyone thought I'd be gone before my time….
Lots of big names you can name, they died young, burned
themselves out….I'm still here."**— John Belushi, two years before
he died from a drug overdose at age thirty-three (in 1982).

**"I'll probably have to keep playing Liesl, or a variation
on her, for a long time, until people recognize me as me."**
— Charmian Carr, of *The Sound of Music*, the most popular movie
up until that time. But the newcomer made no more movies, giving
up stardom to become a housewife.

**"This picture will do for Twiggy what *Mary Poppins* did for
Julie Andrews."**— Justin DeVilleneuve, the skinny supermodel's
manager, on her 1971 musical flop, *The Boyfriend*.
Unlike Andrews, Twiggy couldn't sing.

**"The publicity on this film has gotten out of hand.
It's just unfortunate, it's not bad luck or anything."**
— director Baz Luhrman, during the making of *Moulin Rouge*,
a $50 million movie about Bohemian Paris.

The publicity began when Nicole Kidman fell and broke a rib. But during filming, Luhrman's father was killed, actor Jim Broadbent's wife got seriously ill—thus delaying his arrival from England (to Australia)—and Kidman refractured the same rib while putting on a period corset.

★   ★   ★

"I've written a tell-all biography, unauthorized and sizzling, of Tom Cruise."— author Wensley Clarkson, whose own autobiography was titled *Dog Eat Dog.*

Clarkson made a pretty penny—or English pence—off the book he said he wrote. He aimed to "get to the bottom of rumors surrounding the actor's sex life," including allegations that he was a male escort early on. According to Hollywood columnist Jack Martin, "The Church of Scientology got wind of this and threatened legal action. Clarkson pretended the first print run of the book, which included a chapter on Cruise's sex life, had already gone to press.

"However, if the church were prepared to pay retail for the whole lot, so the story goes, he'd agree to pulp them. So the clever chap ended up pocketing a substantial check before he'd even put pen to paper."

(Immediately after Gianni Versace's murder, St. Martin's Press signed Clarkson to do a biography of the late designer. "I wrote it in 12 days," he boasted, "and have been paid the most incredible amount of money for it.")

★   ★   ★

"I did it for the money, because I had to. But that was then. I wouldn't do it again. One does have one's standards."— Joan Collins, a few years after making the flop bug movie *Empire of the Ants* (1977).

Via television's *Dynasty*, Collins' career hit the heights in the '80s, and perhaps her standards relaxed a bit after she received more monetary offers than ever before. She sold her name to everyone from Jack LaLanne to a rubber-rose manufacturer, and dabbled in perfumes, novels and even stage performances. Ex-husband Anthony Newley, possibly a trifle jealous, stated, "Joan Collins is a commodity who would sell her own bowel movement."

★   ★   ★

"Of course. I am totally against racism."— Bill Cosby.
Cosby was also quoted as saying, "As long as I'm on the screen, I will never hold or kiss a white woman."

* * *

"Hark! I hear a white horse coming!"
—a line from *The Lone Ranger* radio program.

* * *

"If you go on the air with that crap, they're going to kill you dead in the streets!"— Mickey Rooney, to producer Norman Lear, declining to star in the trail-blazing '70s sitcom *All In the Family*.

* * *

"I cannot function in a show that I know is going to go down the drain only weeks after it airs....Who are you trying to kid?"—George Peppard, during a reported tantrum; the show he left was called *Dynasty*, and he was replaced by John Forsythe.

* * *

"This is my chance to wipe Judy Garland off the Hollywood map."— Betty Hutton, after being called in to replace the over-worked and overwrought star in the screen musical *Annie Get Your Gun* (1950)...the once-effervescent Hutton has so far outlived Judy by over three decades but has herself, sadly, been almost forgotten.

* * *

"There were bad kids in our neighborhood in the Bronx, but I had nothing to do with them until I had to sort of study them....They do have a tendency to cast me as troubled teenagers, but I can play a [juvenile delinquent] if I have to, and I guess this proves it."—Sal Mineo (1939-1976), in 1956, referring to his Oscar nomination for *Rebel Without a Cause*.
The two-time nominee was an emotionally open actor but didn't really need to study juvenile delinquents, as he was one. By age eight he'd joined a street gang, and in his teens he stole gym equipment which he hid in a casket at the funeral home where his father worked. He had various run-ins with school officials and the cops. Salvatore was given the option of reform school

or dancing and acting lessons. His mother opted for the latter, which led him to Broadway, then Hollywood, where his specialty was playing troubled teens. His stardom didn't carry over into adulthood, however, and his being openly non-heterosexual in the '70s didn't help Sal's career. Eventually, the ex-star was randomly stabbed to death by a robber with a far longer and more violent criminal record than young Mineo had ever amassed.

* * *

**"You've got it wrong, I think. I did not play Bette Davis'
boyfriend [in *Whatever Happened to Baby Jane?*, 1962]…
I'm too young to play her boyfriend anyway."**
— Victor Buono, Oscar-nominated for the role, as was Davis.
But a few years later, Buono, born in 1938, played Bette's father in *Hush, Hush, Sweet Charlotte*. He was thirty years younger than the screen diva, but hundreds of pounds heavier, and died at the age of forty-three.

* * *

**"I had to ponder long and hard whether to accept [the role of]
Miss Marple (in four 1960s MGM movies)….She solves
murders and is a good, dear soul, but I've always strenuously
avoided anything to do with violence and especially murder."**
— Oscar-winner Dame Margaret Rutherford.
Technically true. But after Rutherford's death in 1972 it was revealed that her mother had hanged herself and her father had killed his own father.

* * *

**"I've played everything but a wife, it seems. I have my
doubts about the public accepting me as a loving, faithful wife,
even this one."**—Carolyn Jones, on playing Morticia in the
'60s sitcom *The Addams Family* (Jones was wife to Aaron Spelling
in his pre-TV-mogul days).

* * *

**"I'm uncomplicated….My biggest problem is
figuring out what necktie to wear."**— Dick Van Dyke,
in the 1960s; only much later did he reveal that at the time of
The Dick Van Dyke Show he was an alcoholic.

"No....The public's not gonna buy me as an alcoholic."
— William Holden, declining a mini-series role in the 1980s.
Technically true for the most part. A majority of the public might have been surprised that the handsome, popular movie star was a *longtime* alcoholic. Supposedly, Audrey Hepburn refused his marriage proposal for exactly this reason.

"...cutting out fatty foods and staying away from red meat."
— Cybill Shepherd, in 1987, listing some of her beauty
tips for *Family Circle* magazine.
Earlier that year, Cybill had chomped on a hamburger in a TV ad for the Beef Association of America.

"Of course I use them. I'm a big believer in what I choose to promote."— actress Nancy Walker, on her sideline as a paper-towel salesperson; but during a local L.A. talk show, the *Rhoda* star let slip, "Sure...my maid uses them every day—I'm pretty certain."

"I think it's wonderful when housewives take an
interest in sewing [and] making their own clothes....
We can all benefit from good, easy to sew patterns."
— Gloria Swanson (*Sunset Boulevard*), who designed and pitched
patterns for many years but privately wore designer originals or
off-the-rack from toney department stores.

"Rita Hayworth voted year's best-dressed actress offscreen
by the Fashion Couturiers' Association of America."
— late-1930s press release from publicist Henry Rogers
(Carole Lombard was best-dressed on-screen).
As the Hayworth biography *If This Was Happiness* pointed out, there was no such Association. Rogers invented it. But the fake publicity led to a *Look* magazine cover that boosted Rita's career. *Happiness* author Barbara Leaming explained:

"Thenceforth scarcely a day went by that the influential columnists and movie magazines of the moment didn't receive items about Rita dreamed up by Rogers. Even better, many of the items about Rita that began to appear in the papers hadn't even been planted by him. 'Once the ball got rolling,' said Henry Rogers, 'it accelerated by itself, it was self-generating.'"

* * *

" ...Florence Lawrence Dead...."
— 1910 *St. Louis Post-Dispatch* headline.

Universal Studios founder Carl Laemmle—notorious for employing many members of his large family—planted the false story about his star Florence Lawrence. It said she had died in a trolley car accident. The next day, Laemmle took out ads that the story was a lie, that Miss Lawrence was alive and on view in his new movie *The Broken Oath*. The paper then ran what is often credited as the first-ever interview with a movie "star," accompanied by several photos of her. Laemmle arranged for her to visit St. Louis, and a near-riot ensued from the publicity, which helped make his movie a hit.

P.S. Generally considered the first movie star, Florence Lawrence was accidentally disfigured on the set. Without a flawless face, Hollywood dropped her, and several years later she committed suicide by ingesting ant poison.

* * *

"Murder, not completely impossible...[but] not suicide."
— Brenda Benet (before the death of her son), frustrated actress and former wife of TV star Bill Bixby. She did eventually commit suicide.

* * *

"I'll never write my memoirs, I'm too busy livin' and lovin' it up....I got a perfect right to sue anybody that tries to write a book about me."— Mae West, 1954.

Later in the decade, her memoirs were published—a ghostwriter penned them for her. As for suing, anyone has a legal right to write a book about a public figure.

"I've always been, I suppose, rather intimidatingly independent," observed Katharine Hepburn, who more than once said she had lived her life like a man, by her own rules.

A big exception to her declaration of independence was the fact that even as an adult and a movie star, Kate was given an allowance by her father. He doled out her own money to her until he died. And she claims never to have eaten in a restaurant—"too expensive"—in over sixty years!

★ ★ ★

"It's such a joy to me," cooed Diana Ross, "to have been the one to discover the Jackson Five and then be able to share them with the rest of the world."

The Jacksons were discovered by singer Gladys Knight, who then put Motown onto them. The record company decided to credit their biggest star—and founder Berry Gordy's personal protégée—Diana "Miss Ross" with the discovery. The fiction went unchallenged until Knight's and other books revealed otherwise, and until a Showtime cable-TV special in which Michael Jackson purposely made Diana out to be something of a liar.

★ ★ ★

"Me in a dress? That's not something you're likely to see, so don't hold your breath," advised Ellen DeGeneres long before she came out of her pants-filled closet.

But when she was tapped to host the Emmy awards, she did—for part of the evening—wear a dress.

P.S. Similarly, Katharine Hepburn detested skirts offscreen. Her ten-time director and platonic friend George Cukor confessed, "The only time Katie wore a skirt was once at a funeral. She was going to wear pants, but I said if she did on this occasion, I wouldn't go with her. So she wore a dress!"

★ ★ ★

"I like all kinds of girls. I don't really have a type," said Leonardo DiCaprio, international sex symbol (of the moment) for the pre-teen set.

He may *like* girls, but the star who moved out of his mother's house at twenty-three doesn't socialize a lot with them. For photo ops, he's seen with female costars or models like Amber Valletta, but he's reportedly been spotted at such "mixed" (straight/gay) hot spots as L.A.'s Akbar and Good Luck Bar, also the gay club Luna Park. And at 360 (on Sunset Boulevard), a regular haunt of Ellen DeGeneres and partner Anne Heche, Chastity Bono, and openly gay actor Rupert Everett. And when Leo visited the Playboy Mansion in 1998, columnist Arlene Walsh noted, "He paid no attention to the bunnies and hung out in the Jacuzzi with his posse of male friends."

★　★　★

**"I think Leonardo is talented…he has a deep soul.
He's so sensitive, Leonardo would stay up all night with the
withering flowers so they don't have to be alone,"
said actor River Phoenix.**

But *Titanic* producer-director James Cameron—and millions of fans—felt that Leonardo DiCaprio was pretty insensitive not to attend the 1998 Oscar ceremonies, which *Titanic* swept (Leo the talented was one of its few non-nominees). Leo had informed Cameron, who'd pleaded with him to go, "That's not me, bro. That's not my style." But it was the deep-pocketed thespian's style, around the same time, to go to Japan to make a multi-million-dollar TV commercial.

★　★　★

**"Olivia Newton-John's Dilemma!!"
— 1970s *TV Radio Mirror* headline.**

The "dilemma" was whether the (dyed) blonde singer should wed Lee Kramer, her handsome young Jewish manager, who'd supposedly proposed. Among the things left unsaid in the fanzine article was Olivia being herself half-Jewish. Fact: If the image seems mainstream, the media and the celebrity almost always play it that way.

★　★　★

**"I was an Arabian princess, but it seems like another
lifetime," explained silent-movie star Theda Bara.**

And well it might. She was really a Jewish tailor's daughter from Cincinnati named Theodosia Goodman, and the first female movie sex symbol. Her stage name was widely publicized as an anagram for "Arab death:" as the original screen "vampire," she lured men to their ruin, and inspired tons of hate mail. The "imported" diva starred in several screen hits a year until she was washed up by the 1920s.

★　★　★

"I was born in Rangoon," Barbra Streisand informed some of her early interviewers.

Of course Barbara (three a's) Joan Streisand was born in Brooklyn. Perhaps she was taking a cue from Theda Bara's publicists? Early on, she handed out assorted fictions regarding her background. Decades later, on Rosie O'Donnell's talk show, Babs disowned Rangoon, the capital of Burma, aka Myanmar. When asked where Rangoon was, she guessed (wrong), "Somewhere near Africa."

★　★　★

"I am proud to represent my country, Egypt."

Omar Sharif, "Egyptian Muslim," was reportedly born Michel Shalhoub, a Lebanese Christian. He attained stardom in the Arab world by marrying Egypt's top actress (Cairo is the Middle East's Hollywood) and converting to her religion. When he went Hollywood, he went single, and in 1968 became a romantic male lead via the hit *Funny Girl*, whose Jewish leading lady, Barbra Streisand, he romanced in real life. Quipped Babs, "You think Cairo is upset? You should have heard my Aunt Rose!"

★　★　★

"I like to talk about America, where my future is. Not about my ancestors in old Spain," said Ricardo Cortez, a movie star of the 1920s and '30s.

Though cast in the Latin Lover mold of Rudolph Valentino, Cortez was in no way Latin: he'd been born Jacob Krantz and was of Jewish-Austrian background. After Latin Lovers were finally out, he traded films for the stock market and real estate.

★　★　★

"Originally, I was Australian. From Tasmania,
off the eastern coast," said movie star Merle Oberon, noted for
her exotic good looks. "We're partly or primarily of Irish
origin and, you know, the ordinary, everyday background....
I always wanted to go to England."

Oberon also wanted to be a successful actress, and in racist England, which ruled over India, she had to pass herself off as entirely European. Her mother was Indian, a fact Merle kept hidden. In the UK she reportedly introduced her mother as her maid, later burying her in an unmarked grave before departing for Hollywood, where anti-Third World prejudice was just as strong.

★　　★　　★

"I do have some Russian forebears, and being other than the
average leading man type, I'd already decided not to use my
own name," said Boris Karloff, king of the horror movies but
born William Henry Pratt and known to relatives as Billy.

Like Merle Oberon, Karloff had some Indian forebears, at a time when any national or racial origin other than European was unacceptable in those vying for cultural prominence. To explain away his "exotic" looks, he concocted a partly Russian background; however, daughter Sara Karloff has asserted on TV that she knows of no Russian ancestors on either side of her late father's family.

★　　★　　★

"Why, he's as Irish as you or me," said Raquel Welch
about a friend in the 1960s.

But she was born Raquel Tejada, via a Bolivian father, and had a nose job to fix what she later called her "Latin nose." Welch was the surname of her first husband, and served to hide the fact that, like another all-American movie sex symbol, Rita Hayworth—née Margarita Cansino—Raquel was half-Hispanic.

★　　★　　★

"The men in Paree, they all go wild for me!
But the men in America, crazee!"—"Parisian" sex symbol Fifi
D'Orsay, who in fact had never set foot in France—

she hailed from Montreal, Canada—besides which she was either gay or bisexual. According to the book *Hollywood Goddesses*, she had an affair with Greta Garbo, who'd seen her in the 1929 movie *Hot For Paris* and been smitten… today Fifi is barely remembered for her once-famous catchphrase, "Allo, beeg boy."

★　★　★

"Cugie's Latin Doll"—nickname for Brooklyn-born Lina Romay, singer with Xavier Cugat's band in the 1940s.

★　★　★

"The Puerto Rican Pepperpot"— nickname for Brooklynite singer-dancer-actor Olga San Juan.

★　★　★

"The Venezuelan Volcano"—nickname for movie performer Acquanetta (born Burnu Acquanetta), who hailed from Wyoming.

★　★　★

"Cuba's Latin Lover Supreme"— a nickname for Cesar Romero, who was of Cuban ancestry but went to high school in New Jersey. He explained, "I was due to be the new Valentino, the latest Latin Lover, a dancing rival to Tyrone Power…they had me speaking with a Spanish accent until they finally realized the Valentino era was over for good." The gay Romero, who despite pressure never wed, and the bisexual Power were lovers for a period and then lifelong friends.

★　★　★

"Now I'm Mexican…okay."—Desi Arnaz, on the new nationality assigned to him by a nervous CBS in his role of Ricky Ricardo, after Cuba went communist in the late '50s.

★　★　★

"Yes, I'm Spanish…I was presented at the royal court."
— Mexican movie star Dolores Del Rio, cooperating (in the 1920s) with Hollywood publicists who felt a European heritage was classier than a Latin American one; in the '30s she dropped being "Spanish,"

and in the '40s returned to Mexico; in 1960 she had trouble with U.S. authorities when she returned to play Elvis Presley's mother in *Flaming Star* because she'd opposed fascist dictator Francisco Franco and helped Spanish refugees settle in Mexico.

⋆　⋆　⋆

"I don't think he likes me, because I am a Latin."
— Maria Montez, from the Dominican Republic, on her frequent movie costar Jon Hall. They didn't get along, but not because of racial bias—he had himself wed former star Raquel Torres.

⋆　⋆　⋆

"…a Christmas tradition at our house."
— Dinah Shore, who kept her Jewishness in the closet and far more often referred to being from Tennessee; however she did choose to be buried in L.A.'s Jewish (last resting place of stars from Al Jolson to Jack Benny, The Three Stooges and *Bonanza*'s Lorne Greene and Michael Landon) Hillside Cemetery, with a female rabbi presiding.

⋆　⋆　⋆

"Frankly I think the part's a little too Jewish."
— David Janssen (born David Meyer), worrying what (some of) the public might think about a made for TV movie role he turned down in 1978. Janssen is best remembered as *The Fugitive* (and is also buried at Hillside Cemetery).

⋆　⋆　⋆

"Being British, I'm dedicated to helping fight the menace posed by Hitler and his ilk."
—Leslie Howard (born Lazlo Steiner).
The distinguished star of *Pygmalion*, *Of Human Bondage* and *Gone With the Wind* was also of Hungarian origin and Jewish (like American Douglas Fairbanks, ne Douglas Ulman). Howard was working secretly for the British government against the Nazis when his Portugal-to-England plane was shot down (1893-1943).

⋆　⋆　⋆

UPPITY ACTORS

"I did not use paint. I made myself up morally."
— Eleanora Duse.

_____

"I never wore makeup."
— Ronald Reagan, who did.

_____

"For the theatre one needs long arms…better too long than too short. An artiste with short arms can never, never make a fine gesture."
— the "divine" Sarah Bernhardt.

_____

"It's pretty hard to retain the characteristics of one's sex after a certain age."
— performer turned writer Colette.

_____

"I do not act. I elucidate."
— John Barrymore.

_____

"I enjoy reading biographies because I want to know about the people who messed up the world."
— #1 box office movie star Marie Dressler.

_____

"Hollywood always had a streak of the totalitarian in just about everything it did."
— Shirley MacLaine.

_____

"If you can't be direct, why be?"
— Lily Tomlin.

_____

"Good notices, dear."
— British stage star Gertrude Lawrence, on arriving in New York City and being asked what she'd most like to see there.

_____

"I'm too good."
— Sophia Loren, on why she declined to play Alexis on _Dynasty_.

_____

"I don't have time for children….I don't have a strong desire to have my own children."
— Richard Gere, who became a father in 2000.

_____

"[Playing] Superman is quite a responsibility…I think it's better to play worthwhile, admirable characters."
— Christopher Reeve, who then played an amoral priest blackmailing bishops and having an affair with a nun in the flop _Monsignor_.

"I'd be real happy if they showed this picture in all the classrooms. It's a big slice of our history, with lots of heart, and a message."
— John Wayne, on *The Alamo*, which he also directed, and which was full of historical errors and propaganda.

———————

"I was at first rather surprised that anyone chose to play [Joan of Arc] after I did."
— Dame Sybil Thorndike, on her critically acclaimed role.

———————

"Every nude scene I have done was really, it was, absolutely intrinsic to that particular plot. I'm not an extrovert, and I'm certainly not an exhibitionist."
— two-time Oscar-winner Glenda Jackson.

———————

"My [topless] scene in *Shakespeare In Love* was not to show me off, it was for the scene, it was for the mood…and to express something."
— Oscar-winner Gwyneth Paltrow.

———————

"Yeah, I'd date me."
— Brad Pitt, confirming his hunk status. (But would he go all the way?)

———————

"Actors are priests. They are a conduit from something very powerful to the people. That's why when you go to the theatre or to the movies you are moved in some way—to laugh, to get a hard-on, to feel compassion."
— Christopher Walken.

———————

"I don't know. I guess fate chose me for success, and then I became a slave to it. I never worked so hard in my life."
— Steve McQueen.

———————

"Don't judge by critics….Regardless of my movies, I was always at my very best."— Ginger Rogers (the French say that only the mediocre are always at their best).

———————

"It was a classic, and it was #1 —and for a long time too….How many people ever saw *Hamlet*? Did a hundred million people ever see *Hamlet*? I don't think so."
— Max Baer, Jr. (aka Jethro), comparing *The Beverly Hillbillies* to Shakespeare (no comment).

———————

"Of course I'm Jewish."— Paul Newman, who is half-Jewish…by contrast, Robert De Niro is as well, but instead emphasizes his father's Italian-American heritage.

★　★　★

"I wanted to do everything I could for the [World War II] war effort."

Nonetheless, John Wayne did not serve. He could have—most Hollywood male stars did sign up—but instead claimed a waiver as a father and fought on the screen, for a star's pay.

★　★　★

"I prefer not to talk about it," demurred British screen star Trevor Howard (*Brief Encounters, The Third Man*), referring to his Military Cross and record as a war hero in the invasions of Sicily and Norway in WW II.

Ten years after his death, Britain's War Office released files declaring that Howard had never received the Military Cross and had fabricated his heroic war record.

★　★　★

"Serving during the [Second World] War was a duty and, in its way, a privilege. But where a lot of us lied was when we said we were happy to do it. Many of us actors hated to do it, because our careers were gaining momentum, and taking years off to serve interrupted that, sometimes stalled it badly.…Without naming names, but many who served rarely speak of it nowadays, and many who didn't really serve, well, you'd think from their reputation or boasting that they were out there, in Europe or the Pacific, engaged in hand-to-hand combat."
— Richard Denning, film and radio actor who played Lucille Ball's mate in her pre-*Lucy* radio series *My Favorite Husband* and later portrayed the governor in *Hawaii Five-O.*

P.S. Among those not named: Ronald Reagan, who chose to stay home and make training films stateside.

**"My family fascinates me. But I'm not going to
talk about them to an indifferent public. I'm a comedian,
not a genealogist."—Bob Hope.**

For one reason or another, sometimes ego, most celebrities don't shed the spotlight on their families. Hope may have had image concerns, for his Italian-American nephew was gay and died of AIDS, and his two (adopted) daughters are both openly lesbian. (Hope's wife Dolores is Italian-American.)

☆　☆　☆

"Boring Englishman…very boring."
**— Denholm Elliot (*A Room With a View*, *Raiders of the Lost Ark*),
discouraging an interviewer from questions about his private life.**

A closeted gay or bisexual, Elliott died of AIDS in 1992 at the relatively advanced age of seventy. His widow (his second wife) speculated in a posthumous book that he may have contracted the disease during an orgy while on location in the South Pacific.

☆　☆　☆

**"We were very in love, devoted to each other…
though it was brief."— Angela Lansbury, in the '60s, on her first
marriage, to actor Richard Cromwell.**

Decades later, Lansbury admitted Cromwell was gay. They'd lived together nine months, and she was 19. Previously, she'd said they divorced because she was "too young." And in 1947 she tellingly informed the *New York Post*, "The Hollywood men are so darned keen on themselves….They adore themselves so much, they make love to themselves constantly. When I get married again, I expect to marry somebody who isn't an actor at all."

Angela met her second and current husband at the home of her gay costar and friend, Hurd Hatfield (*The Picture of Dorian Gray*), and they wed in 1949.

☆　☆　☆

**"The two loves of my life…Ava Gardner and Greta Garbo."
— MGM hairdresser Sydney Guilaroff.**

Despite his profession, Guilaroff was deeply closeted. In his 1996 autobiomythography *Crowning Glory*—preface by Angela Lansbury—he concocted affairs with the late heterosexual Gardner and the late lesbian or bisexual Garbo. He also, over the years, misrepresented certain of his younger lovers as his adopted sons or grandsons. A traditionalist, he abhorred women in pants and did not get along with most gay men, feuding, for instance, on the set of *Gigi* with designer Cecil Beaton (who later feuded with gay director George Cukor on *My Fair Lady*, as described in the book *Celebrity Feuds!*)

"I think I have a humorous point of view…[but] I don't know that I'll ever get the chance to do comedy. They judge you by your looks—so probably never."— Candice Bergen, in 1972, after starring in a string of dramatic flops; she made her screen bow in 1966 as a lesbian named Lakey in *The Group*, but not until *Rich and Famous* (1981, directed by George Cukor) was her flair for comedy widely recognized.

"Women can be just as funny as men…. I don't think we're as good at directing comedy as men." — Lucille Ball, at a comedy seminar.

Known for virtually directing her own post-*I Love Lucy* sitcoms, Lucy also told Garry Marshall, one of her writers, that no woman would ever direct a film that would gross over $100 million. His sister Penny Marshall was the first female to direct two $100 million movies.

"It's a lie! I'm rich…successful. I've never had to steal in my life."—Hedy Lamarr, in 1966, after being arrested for stealing $86 worth of May Company department store merchandise in L.A. (she retaliated by suing the store for $5 million damages; she was acquitted, and her suit was dismissed).

Decades later, after a Florida arrest for shoplifting, the ex-movie star again declared her innocence and again sued for defamation. (Of course, many shoplifters don't need to, but do.) Born in Austria in 1913—she claimed 1918 and 1920—the raven-tressed star who retired in 1957 was called "the most beautiful actress ever to appear on screen." Despite her looks and rather shallow image, Lamarr (real surname: Kiesler) held several patents on her own inventions and possessed a lofty I.Q.

"Joan Rivers, Plastic Surgery Fan, Declares, 'I Was Born in 1962!'"—tabloid headline; but it was the paper that prevaricated, for surely they knew the second line of Rivers' joke: "And the room next to mine was 1963."

"Gary [Morton, ne Morton Goldapper] and I are about the same age. Little difference—closer than Desi and I....But he's a lot more mature than Desi was."
—Lucille Ball, on her second and final husband.

Lucy was born in 1911, Morton in 1917, which is also reportedly the year Desi Arnaz was born. (By "mature," Lucy apparently meant he didn't chase after women.)

"Yeah, I'll be forty next year. But don't quote me on that —even actors are vain!"
— Desi Arnaz, in 1954, during the run of *I Love Lucy*.

Though apparently born in 1917, Arnaz gallantly tried at times to diminish the age gap with his wife by claiming a birth year of 1915. Of course, in the '50s, the couple's biggest deception was their image as a happy couple, devoted to each other for years. They considered divorce more than once, and *I Love Lucy* was Ball's last-ditch attempt to save the marriage by keeping her younger husband with her at home and at work. ("even actors"??)

"Jackie was fifty-three."—Jacqueline Susann's widower and manager Irving Mansfield, who shaved three years off the novelist's age and didn't admit she'd had cancer and they had an autistic, institutionalized child.

"I was born on the Fourth of July. Don't ask what year,"
said MGM chief Louis B. Mayer.

Don't ask what day he was really born, for he didn't know, and neither did his relatives. In czarist days, record-keeping was scant. But the super-patriotic immigrant created a July 4th birthday for himself and stuck with it.

"I was born November 8th, and I don't volunteer the year!"
Katharine Hepburn's "birthday" belonged to her older brother Tom, who committed suicide in 1921. According to her most frequent director, George Cukor, "She identified very strongly with her brother…she was always quite the tomboy." As a girl, she was nicknamed Jimmy. As a star, she only occasionally volunteered her year of birth as 1909. When she finally published her (incomplete…) memoirs, titled *Me*, she admitted, "I was born May 12th, 1907, despite everything I may have said to the contrary."

"Oddly enough, I was born on October 31st," said Elsa
Lanchester during filming of *The Bride of Frankenstein*,
in which she played the monster's intended mate.

After the Englishwoman discovered that Universal meant to hold her to a Halloween birthday date—the better to promote the 1935 horror classic—she refused to continue the pretense. "Some people already think I'm a witch!"

P.S. A bigger lie was her longstanding contractual marriage to star Charles Laughton, who was gay (as was his brother). Which she revealed after he died, claiming that she herself was heterosexual—which several insiders later disputed.

"I always tell my real age. I have nothing to hide,"
shrugged movie costume designer Edith Head, who had
eight Academy Awards to her credit.

But she hid plenty. To begin with, it was eventually found that she had subtracted a decade from her age; she was born in 1897, not 1907. She also hid that she was half-Jewish, as well as lesbian, bisexual or asexual (take your pick). And that she'd claimed credit—often—for designs which weren't hers, even winning Oscars that, as biographers would point out, she didn't really merit.

**"Darling, I vasn't even born ven it vas silent movies!"
said Zsa Zsa Gabor.**

The Jazz Singer in 1927 is generally credited as the first talkie. But the woman who also claimed to have been Miss Hungary—pretty convenient that the communists "destroyed" records of such things—rarely gave a year, or even a decade, for her birth. A year frequently cited by record books is 1919. Zsa Zsa has also always insisted that she's never been near a plastic surgeon, despite long ago having discovered the secret of perpetual middle age.

"Bette [Davis] and I are the same age," beamed Joan Crawford—born 1904—during filming of *Whatever Happened to Baby Jane?* The two were playing sisters, Joan's character being the elder.

Davis was actually four years younger, though not being as self-disciplined or prone to plastic surgery, she looked older. When Bette heard of Joan's public remark about their age, she exploded, "The bitch is years older than me! My God, she began in silent movies!" (Crawford made her screen bow in 1925; Davis also later referred to her as "Hollywood's first case of syphilis.")

**"I can play this role because of how I look.
No one else can do it….I've got the skin of a
twenty-six-year-old," cooed Mae West in her mid-eighties
while playing a blonde sexpot in her final film, *Sextette*.**

The reviews—which she was kept from reading—were not kind. Her appearance was more than once compared to that of a mummy.

NUMERICALLY CHALLENGED

"I'm glad we don't have to play in the shade!"
— golfer Bobby Jones (1902-71) on being told it was 105 degrees in the shade.

———————————

"Suddenly, at age thirty-seven, I have acquired sensuality and woman-ness."
— Whoopi Goldberg in 1993.

In 1983 she told an interviewer she was thirty-three.

———————————

"Baseball is 90% mental. The other half is physical."
— Yogi Berra.

———————————

"…my community, the African-American community."
— Halle Berry in 2000, accepting an Emmy Award. She's half black and half white.

———————————

"*Chariots of Fire* is Mr. Charleson's first film."
— official bio of British actor Ian Charleson, star of the Oscar-winning 1981 film.

The secretly gay actor (who eventually came out) had made his movie debut in 1977 in openly gay director Derek Jarman's *Jubilee*. The two were friends through the 1970s. "Then everything changed," recalled Jarman many years later. "[Producer] David Puttnam…told him to have his association with me struck off his CV. And that from henceforth *Chariots of Fire* was his first film.

"Ian apologized to me for doing this, but complied. Until two years ago he was denying his sexuality and his friendship with me in the yellow press." Charleson died of AIDS in 1990.

———————————

"I went to live with him when I was twelve."
— Richard Burton, born Richard Jenkins, on moving in with gay instructor Philip Burton, whose surname he adopted.

He actually moved in with Burton at age seventeen, but gave the younger age to give the relationship a platonic gloss. His family later admitted it was at seventeen and by choice. Richard Burton eventually informed *People* magazine, "Perhaps most actors are latent homosexuals and we cover it with drink. I was once a homosexual, but it didn't work." (Elizabeth Taylor's latest biographer claims Burton had an affair with bisexual Laurence Olivier a few years before meeting Liz.)

"Five feet nine inches."
— Tom Cruise's height on his official biography.

Columnist Jeanette Walls wrote, "The word was that Cruise stood on a 'cheater box' to make him as tall as Nicole Kidman. He also allegedly used one to stand above his *Top Gun* costar Kelly McGillis. He also had to use one in *Interview With a Vampire* so that the six-foot-tall Brad Pitt wouldn't tower over him."

The "urban legend" that Humphrey Bogart, whose mother was an illustrator for various companies and magazines, was the original model for the Gerber baby food baby. Bogart was born in 1899. Gerber was born in 1927. (When Bogart moved from gangster roles to Warner Bros. movie leads, the studio assigned him a new birthday for public relations reasons. Born January 23, 1899, he was now "born" December 25, 1900.)

"Well, I'm 3/4 Irish and a quarter Mexican, and proud of it."
— Anthony Quinn. In fact, it was the other way around. The actor's paternal grandfather drifted from Ireland to the U.S. to Mexico.

"In two words: im possible!"
— producer Samuel Goldwyn.

"She's a clot. But you won't print that anyway, of course, because *Playboy* is very pro-Mansfield. They think she's a rave. But she really is an old bag."
— Beatle Paul McCartney (born 1942) in 1965 in *Playboy* magazine, about Jayne Mansfield, then in her early thirties but nearly ten years his senior.

Playboy, which had regularly featured the buxom Mansfield, never did again in her lifetime after McCartney's sexist pronouncement (she died two years later, in a notorious 1967 car crash).

"She is not too young for me. Although I might be too young for her."
— Frank Sinatra, upon marrying Mia Farrow, thirty years his junior (and the daughter of actress Maureen O'Sullivan).

In June, 2000, *In Los Angeles* magazine ran a blind item asking, "Could it be that a certain legendary entertainer married his own daughter? This rumor, which first surfaced decades ago," revived with the entertainer's death. "The story goes that when this crooner first came to Hollywood, he had an affair" with an actress who later gave birth to a daughter who would eventually marry the entertainer. "Of course there is no proof about this…but the alleged father and daughter/wife both had similar blue eyes."

_____

"The size of the check isn't important. Following your heart is."
— Laura Dern, declining to costar with John Travolta in *The General's Daughter* so she could appear in a "little" film written and directed by long-time beau Billy Bob Thornton, who (after the film) suddenly dropped her and married Angelina *"Tomb Raider"* Jolie.

_____

"Many a man owes his success to his first wife and his second wife to his success."
— Jim Backus (*Gilligan's Island*), pointing out an established marital pattern.

_____

"A few hundred dollars one way or the other shouldn't make much difference."
— friend-of-Reagan Alfred Bloomingdale on wife Betsy being caught in 1975 trying to smuggle tens of thousands of dollars' worth of Dior gowns into the U.S. via the "doctored invoice ploy."

A member of President Reagan's "kitchen cabinet," Bloomingdale recalled of his 1946 marriage to Betsy (later Nancy Reagan's best friend), "One morning I was a Democrat and a Jew. The next morning, a Catholic and a Republican!" The judge in the smuggled-gowns case told

Betsy, "You deserve the contempt of this court and of the society which has served you so well!"

———————

"Two's company. Three's five hundred bucks."
— Will Smith.

———————

"For three days after death, hair and fingernails continue to grow but phone calls taper off."
— Johnny Carson.

———————

"After three days, fish and houseguests stink."
— humorist Robert Benchley (father of novelist Peter, who wrote *Jaws*).

———————

"The 100% American is 99% an idiot."
— Irish writer and curmudgeon George Bernard Shaw, who lived in England.

"They say that forty is the old age of youth, and fifty is the youth of old age."
— former French sex symbol Brigitte Bardot.

———————

"Some time after forty you finally realize that marriage is not a word, but a sentence."
— Elizabeth Taylor, after her eighth marriage.

———————

"After forty, it takes at least ten years to get used to your real age."
— fortysomething Madonna. (And how would she know?)

———————

"Any two people, either sex. If you stare at somebody else for as long as thirty seconds and they return your stare, you'll either end up fighting or having sex."
— Madonna (she should know).

"But who could be convinced, me as some old, washed-up silent movie star going crazy?"— Pola Negri, in 1963, referring to *Sunset Boulevard* (1950).

The answer to the Pole's question: only audiences. The plum role of Norma Desmond was said to have been offered to three aging divas— Mary Pickford, who felt intimidated, and Negri and Mae West, who felt insulted. Both Pickford and Negri were washed-up old silent stars; Mae was no younger but didn't make Hollywood till early talkies. Negri faked an affair and engagement to gay or bi Rudolph Valentino after he died, and preferred the press to think she'd had an "affair" with Hitler than that she was bisexual or lesbian. Tallulah Bankhead, openly bi, termed her "a lying lesbo, a Polish publicity hound!"

"A hero has to look the part."—William Shatner, on the importance of tailoring to his *Star Trek* movie costumes.

But a seaside Photo of the Week in an early 2000 issue of the *Globe* was captioned "It's William Fat-ner!" Actor turned columnist Charlene (*Dallas*) Tilton noted, "I love William Shatner, but it looks like his waistband has gone where no bathing trunks have gone before."

"They have to pick on you…if you don't do drugs, it's something else….Now I have a reputation for being this mad, out-of-control spendthrift. There's no real basis for that."— Elton John.

In late 1999, while on a brief visit to Toronto, he bought twelve suits, twenty sweaters and eighty ties at a Versace boutique, totaling $114,000. On the other hand, he could well afford it.

"I've never been afraid of anything, and I have no phobias."— Donald Trump, author of *The America We Deserve*; but at book signings the possibly germophobic tycoon had bottles of hand sanitizer within arm's reach.

"Hollywood and the pictures have been generous to me....
I've given a lot to my business, but I've received far more."
— silent star Harold Lloyd.

Actually, he gave more than he got. Even stars weren't sensibly protected in the silent era, and Lloyd lost the thumb and index finger of his right hand to a faulty explosive prop (he later wore latex prosthetic fingers when not in his perennial gloves).

★ ★ ★

"I plan to make acting a long-range goal where I keep measurably improving and growing."—Dolores Hart.

But movies like *Where the Boys Are* weren't meant for improving one's craft, and the attractive but serious blonde abandoned Hollywood for a nunnery, first as a sister, eventually as Mother Superior.

★ ★ ★

"Maybe you can't do big leading parts when you're past forty, but it's an interesting business to age in...I admire several elderly and talented actresses."—Jean Peters.

However, before she was thirty, Peters (*Three Coins in the Fountain, Viva Zapata!, Niagara*) had retired. She wed Howard Hughes, who insisted she not make movies while married (for fifteen years) to him. Peters was one of a mere handful to give up Hollywood before Hollywood gave them up; another was Grace Kelly. In one case, it took a billionaire's wealth, in the other, a (mini) kingdom.

★ ★ ★

"...some of my men, but one thing I can't complain about is my figure!"—Carole Lombard.

But the beautiful blonde movie star was not amply endowed. One trick was to pencil in a shadow to make her cleavage seem deeper and lighten the top of her breasts to seemingly enlarge them. At times when her form-fitting '30s gowns didn't reveal cleavage, she simply wore a molded bust underneath—she was famous for yelling to her costumer, "Bring me my breasts!"

★ ★ ★

FACTUALLY CHALLENGED

"There is no capital of Uruguay,
you dummy. It's a country."
— Lorenzo Lamas in 1999 on
The Daily Show.
Surprise: most actors never go to
college. (Lamas' movie star father
Fernando was from Argentina,
which borders Uruguay—no
wonder he knew it's a country.)

———

"I had to wait until my
sixties before I finally found
my own voice."
— Jane Fonda (born 1937),
upon separating from
TV mogul Ted Turner.
She seems to have forgotten
she had quite an outspoken
voice in her thirties and forties,
before she wed Turner and
became, by choice, a Stepford
billionaire's wife.

———

"If you misuse your microwave,
it's more dangerous than a gun."
— Sen. Ray Haynes,
GOP gun-supporter.

———

"Outside of the killings,
we have one of the lowest crime
rates in the nation."
— Marion Barry, mayor of
Washington, D.C.

———

"I came right out and asked
[Pres. Jimmy Carter] why he
had homosexuals on his senior
staff at the White House."
— preacher Jerry Falwell
at a conservative Alaska
election gathering.
White House transcripts
later proved no such question
was asked.

———

"We simply picked the most
talented actors available."
—Jackie Gleason, regarding the
casting of *The Honeymooners*.
The other deciding factor, during
the McCarthy witch-hunt era,
was politics. Movie comedienne
Pert Kelton, who'd originated the
role of Alice Kramden on TV's
Cavalcade of Stars, was blacklisted by CBS for being too liberal.

———

"I'm on a diet."
— Oprah Winfrey in a
San Francisco restaurant in
1993, explaining why she'd
just refused dessert.
However, she'd already consumed
a dozen oysters, crabcakes,
tuna tartare, stuffed calamari,
salmon with mushrooms, and
risotto with truffles.

"Your honor, I would like the
court to know that I have taken
this matter very seriously from
the very beginning."
— actress Halle Berry in
court, in 2000.
She was fined $13,500 and
placed on three years' probation
for a hit-and-run accident which
left another woman with a broken wrist and other injuries.

"He died of a drug overdose."
— Austrian actor Helmut Berger,
when asked whatever became of
Swedish actor Bjorn Andresen,
who costarred in Luchino
Visconti's *Death in Venice*
(1971).
Years later, Andresen (still alive
as of this writing) was asked why
Berger—who starred in Visconti's
The Damned and *Ludwig*—
would say such a thing. He

explained that Berger had had
his heart set on playing Tadzio in
Death in Venice.

"New Oprah Shocker!
Fiance Stedman Had Gay Sex
With Cousin."
— the March 24, 1992, issue of
News Extra.
A private investigator hired by
Oprah Winfrey found that
particular tabloid had never
interviewed Carlton Jones,
Stedman Graham's gay cousin.
He had been interviewed by
another tab that "plied Jones
with liquor and agreed to pay
him money in exchange for his
statements." Winfrey and
Graham sued *News Extra*, which
soon after fired its
staff, disconnected its telephones
and ceased publishing. Nobody
from the tabloid showed up at
the trial, and the happily
unwedded couple won the case
by default.
P.S. *News Extra*, founded by
the younger brother of the
original founder of the *Globe*,
had also declared Sylvester
Stallone had received a penile
implant after steroid used rendered him impotent. He sued.
And it claimed that Bill Clinton

had fathered a child with a black prostitute, which was disproved when the *Star* tabloid paid the alleged child to take a blood test.

"It's a lie."
— Laura Schlessinger on the existence of any nude photos of herself, the ones she later sued in vain to get off the Internet (they were taken at the time of the holier-than-thou one's adulterous affair).

"I love you, Spain!"
— Whitney Houston, opening her concert in Lisbon, Portugal (where people admit to being Lisboans).

"I love Albuquerque, where I was born and reared."
— Vivian Vance, who was actually from Kansas (her TV character Ethel Mertz on *I Love Lucy* was from Albuquerque). Vance eventually said, "Dorothy [Gale in *The Wizard of Oz*] was so happy to wake up in Kansas. Not I! I'd have looked for another cyclone and stood right in its path!"

"'Ex-Gay' Poster Boy Sneaks Into Gay Bar!"
10/13/00 headline in Los Angeles' *Fab!* newspaper. "Ex-gay" John Paulk was photographed inside Mr. P's, a Washington, D.C. gay bar. (His contractual wife, a self-described ex-lesbian, is rumored to be a posing heterosexual.) The media seldom reveal that nearly all "ex-gays" are religious fundamentalists. The 1993 documentary *One Nation Under God*, available on video, is about the founders of the leading "ex-gay" ministry who met, fell in love, then departed the anti-gay group they'd helped establish in order to fight it.

Jane Wyman's fan magazine *P.R.* claimed that she was "lonely" without hubby Ronald Reagan, just like millions of wives during World War II. The 1988 book *The Peter Lawford Story* noted, "The fact that Reagan slept at home each night was ignored." The fanzines made references to the actor being "on leave." "In reality, his war work might take him to the Disney studio to narrate an animated film on the war." (The book was cowritten by Lawford's widow; Peter was pals with actor Robert Walker, a pre-Reagan boyfriend of Nancy Davis.)

"During the war, nobody not actively engaged did more to oppose the Nazis… than we in Hollywood."
—Walt Disney, one of two non-Jewish studio heads at the time, and the only studio head willing to welcome and entertain "Hitler's golden girl," director Leni Riefenstahl, when she visited Hollywood in 1938.

"Like many couples, we have our ups and downs, but Brynn is undeniably a wonderful, devoted mother."
— Phil Hartman, whom Brynn shot dead in 1998 before shooting herself, thus orphaning their two children.

"Motherhood is the most important thing to me. I'm not sure every actress today feels that way, but certainly I do."
— 1930s MGM superstar Norma Shearer, who'd wed the studio's #2 executive, Irving Thalberg. As with many actresses and actors, Shearer's career took

precedence, though not publicly. Most stars wish to seem enough like their fans so the fans can identify with them while simultaneously idolizing them.

But as Irving Thalberg, Jr. admitted, he was virtually reared by his governess. "My mother would tell her to go see to the luggage when we'd return from a trip, so she would be out of sight while the reporters and more particularly the photographers came around." Most stellar actresses still have nannies or governesses for their child or children, and sometimes there's more deception involved than in Norma Shearer's more typical case. To wit, a gay or bisexual married actor (superstar) and lesbian or bisexual actress (star) are occasionally seen with their adopted offspring and the attractive young nanny who is actually the wife's lover. Then as now, Hollywood on-camera is not necessarily Hollywood off-camera.

> **"I know there are jokes. They don't mean anything,**
> **because there's no basis in truth to them."**
> **— petit hunk movie star Alan Ladd, on short jokes**
> **(Robert Mitchum teased him about his height publicly).**

At 5'6" or less, Ladd wasn't tall enough to dominate all actresses. Most at the time were quite petite—among others, Norma Shearer, Liz Taylor, Lana Turner, Carole Lombard, Judy Garland and frequent Ladd costar Veronica Lake were just a bit over five feet tall. But with some of his later costars, like statuesque Sophia Loren, the little Ladd had to stand on phone books during kissing scenes.

    P.S. More recently, Sylvester Stallone is known to hire mostly actors shorter than he—he's not tall—except for gargantuan villain types. It's no secret that Brooke Shields' height is the other reason she didn't become a movie star, and that Hollywood actors shy away from working with the tall and talented Vanessa Redgrave.

> **"I think this picture, this role, will, to digress for a moment, be**
> **very good for me as an actor....They've tried to make it more**
> **real to life, for today's audiences, and more...naturalistic."**
> **— Jeffrey Hunter, on playing Jesus in *King of Kings* (1961).**

But some critics dubbed the non-hit *I Was A Teenage Jesus*, and two of his next five movies were made-for-TV. As for "naturalistic," in the crucifixion scene, Hunter's underarms were shaved.

> **"From his lips to his hips to his tips on wowing**
> **the girls, the Presley boy is the genuine article."**
> **— columnist Dorothy Kilgallen.**

Elvis' naturalistic hips were genuine, all right, but his hair was something else. As writer Penny Stallings put it, "When he arrived in Hollywood, he was a boyish blond....By the time he returned to the screen after his tour of duty in Germany, his hair color had gone from blond to bluish black, and he was sporting more mascara and pancake than his leading ladies." Several insiders said Elvis didn't feel blond was a masculine enough hair color. (In several movies, he also dyed and shaped his eyebrows.)

"Some people want to write that I am a bitch, but I am not."—Diana Ross, not aka Miss Congeniality.

Perhaps middle age has mellowed her, but Jon Bon Jovi recalled a not untypical incident to *Musician* magazine from when he worked as a gofer at a recording studio and had to deliver a message to the former Supreme being: "She chewed me out big-time when I called her 'Diana.' She said, 'Can't you read, you moron? It's Miss Ross to you. Now get the (bleep) out of my studio.'"

**"It's all untrue, and I wouldn't lower myself to her level."
— Madonna, denying she dissed Jennifer Lopez, who
has been calling the singer/actress (eleven years her senior)
a has-been and untalented.**

Madonna may not have hurled insults publicly, but the enmity reportedly began when Lopez arrived ninety minutes late at the Miami party hosted by late designer Gianni Versace's sister Donatella. Upon her arrival, Madonna stood up and declared, "Dinner is now over!" She left, and so did pal Gwyneth Paltrow, whom Lopez offended a few years before by stating in an interview that Paltrow only became famous— pre-Oscar—because of her relationship with Brad Pitt. In the same interview, Lopez said that Madonna couldn't act.

**"Singer Cass Elliott Chokes to Death on Ham Sandwich"
— headline.**

When "Mama" Cass died at thirty-one in London, the coroner's spokesman foolishly offered a theory to the press, which ate it up. The obese singer's death thus became colorful and dramatic. A week later, the coroner declared Elliott a heart attack victim, adding that the "heart muscle had turned to fat due to obesity." The media mostly ignored the death solution—as they did with Sal Mineo's murder solution.

Further obscuring the situation, another member of The Mamas and the Papas, John Phillips, told the press she had died from a heroin overdose. Those who knew her cried foul and said Phillips was trying to spread the blame and create a diversion; at the time, he was facing a possible 15 years in prison for conspiracy to distribute narcotics (his daughter, former TV star Mackenzie Phillips, had gotten hooked on drugs partly due to his influence). Former Mama Michelle Phillips (John's ex-wife) discredits the drug death story and supports the coroner's verdict of heart failure. However it's the ham sandwich story that has stuck.

P.S. Joan Rivers joked that both Cass Elliott and anorexic singer Karen Carpenter might be alive today if only "Mama" Cass had given her ham sandwich to Karen.

★   ★   ★

"Lana Turner was discovered having an ice cream soda at the famous Schwab's drugstore."—misinformation included in hundreds of articles about the blonde movie star.

Which came first? Schwab's' fame or the myth about Lana's (née Julia and nicknamed Judy) discovery? Turner herself eventually discredited the story, but by then it was "common knowledge." A student at Hollywood High at the time, she was playing hooky when she was "discovered" sipping a Coke at a malt shop across the street from her school. Which makes far more sense: Schwab's would have been far too long a walk.

But apparently owner Jack Schwab, who bought the drugstore in 1932, was quite a publicist, and may have even employed one. Another myth had it that composer Harold Arlen was walking by when the lights coming from Schwab's' windows inspired him to write *Over The Rainbow*. Can you believe it? (Schwab's closed down in 1983.)

★   ★   ★

"Only the fans can make a star. That's why they're the ones you court, not the know-nothing talent agents."— actor turned director John Derek, best known for having been married to Ursula Andress, Linda Evans and his widow, Bo Derek.

What Derek didn't add was that if the fans—with a little help from the studios—didn't make you a star, you turn your back on them. After he failed to become famous, he reportedly never gave another autograph. Once, he confronted a teenage girl seeking an autograph for her photo of John and Bo with, "Don't you have anything better to do with your life than this? Buzz off!"

"I'm okay [to] the fans."—Richard Gere.

Gere was known as a difficult, even hostile interviewee. Once, when a female reporter for a women's magazine asked him about being a sex symbol, he allegedly pulled down his pants and pointed: "This is a sex symbol." The reporter declared herself quite unimpressed. Gere has credited Buddhism with mellowing him toward interviewers, fans and stardom. But he has occasional lapses. One paper reported that while he was filming *Autumn in New York* on location, "Chilled Big Apple fans waited for hours in front of [his] trailer to get his autograph. But when the actor finally emerged, he suddenly ducked around the back of the trailer to avoid the adoring crowd. Guess Richard briefly forgot who made him rich and famous."

★　　★　　★

"For the money men, the financiers and businessmen, I care nothing....Only the fans, the people who see my movies." — Brigitte Bardot.

French sex symbol Brigitte Bardot retired at age forty, and although she champions animals tirelessly as an animal rights activist, she seems to have since soured toward human beings. In 1992 a fan from California wrote to inform *Hollywood Studio* magazine that he'd sent Bardot a photo to sign—all the way to St. Tropez—and she returned it with "No Pushover" written across it.

★　　★　　★

"My father used to hunt when I was growing up in Vancouver....Ever since then, I've been driving people nuts about animal rights."—Pamela Anderson, in 1999, accepting an animal rights activism award in front of some two thousand people.

Weeks later, she was seen in British *Cosmopolitan* wearing lambskin coats and leather boots (she had reportedly banned rocker husband Tommy Lee from sporting his leather jackets and her kids from wearing leather or wool). When animal fans complained, Anderson claimed she'd been assured the hides she wore during the fashion shoot were fake. A spokeswoman for PETA (People for the Ethical Treatment of Animals) said, "Pam has done a lot of great work for the organization. We're sure this was a genuine mistake." And all was fur-given.

"Just because I have my standards they think I'm a bitch."
— Diana Ross, in 1984.

She made that comment after personally inspecting the marquee at Caesar's Palace, to insure that her name, and her name only, was on it. Her contract stated there should be no other name or words on the marquee, and Ross refused to begin her concert until "Sheena Easton Appearing in Two Weeks" was removed.

Another time, to improve her image, "Miss Ross" gave a charity concert in Manhattan's Central Park for a children's playground. But the diva spent $12,000 on limousines, over $47,000 on catering, almost $56,000 on security, and $64,000 on airline tickets. So the "charity" event ended up $500,000 in the red. To save face, Diana had to donate $250,000 of her own money.

"You won't catch us!"

—Henri Paul, the purportedly uninebriated chauffeur driving Princess Diana the night of her death in a car accident in 1997, to the paparazzi chasing them, according to the *New York Daily News*.

★★★

Romance vs. Reality

"I could stay in love with Brad Pitt forever."— Juliette Lewis.
Years later, she admitted, "It didn't last very long….I'm not sure I was
ever really, you know, factually in love with him."

★   ★   ★

"Who wouldn't dream of a date with Elvis—how exciting!"
— costar Ursula Andress (*Fun in Acapulco*), who later
revealed, "He had no conversation, and I think he would much
rather be alone watching the television."

★   ★   ★

"Elizabeth [Taylor] was abused by Nicky Hilton, who was a
spoiled little rich boy."— Taylor's pal Roddy McDowell.
Indeed Liz was reportedly beaten by her first husband. However, Zsa
Zsa Gabor, who was married to Nicky's hotelier dad Conrad, told the
press, "Nicky Hilton begged his father to allow him to divorce
Elizabeth. He said he would kill himself if he had to stay married to her
one more hour." Hilton Sr. was a staunch Catholic.

★   ★   ★

"Tom and I patched the whole thing up. It's cool now."
— Roseanne, in 1998; the following year she asked him
on her TV talk show (reportedly to boost the sagging ratings),
then *un*invited him, claiming her psychic said the
appearance would be ill-timed.

★   ★   ★

"The guy cost me a fortune!"— Roseanne, on ex-husband Tom Arnold, who declares, "I never got any alimony but received one-half the value of the house, and I never received my clothes back because she burned them."

★   ★   ★

"Gore Vidal is so full of it. Ask him about his latest boyfriend, and he'll always say, 'Oh, we're just friends.' Like he only sleeps with his enemies?"
— Vidal adversary Truman Capote.

★   ★   ★

"I just wrote a book and told it like it is….If the truth hurts…."— former singing star Eddie Fisher on his memoir *Been There, Done That,* which ex-wives Elizabeth Taylor, Debbie Reynolds and Connie Stevens claim is mostly fiction (e.g., Fisher asserts that Liz had sex with her gay pals and costars Rock Hudson and Montgomery Clift).

The book also alienated Fisher's four kids, including daughters Joely Fisher of *Ellen* fame and thespian/scribe Carrie Fisher, who stated on TV that her mother Debbie Reynolds' crush on Jack Lemmon was "the only time my mother ever displayed good taste in men."

★   ★   ★

"Liz Taylor Busts Up Hollywood's Happiest Couple!!!"
— 1950s *Photoplay* headline. (Decades later, Eddie Fisher said his marriage to Debbie Reynolds, whom he'd previously alleged was a lesbian, was on the rocks before his affair with Taylor.)

★   ★   ★

"Eddie is so much fun to be with…we have a great time."
— Elizabeth Taylor in London, preparing to make *Cleopatra* (1963).

Pal Truman Capote recalled, "We used to make bad jokes about [Fisher]. We called him the Bus boy. He was so boring! But I felt sorry for him too. He was so much in love with her, and she was so rude to him."

LIZ TAYLOR SIDEBAR

"I look forward to growing old with him."
— Elizabeth Taylor, during marriage #1 to Nicky Hilton, Conrad's wife-beating son who died young.

———————

"We're truly and deeply in love."
— Taylor, during #2 to bisexual actor Michael Wilding.

———————

"This marriage is forever."
— Taylor, #3 to producer Mike Todd, who died in an airplane crash.

———————

"I'm working to make this last."
— Taylor, #4 to Eddie Fisher.

———————

"I know this will last forever."
— Taylor, #5 to Richard Burton.

———————

"This time will be better than the last."
— Taylor, #6 to Richard Burton *again*.

———————

"We're going to make this marriage work."
— Taylor, #7 to Senator John Warner.

———————

"I'm getting married for good this time."
— Taylor, #8 to truck driver Larry Fortensky.

———————

"I don't know why anybody would ever want to get married!"
— Taylor, in 1998, when asked about gay marriage.

———————

"When a man is married to Elizabeth Taylor, he need never look at another woman."— husband Richard Burton.

Truman Capote: "I spent several days and evenings with her and Richard Burton. That's when they used to sit up all night, drinking champagne. Theirs was an affair based entirely on tension. They would have terrific but at the same time sort of affectionate rows. They really riled each other up, and I always felt they did it on purpose so they could have a big make-up in bed. She was faithful to him, but he was never faithful to her. He flirted with everything and made dates with waitresses practically in front of her. She put up with an awful lot from him. He was terribly indiscreet."

★　　★　　★

"Raquel Smolders!!...Burt Reynolds Comes Hither!!... An Affair of the Heart, or...?!!"—tabloid headline during filming of *100 Rifles* (1968).

The handsome costars were passionately in hate, not love. Reynolds eventually wrote, "She said, 'Why haven't you made a pass at me?' Without the slightest pause, I replied, 'Because I'm positive that I'd pull up your dress, pull down your panties, and find an 8 x 10 glossy of your c—t.' Needless to say, she refused to go anyplace near me, though three years later we ended up starring together in the movie *Fuzz*.

"Raquel signed to do the picture only after the producers and director agreed she didn't have to appear in any scenes with me. Although we had four scenes together in this movie, we never exchanged one word. Never even saw each other. Her double stood in the wide shots with me, and after I did my closeup, I got in my car and drove off the lot. When I was good and gone, they called her, she drove on, and my double repeated the same shenanigans with her." So much for those smolderingly convincing scenes "together."

★　　★　　★

In her memoirs about life with mom Judy Garland and half-sister Liza Minnelli, Lorna Luft implied but didn't openly declare a not too convincing affair with singer Barry Manilow. She wrote that it was his music that turned her on.

"Tom Cruise is like the boy next door, only handsomer and more appealing."— record producer Ben Bagley.

Star columnist Janet Charlton told *In* magazine, "Tom Cruise is scary. Very threatening, very controlling. You don't dare do or say the wrong thing around him, because bad things might happen to you. He's very powerful."

★　★　★

"I love the ladies, bless the dear little things."—W.C. Fields.

In real life, the comedian tended to avoid women, though apparently he was heterosexual. In his films, female characters his age or near it, and of course older, were invariably harridans. He used to tell male friends, "Never try to impress a woman, because if you do she'll expect you to keep up to the standard for the rest of your life."

★　★　★

"It was Sonja Henie that inspired me to take up ice-skating." — Liberace.

There is no evidence that the pianist ever ice-skated. He also claimed, after her death, that he'd been engaged to the Norwegian skater turned movie star.

61

★　★　★

"Capucine—French Iceberg's Heart Melted By William Holden!"—*Coronet* magazine headline.

The media tends to romantically link any two stars of the opposite sex who make a movie together, and Holden and Capucine made two forgettable '60s flops. They may have had an affair, and Holden did remember the model turned actress in his will, but the fact remains that she was bisexual or gay, as she allowed in the book *Hollywood Lesbians*. Holden, who returned to his wife after filming, later admitted that his "close friendship"—perhaps she nursed his alcoholism the way Kate Hepburn did Spencer Tracy's—with Capucine might have lasted longer "if those two pictures we made had been successful."

Lesson: Hollywood romances, whether real, exaggerated or phony, tend to wither when the box office doesn't bloom…example: that much media-hyped couple, Whoopi Goldberg and Ted Danson.

"I want to get married and stay married."— Stefanie Powers.

But then she filed for divorce from her handsome French husband, cleverly noting, "A man leaves a woman for another woman, but a woman leaves a man for herself."

P.S. Powers was also remembered in Bill Holden's will. They were good friends and reportedly ex-lovers, said to be still "very close," yet Holden, who bled to death after an alcohol-induced accident in his apartment, wasn't found for several days. Neither friends nor exes had gotten in touch with him for some time.

"Some people find it surprising how many movie star actors I knew intimately. But I don't find it surprising…I'm just heavier now." And the polar ice caps have receded.— Shelley Winters, actor/author (few remember her then; it was decades ago that comedians began commenting that they'd seen Shelley Winters shopping for stretch jewelry).

Myth: Romances between an older woman and a younger man end more gracefully than those between an older man and a younger woman.

It depends, though there's less likelihood of a lawsuit to get money from an older female partner. In 1997, fifty-seven-year-old Raquel Welch ended a ten-month affair with British boxer Gary Stretch, thirty-two. She dismissed him as "immature," and he sniffed that she was "too old and too boring."

"Sean's a sensitive guy…sometimes he's quite poetic."
— Madonna.

At the start and, oddly, long after their marriage, Madonna waxed rhapsodic about the pugnacious Penn, who after a big fight at the end of their marriage walked out on the blonde, leaving her tied to a chair (she still declares her "great respect" for him). Also helping end the marriage was Penn's ire over her commercial success. The poetic one warned, "You can continue to suck the big dick of Hollywood if you want to, but you can count me out!"

P.S. Penn also ended his friendship with actor Nicholas Cage—after Cage won an Oscar—by publicly declaring his opinion that his pal had sold out to Hollywood and wasn't a true actor anymore.

**"I'm quite happy to be going to Hollywood.
I think there is more I can do there, and I know it will be
happy, because Elizabeth and I are deeply in love...
she is a very passionate girl."—Michael Wilding, 1952, on
leaving England, where he was a movie star.**

But in Hollywood, Wilding went from male lead to supporting actor. He was English and a bit effete, which in Tinseltown is redundant. And he became Mr. Elizabeth Taylor. As for the marriage, the couple had two sons, but the passion soon fizzled.

**"Daryl's wonderful....I won't comment on the future,
but...yeah, it's great, like the real thing."—John F. Kennedy, Jr.,
on longtime girlfriend, actress Daryl Hannah.**

"I feel sorry for Daryl Hannah," offered talk show host pioneer Virginia Graham, who was New York correspondent for *The Roseanne Show* in 1998. "The Kennedy boy didn't marry her, after all that long romance, and he was seen hitting her in public no less...usually it's anywhere....The beau she had before the Kennedy boy, the singer [Jackson Browne], when she left him, he punched her face and broke her finger. I think she should change her taste in men or just lay off them for a while. A long, restful while."

* * *

**"He's everything I've ever wanted."
— Whitney Houston, on husband Bobby Brown.**

Brown is often called a "bad boy" in the media for his run-ins with the law, and for his alleged spousal abuse. Choreographer Michael Peters (*Thriller*): "I don't get it with these strong, powerful ladies, they throw tantrums, boss everyone around...[but] when it comes to a man, the one guy in their life, they go all meek and jelly-like. Like Whitney, with her man—where's her self-respect? What's he got on her? What she's taken from that guy! And she won't take nothing from nobody else.

"Or Halle Berry…she said she lost 80% of the hearing in one of her ears after one of her famous boyfriends knocked her around. She's not saying who, so we don't know; we just know she's dated Eddie Murphy, Wesley Snipes, Spike Lee, and some others….It's a crying shame, literally."

★   ★   ★

"My wife's not only one of the great beauties of our day, she has the most personality of any woman I've met."
— actor Jim Backus (*Gilligan's Island*).

Beauty is in the heart of the beholder, and Henny Backus has personality-plus. But Jim often told the story of when they were staying in Rome and Henny was still getting dressed, so Jim chose to stroll on the street while waiting. A hooker approached him and offered her services for $50. To humor her, Backus said that back in the United States, the going rate was $5. He smiled, and went back to the hotel. When he emerged, he had Henny on his arm, and the hooker was still there. She strolled over to him and whispered, "See what you get for five dollars?"

★   ★   ★

Myth: If a woman can latch hold of a movie or TV star, she'll be set financially for life.

The few cases where a woman, usually a wife, wins or earns a bundle are publicized out of proportion. Most females involved with male actors end up with precious little. Examples: Michelle Triola Marvin, who sued longtime boyfriend Lee Marvin for palimony but lost (she has however found happiness with Dick Van Dyke). And Jack Klugman's girlfriend of eighteen years, Barbara Neugass; they met in 1971 when she was an extra on *The Odd Couple*. He says it was on-and-off, she says they were a married-couple equivalent. Neugass, twenty years Klugman's junior, sued and lost. Besides which, Klugman publicly maintained he never loved her.

When Neugass' lawyer asked during the trial, "You love your pets as companions but not the woman you are dating for eighteen years?" Klugman replied, "Now you got it."

Myth: Those few Tinseltown marriages that really last are really special.

More than in any other business, in show biz there are marriages and there are marriages. A large percentage involve one or two non-heterosexual partners. Many such cases of, uh, matriphony are loving or amicable, but platonic (like many hetero marriages become). There are other factors too, some involving money, other coverups or instances of image, blackmail, practicality, etc. Jack Klugman, ex-star of *Quincy, M.D.*, wed actress/game-show panelist Brett Somers in 1956. In 1974 they legally separated. As Klugman explains it:

"I've always married purposely so that some Friday night I don't get drunk and say, 'Let's go to Vegas,' and marry a younger woman." In 1989 Klugman began dating a younger actress, whom he says he loves. He and Somers are pals, but he and his girlfriend will remain non-legal lovebirds—and that's Hollywood!

★　　★　　★

Myth: Hollywood's love goddesses are great lovers, more uninhibited and self-confident, because they're so beautiful and desirable, and they grew up as beauties.

As non-beautiful director Tim Burton (*Pee-Wee's Big Adventure*) has said, a lot of getting into show business has to do with not having been able to get a date in high school. Nor were all of today's beauties desired then. Kim Basinger recalls, "When I was a young girl I didn't see myself as pretty or attractive. Boys used to tease me about my big lips and I'd run home in tears."

Much of Hollywood beauty is manufactured. As with Rita Hayworth, born Margarita Cansino, who had electrolysis and her hair dyed red. She had no dates in high school, for she worked as a dancer with her watchful, jealous father, who may have sexually abused her. And although she wed rich and famous men, Hayworth observed sadly that the woman they desired and went to bed with was her celluloid alter ego, Gilda—but the girl they woke up with was Rita.

★　　★　　★

Myth: Hollywood actresses have no romance left in them.

It depends on the individual. Some are romantic yet practical; Glenn Close believes, "I don't want to be chauvinistic but I think women can get along without men easier than men can get along without women." TV star James Franciscus said, "This business is even harder on the gals than the guys. The way a producer friend explained it is this: aspiring actress Farrah Mount comes to Hollywood, meets guys like Horace Zontal and Jim Nastick—her potential employers—and she either decides to leave town or become Selma Soul and then Shirley I. Wood. Then she either makes it big, not so big, or not at all, and at some point meets Morty Feid before finally becoming Phyllis Sophical, an actress of a certain age who has no official past except marital. Tough, rough business."

In 1979 Austrian star Romy Schneider (*What's New, Pussycat?*) told *Paris Match*, "In and out of the movies, with the ups and downs, and even for an actress, I still believe that most men want to be a woman's first love, and most women want to be a man's last love." In 1982 she took her own life.

Myth: Actresses of "a certain age" take on younger men because of their greater sexual potency.

That may be a reason. Others include "A young man is less set in his ways, less apt to be a male chauvinist pig."—comedian Elayne Boosler. "Younger men can't usually afford the best cars, and darling, they're so grateful."—Zsa Zsa Gabor. "Young guys are used to fast-food and eating out...old ones want you to cook for them!"—comedian Judy Tenuta. "Younger men look better, darling."—Eva, another of those Gabor comediennes.

Perhaps most practically, Jolie Gabor, who lived to 97, advised her three daughters, "Girls, if you marry an older man, eventually you'll become a nursemaid."

"I don't believe in divorce, because I was raised a strict Catholic."—Madonna.

But the Material Woman makes her own rules, and did divorce, and had her first child out of churchly wedlock.

"If any couple is in love, they'll have a happy marriage and no amount of gossip will ever break it up."—Janet Leigh, in 1953, on rumors about her marriage to Tony Curtis; they divorced in 1962.

I learned from my first marriage that talking about it in public does nothing to strengthen it, and quite the contrary....Now I don't discuss my marriage to Ted [Turner], and I think it's a smart policy for keeping it strong and inviolate."—Jane Fonda, in 1996; in 1999 her third marriage unraveled.

"We just felt pressured into it...we didn't feel we had a choice, finally."— Richard Gere, on the full-page ad in a British newspaper which proclaimed that he and wife Cindy Crawford were each heterosexual and monogamous and happy together, etc.
Mere months later, they divorced, and Crawford finally disclosed that the desperate ad was Gere's idea and she just went along with it.

"Renate and I, we're so happy, we really are."— Elton John, who may well have been happy with his contractual wife as a friend, but who later admitted he was gay, before, during and after the "marriage."

"My wife and our two kids come first in my life... my career comes a close second."—Anthony (*Psycho*) Perkins. Perkins was also gay before and during his marriage, and kept having same-sex affairs during it; he died of AIDS in 1992, his career peak over three decades behind him.

> **"Well, ya know, I like having lotsa men in my life, but I let Paul stick closer to me than mosta the boys."**
> **— Mae West, in her eighties.**

Though she sometimes used other escorts, usually bodybuilders, some of them gay, the old West actually had but one man in her life, ex-bodybuilder Paul Novak. It may eventually have been a purely platonic relationship. Nonetheless, Novak devoted some two decades of his life to caring for West, including playing her nursemaid. Some insiders said they were married in all but name. West, however, eschewed the image of a one-man woman, let alone a wife. And she willed him a paltry sum—a reported $10,000—which led to his suing her estate for a bigger legacy. He got it, allegedly in return for never discussing or writing about the miss behind the myth.

★ ★ ★

> **"Will Wedding Bells Ring For Esther Williams and He-Man Jeff Chandler?"**— *Motion Picture* magazine headline after the two completed *A Raw Wind in Eden* (1958).

Over four decades later, ex-star Williams wrote in her memoirs that heterosexual Chandler (ne Ira Grossel, 1918-1961) was a secret cross-dresser. She declined his marriage proposal, particularly objecting to his "plethora of polka dots…nightgowns of polka dots, paddy girdles. I didn't know you could buy a paddy girdle of polka dots! The volume of possessions! Suddenly I'm looking, and he's got more clothes than I have. He's got a better wardrobe—all custom-made because he was six-foot-four."

It was widely known in Hollywood that Chandler's hairy chest was routinely shaved for his numerous topless scenes. That was standard practice in the prudish '50s, but now one wonders, if Williams' revelation is true, whether he didn't encourage the smooth, hairless torso? On radio, Chandler played the marriage-shy biology professor Mr. Boynton in *Our Miss Brooks*; when the show transferred to TV, another actor replaced him. Star Eve Arden later explained, "Jeff was a pussycat in real life, and could sound like one. But he didn't look anything like our Mr. Boynton should." Image versus reality.

"I love all women...I love to love all women."— Warren Beatty.

But before finally marrying, he was selective. "Whenever I...turn on the TV I am reminded of the millions of women who have stringy hair, large pores, overweight figures, and rough hands." His playboy image was enhanced by the fact that most of his "conquests" were famous women; such dates and/or affairs were more likely to be reported than an out-on-the-towning with Lois Commondenominator. And although Beatty was a beauty, reportedly well-endowed and seemingly insatiable, some of his celebrity beauties described him as a selfish or unsatisfying lover.

Finally, his Oscar-winning *Shampoo* costar Lee Grant disclosed, "Warren's conquests of women are not totally successful. His percentage is about 50-50."

Myth: Hollywood women are proud of the Big Names they've had.

But many are proud of not having had them. Farrah Fawcett claims to have made it without sleeping with anyone on her way up, adding, "I'm not in Warren's book and I'm not in Jack's [Nicholson] book, and I am proud of that."

"We're just friends."—Jennifer Lopez, on singer Sean "Puffy" Combs; months later, they admitted their affair and revealed wedding plans.

"What we are is happily engaged."— Judy Garland, in 1967, regarding her publicist Tom Green (a publicity stunt?), whom she soon after denounced for having "stolen" her jewelry; in fact, at her behest he'd taken it to a pawn shop to help settle a bill. (The two never wed.)

★   ★   ★

"If she wasn't married, I could really see falling in love with Florence [Henderson]."— Robert "Mr. Brady" Reed, on his *Brady Bunch* costar and "wife"; Reed was gay.

"She's almost like a mother to me."—Barry Williams, aka "Greg Brady," on his TV stepmom Florence Henderson, whom he later dated (he also had the hots for TV stepsister Maureen "Marcia" McCormick).

★　★　★

"He was a father figure to me."—Natalie Wood, on *Rebel Without a Cause* director Nicholas Ray; several biographers have noted her affair with him; she was seventeen at the time.

★　★　★

"There was no impropriety whatsoever in my acquaintance-ship with Miss [Christine] Keeler."—John Profumo, British minister of defense, lying in the House of Commons, 1963. The ensuing sex scandal toppled the Conservative government of Prime Minister Harold Macmillan, who was secretly bisexual.

★　★　★

"Marilyn Monroe Denies She's More Than a Constituent to JFK."— Australian tabloid headline, after MM flew to JFK's birthday party to sing to him (American and British papers wouldn't touch the issue of a president's sex life at the time).

★　★　★

"Kemal Ataturk, the founder and president of modern Turkey, was the man who took my virginity."—Zsa Zsa Gabor. Her first husband was a Turk (not a young one either), but it's extremely unlikely the publicity-hungry Hungarian was deflowered by Ataturk (being the "father of his country," the icon is virtually never referred to as homosexual, though many biographers believe he was; likewise, "Uncle Ho" Chi Minh is an honorary heterosexual in Vietnam's culture and mythology).

P.S. Zsa Zsa claimed she lost it at fifteen; according to one of her dating (chronological, that is) systems, Ataturk may have been dead (1938) by then!

★　★　★

"He's been the only man in my life."
— Nancy Reagan, on Ronald.

According to periodicals and publicity releases on actress Nancy Davis, she dated many men. Patricia Lawford, the widow and biographer of actor and some-time Kennedy husband Peter Lawford, wrote, "By the time she was engaged to Ronald, the studio had even restored her virginity. An effort was made to give the impression that she had been working so hard on her career that she had had no time for men until Ronald Reagan came along." The future First Lady was described as "rather wild, the delight of a number of men, and the regular lover of the alcoholic actor Robert Walker (*Strangers on a Train*)."

"I believe in romance, that's why I wrote it," said Robert James Waller of his novel *The Bridges of Madison County.*

But the best-selling middle-aged romance was of course fiction. Off the printed page, Waller (at the age of fifty-eight) left his wife (fifty-six) for a woman twenty-two years younger. Clint Eastwood starred in the film version, and in 1994 the sixty-four-year-old left his latest younger woman—his lover of six years and mother of their child—to wed, in 1996, a female less than half his age.

"Peter's a very romantic guy. Imagine having a
husband who can sing to you or compose for you!"
squealed Liza Minnelli about her first husband, Aussie
singer/composer Peter Allen (*I Honestly Love You*).

What Liza didn't say was that Peter was gay, and their wedding night was not spent together. She claims not to have known he was gay, and says she found out "one day when I unexpectedly arrived home early. He was not alone....All I can say is, always call first."

"Romance is better cold-sober," Spencer Tracy told
friend and writer Garson Kanin.

So is sex. A biographer of Lana Turner quoted the blonde as saying that their affair was a bust because Tracy was drunk so often he couldn't get it up.

**"A good and frequent love life can keep any marriage going,"
said Mickey Rooney during marriage #4.**

With more perspective, Rooney wrote during marriage #8, "I think that many marriages die because couples get flabby in the head. They need to exercise their brains, read books, perform mental aerobics—daily. Otherwise, they have nothing to talk about."

★   ★   ★

**"Yeah, I like romance," allowed playboy Charlie Sheen
during his brief marriage.**

His ex later said that Sheen's idea of foreplay was "beer and TV" before sex.

★   ★   ★

**"Marry a model, and the whole world envies you,"
rasped Rod Stewart.**

In between blondes, Stewart later admitted that "A model doesn't usually make a model wife....But I love 'em tall and leggy."

★   ★   ★

**"The reason Mary's and my marriage has lasted is that I
always have the last word," offered comedian Jack Benny.**

There are a few reasons why Hollywood marriages don't last, and several why they do. Benny's marriage to associate Mary Livingstone (née Sadie Marks) may initially have been for convenience; they later adopted a daughter. Known in show biz as something of a tyrant, Mary may have had something "on" Jack, who was rumored to be gay. The book *Lucy in the Afternoon* by Jim Brochiu, about Benny's next-door neighbor Lucille Ball, describes how in later years Mary forced Jack to sleep routinely in a tiny room downstairs and how he meekly complied.

★   ★   ★

**"Yes, we're together...it is wonderful. But I don't talk about
Michael [Douglas]. And being a gentleman, he doesn't talk
about me," said actress Brenda Vaccaro in the 1970s during
her big affair with Kirk Douglas' son.**

However when Michael left her (he was still romancing women her age then…), he ungentlemanly forced her to buy his half of their house, which was a considerable financial burden for Vaccaro, who never became a big star.

"I already felt married to Clint [Eastwood]…I don't think having a contract between us would really change anything," said the superstar's frequent blonde costar, Sondra Locke.
But when Eastwood left her for another woman, by whom he'd secretly had two kids, he changed the locks on their house and in order to pay less palimony declared that he and Locke were just friends. For the first several years of their affair, both were still legally married (he to the mother of his two prior children). Sondra remained married to her best friend, a gay artist she didn't live with. Eastwood was counting on the man to not admit being gay, so it would look like Clint was simply the friend of a married woman. But the artist came out of the closet to help Locke, who eventually lost her acting and directing careers and had a double mastectomy.

"It's hard to generalize, but I think most women are color-blind. You know, except about the color of [wedding] rice and, more to the point, greenbacks….When you're an actor, you're fair game. Depends how successful you are."
— Richard Kiley, stage and TV actor (*Ally McBeal*).
Actresses are also fair game, but since male actors earn more, they're *more often* fair game. (Also, for every literally color-blind woman, there are 20 color-blind men.)

"I love the menfolk, and I loved getting married. But I can't seem to avoid choosin' some of the wrong ones."
— Hattie McDaniel, an Oscar-winner for *Gone With the Wind*.
What McDaniel couldn't reveal in those days was her bisexuality. Nor that most of her husbands lived off her and caused her grief. Of one, she declared, "He paid me lots of compliments, which is about all he ever paid."

"I'm single because I was born that way,"
purred Mae West in the 1930s. She often stressed that she
preferred to play the field rather than be tied down to a
husband. Her philosophy was "Don't ever let a man put
anything over on you, outside of an umbrella."

But once she was a superstar, Mae's long-lost husband from vaudeville days—in need of cash—contacted the newspapers and sued her for maintenance, which he didn't get. Embarrassed, Mae claimed to have "forgotten" she'd been legally wed, partly because they hadn't lived together as husband and wife.

★   ★   ★

"I have had three wives and one son, who died,"
Raymond Burr, aka *Perry Mason*, told interviewers over the years.
But the secretly gay actor had had one wife and no offspring. Eventually he was survived by his male life partner of over three decades—a fact ignored in his obituary in *Variety*, "the show biz bible."

★   ★   ★

"Gala and me, it is always the great honeymoon! Means this
moon of honey [in English]? It is very sweet."
— Salvador Dalí.

Dalí's often surreal marriage to the older Russian woman was contrived for his image, and perhaps to convince himself he wasn't homosexual. Neither partner was sweet, but Gala was a grasping, manipulative lover of young men, indulging on the side much more often than her frightened spouse.

P.S. Once, when Dalí was offered his first raw oyster, he shuddered and said, "I'd as soon eat a piece of Mae West!"

★   ★   ★

Myth: The real romance and marriage in
The Sound of Music, as depicted in the movie starring
Julie Andrews and Christopher Plummer.

At age twenty-two, Maria Kutschera wed Georg von Trapp, who was twenty-five years her senior. The marriage took place in 1927, long before Nazism inundated Austria and Germany and led to World War II. On screen, the von Trapp children were delighted with their stepmother and Maria and Georg were deeply in love. In reality, the kids weren't enthusiastic, Georg—who never worked after age thirty-eight—may or may not have married for love, and Maria had no inclination toward sexual married life.

Some insiders speculated that von Trapp married his children's governess to avoid paying her a salary. Daughter Agathe declared, "I can't say I know it or I don't know it," about whether Georg wed for love. "But since he did what he did, he must have liked her." Maria, who'd dedicated herself to a convent-like life of asexuality, later stated, "I married the children." In her memoirs she admitted her shock at learning that husband Georg expected her to go to bed with him; she wrote, "I felt betrayed—betrayed by the One to whom I had vowed my life and my future." Presumably she'd expected God to shield her from sexual intercourse.

P.S. In the movie (wonderful on its own semi-fictional terms), the von Trapps escape the Nazis by actually walking across the Alps. In reality, they took a train to Italy.

"You gotta live your life for romance some of the time."
— Dean Martin.
The rest of the time, the singer-actor was decidedly non-romantic, as when he explained, "Now, for a fella that's rich and famous and a star and all that, he can afford to hire anyone he wants…money's no object. But for the average working joe, marriage makes a lot more sense. How else you gonna get free sex and housekeeping?…The little woman'll work for free if she thinks she's part of the corporation."

"I believe it, in love at first sight."—Desi *"I Love Lucy"* **Arnaz.**
Possibly—he wed twice. But according to most who knew him, when the Cuban met a woman it was more often "love" at first site. After divorcing Lucy he told friends if he re-wed it would be to a more submissive woman, preferably Latina. But he married another American.

"I resolve if I ever get hit in the face again with rice, it will be because I insulted a Chinese person.""—TV talk host Johnny Carson, in 1984, after his third marriage and before his fourth one.

* * *

"If you don't believe me, just follow me."—presidential aspirant Gary Hart, in 1988, denying that he was involved extra-maritally; reporters did follow him, and discovered his affair with Donna Rice, which ended his campaign.

* * *

"I want to say one thing to the American people. I want you to listen to me. I'm going to say this again: I did not have sexual relations with that woman, Miss Lewinsky."
— President Bill Clinton, on January 26, 1998.

"I did have a relationship with Miss Lewinsky that was not appropriate. In fact, it was wrong."
— President Clinton, eight months later.

* * *

"Even a president should make time for romance."
—Richard Nixon, whose confidant Bebe Rebozo told more than one mutual friend that Nixon had admitted to not sleeping with Pat for more than 15 years.

* * *

"Mr. Onassis is a good friend…he is just a friend."
— Jackie Kennedy, weeks before wedding Aristotle Onassis.

* * *

"Aristotle Onassis and I are just good friends."
— diva Maria Callas, several times in the early 1960s when she was his paramour and before he was wooing JFK's widow.

* * *

"John and I are friends....It's not as serious as the press wants to believe."—Caroline Bessette, months before marrying JFK Jr.

★   ★   ★

"I'm just friends with her, that's all."
— JFK Jr., commenting on girlfriend and actress Darryl Hannah, whom many expected him to wed.

★   ★   ★

"I've found the person I'm complete with."
— Gwyneth Paltrow, in late 1996, about her future fiancé Brad Pitt; less than a year later, the unmarried couple had split.

★   ★   ★

"You can bet on it. We are going to get married."
— magician David Copperfield, whose long-term engagement to model Claudia Schiffer outlasted many celebrity marriages.

★   ★   ★

"We work so well together because we're married."
— Sonny Bono, in 1965; however, he didn't legally wed Cher until 1969, for the birth of their daughter Chastity (as a Congressman, he voted against legalizing gay marriage, despite Chastity being openly gay).

★   ★   ★

"Martin [Lawrence] is like my brother."
— Tisha Campbell, in 1994, on her TV costar, two years before filing sexual harassment charges against him.

★   ★   ★

"Being married to an Englishman is very exciting."
— Elizabeth Taylor, on second husband Michael Wilding; the actor was bisexual, and Taylor later described their eventual relationship as resembling "brother and sister."

★   ★   ★

"I feel like Cinderella. I married Prince Charming."
— Loni Anderson, upon wedding Burt Reynolds in 1988.
The bitter divorce five years later marked "the end of my lifelong belief in the Prince Charming myth. And about time too....I learned the hard way that just as I no longer have to save anyone, neither do I have to be saved."

"David and I have too much in common ever to divorce."
— Angela Bowie, on David, who admitted in *Playboy* that they met because they were dating the same man.

"Where I am now is where I will remain for the rest of my life. The family is solid."— Jane Fonda, 1984, on her marriage and politically committed life with Tom Hayden...before she became "Fonda" Turner, as in Ted.

"Now I have what I always wanted...my knight in shining armor."— ex-Miss America Phyllis George, in 1981, on marrying the governor of Kentucky; in the '90s the armor had dulled and divorce ensued.

"When elected, Newt will keep his family together."
— ad for Gingrich's 1978 congressional campaign; less than two years later, he filed for divorce.

"We're sparring partners, the best of friends and ex-lovers. Why should we wish to spoil that?"—Richard Burton, denying rumors that he and Elizabeth Taylor would remarry.

★   ★   ★

"If you love a girl, you love her forever."
— bodybuilder Mickey Hargitay, on ex-wife Jayne Mansfield in
1963; they remarried, and in a year's time had divorced for good.

"He's always been the fun I never had in my life."
— Roseanne, in 1993, describing life with hubby Tom Arnold;
in her divorce action, she cited physical abuse.

"I'm happier than I've ever been."
— Doris Day, on her first marriage…she later admitted he
beat her and was insanely jealous.

"Every woman should be married, she really should."
— Bette Davis, who later admitted all four husbands beat her.

"We have more fun than a barrel of monkeys."
— movie tough-guy Humphrey Bogart, quoted in a 1941 movie
magazine; then-wife Mayo Methot often used to beat him,
requiring extra facial makeup for the screen (he eventually divorced
Methot to wed much younger Lauren Bacall in 1945).

"You know what they say: Third time's the charm."
— actor Tom Neal (*Detour*), upon his third marriage; after he shot
her to death, he was sentenced to ten years in prison. He died in
1972, eight months after his release, of apparent natural causes.

"I'm an Irishman, and I'd rather drink than fight."
— actor Paul Kelly (*Crossfire*), in 1925; in 1927 Kelly (1899-1956)
was jailed on manslaughter charges for the killing of his
paramour's husband after a brawl. (He wed her in 1931 but she
died in a 1940 car crash.)

"I finally found a broad I can cheat on."
— Frank Sinatra, in 1966, on new wife Mia Farrow;
a year and a half later it was finished.

"...for years, Clint [Eastwood] and I were married in all but name. Our personal lives revolved around each other."
— actress Sondra Locke, who later discovered that in
his final years "with" her, Eastwood had another girlfriend,
by whom he sired two children.

"Incredibly monogamous."—opera divo Luciano Pavarotti, in 1995, on his marriage; five months later he confessed to an affair with his twenty-six-year-old assistant.

"He is utterly and completely devoted to me, and vice versa."
— distinguished stage and screen actress Geraldine Page,
on her marriage to actor Rip Torn, who nonetheless had
a child by his girlfriend.

"The best thing I've ever done in my whole life."
— TV star Pamela Anderson Lee, in 1995, on marrying volatile rock star Tommy Lee; in 1996 she filed for divorce, then changed her mind, then filed for divorce again in 1998, alleging spousal battery, then changed her mind....

"[Billy Bob Thornton] would never do anything to make me question the integrity of our marriage."
— actress Pietra Dawn Thornton, the year before she
sought a 1997 divorce from the actor/director and requested
a restraining order against him.

"…the coolest guy in the universe."—1986 Madonna album dedication, to husband Sean Penn, whom she left after a fight which ended with his tying her to a chair; a police report was filed.

⋆　⋆　⋆

"…it really is like Cinderella."
— singer Mariah Carey, in 1993, on her marriage to a record mogul; four years later she dumped her prince.

⋆　⋆　⋆

"I couldn't have married any other kind of woman."
— Prince Charles, in 1991, on his crumbling marriage to the former Lady Diana Spencer; insiders felt he would have been more compatible with an older, worldlier non-virgin whom he wouldn't have looked down on.

⋆　⋆　⋆

"I just knew she was the one for me. My happiness is complete."—Diana's brother Charles, the ninth Earl Spencer, in 1990, explaining why he wed a model whom he'd known only ten days; they later broke up.

⋆　⋆　⋆

"Marriage has been everything I imagined it would be."
— Princess Diana, in 1990; in 1995 she declared on television, "Well, there were three of us in this marriage, so it was a bit crowded," referring to Prince Charles' mistress.

⋆　⋆　⋆

"I marry for companionship…and not to please the status quo."—Charlie Chaplin.
The comic genius had a definite preference for much younger women, often in their teens. His private life was sometimes publicly scandalous, but his final marriage lasted decades until his death. It's said that after one of his child-brides left him for good, a friend tried to console Charlie by saying, "But that's what happens: when little girls grow up, they leave home."

"Romance is somewhat easier to believe in than religion."
— Woody Allen, who said he wed his lover Soon-Yi,
ex-companion Mia Farrow's adopted daughter, for love.

Once, when asked to whom he would be dedicating an upcoming book, Allen replied, "To the one woman that destiny meant just for me, who so far I've been lucky enough to avoid."

Referring to a past love, he noted, "We were almost as one—less, even." But his premarital contract with Soon-Yi is said to be a model of husbandly control and aloofness.

★   ★   ★

"My songs kind of demonstrate how romantic I am."
— John Denver.

In 1965, the out-of-towner approached an attractive woman in Manhattan and inquired, "Are you a model?" She answered, "No, I'm full-scale." He later explained, "If they were available and a little challenging in their availability, and soft and warm, that spelled romance for me." However, after Denver and wife Annie had sex, she complained of chest pains. She went to a doctor and learned hubby had broken one of her ribs. He stated, "I had become ardent, but I was still dumb about ordinary life."

Before his second divorce, Denver consulted a New Mexico shaman. "(He) found three pieces of me that had been missing." In 1993, after the final hearing of his second divorce, Denver got drunk and was arrested for driving under the influence. It happened again in 1994.

★   ★   ★

"I'm an ordinary bloke."—David Bowie.

Not quite. Apart from coming out of the closet in the '70s and going back in in the '80s, when he proposed to look-alike wife Angie he reportedly asked, "Can you handle the fact that I don't love you?"

★   ★   ★

"Sex...it's very important, yeah."
— Roseanne, on one of the ingredients of most marriages.

But so, she informed the press, are separate bedrooms. In order to keep the spark in her third marriage, to ex-bodyguard Ben Thomas, she advocated sleeping apart so that each "reunion" could be like with someone new.

"Pigs."— what intolerant (and hypocritical) radio host Laura Schlessinger termed senior citizens who for reasons of companionship or finances choose to live together without state-sanctioned marriage contracts.

"It's love!"—Jerry Seinfeld's bride, Jessica Sklar.

Quite likely, but not without some financial security. A few weeks after her prior marriage's honeymoon, Sklar met and fell in love with Seinfeld, seventeen years her senior, at the gym. Though well-off via her divorce to theater heir Eric Nederlander, Jessica was reportedly loath to sign a prenuptial agreement. But Jerry's pals persuaded him to insist (he's worth some $250 million, at forty-five). Wrote columnist Arlene Walsh, "He convinced her to sign it by telling her they would be married forever so who cares. But it aggravated her so much, she uninvited the lawyer at the last minute."

* * *

Myth: It was virtually love at first sight for Barbra Streisand and second husband James Brolin.

On their first date: "I resented the fact that I had to drive to this party to meet him, because it took me away from my work." But she found "he was interesting enough for me to let him take me home," allowing that "It is very unusual for me to like a date."

Yet when she found her attraction deepening, Babs "ate a lot of ice cream and said, 'I can't deal with this.' And my son said to me, 'Ma, call him.'" She did, but informed Brolin, "This is very awkward." Then:

"The next time we went out he brought me a movie to see. And this was a great test, to see if he would bring me one that I'd like. It was a French movie called *The Hairdresser's Husband*." Fortunately for Brolin, Streisand liked the movie.

P.S. In between her two husbands, Barbra's longest relationship was

SEXPERTS

"The first thrill of adultery is entering the house. Everything has been paid for by the other man."
— author John Updike.

"I regret to say that we of the FBI are powerless to act in cases of oral-genital intimacy, unless it has in some way obstructed interstate commerce."
— J. Edgar Hoover.

"Hell, it is part rattlesnake!"
— President Lyndon B. Johnson, answering a CBS reporter observing him urinate into dense undergrowth who wondered, "Aren't you afraid a rattlesnake might bite it?"

"Treaties are like roses and young girls—they last while they last."
— French President Charles de Gaulle.

"Marriage always demands the greatest understanding of the art of insincerity possible between two human beings."
— writer Vicki Baum, author of *Grand Hotel.*

"I only read my own books."
— Barbara Cartland, non-diabetic.

"Women fake orgasms because men fake foreplay."
— talk show host/author Virginia Graham.

"Romance is the effort or illusion people, chiefly women, create in order to pretend sex is… not entirely sexual."
— author Patricia Highsmith (*The Talented Mr. Ripley*).

"To be loved is very demoralizing."
— actress Katharine Hepburn.

"Women who marry men they don't love or aren't attracted to, men who are older, unattractive or unlovable, such women cannot validly look down on prostitutes. That is to say, on honest prostitutes."
— stripper/actress Gypsy Rose Lee.

"[American] voters as a whole like to think that their president has sex with his wife. Like the Kennedys…. [Voters] don't like to think he's having sex with other than his wife—like Clinton—or he's too old for sex—like Reagan—or his wife is—like Bush."
— UK actor/producer Derek Nimmo.

"Despite the sexual revolution, we still hate to think of our parents or elderly politicians doing it. Or priests— unless you're Protestant."
— Bob Kane, creator of Batman.

"It's very valid, what Roseanne said about men mostly disliking women's faces and bodies. All the makeup, shaving,…the fact that most men apparently find a woman less sexy naked than if she's wearing some flimsy, fetishistic thingamajig. It's like food, really: if you enjoy the taste of a given food, you don't need to cover it in sauce or gravy or ketchup or whatnot."
— Congresswoman Bella Abzug.

"If heterosexuality was as universally appealing and natural as they pretend, they wouldn't have to be frantically inculcating it—or trying to—into all the kids via TV, movies, ads, books, preaching, sports, socializing, psychologizing and parental hysteria."
— actor Keith Christopher (*Another World, Guiding Light*).

"Sex is natural; trying to shape or direct someone's sex life is not."
— saxophonist and composer Gerry Mulligan.

"Folks who criticize others' sex lives are invariably folks without a sex life or unhappy with the one they do have."
— Chris Farley (*Saturday Night Live*).

"Sex can be nice. Good food is always nice, wonderful even. Sadly, if you have too much food, it shows. Too much sex doesn't show. Unless it's fatal."
— comedian Corbett Monica (*The Joey Bishop Show*).

with hairdresser (at the time, later a producer) Jon Peters. More than one book about the überdiva incorrectly refers to Peters as her then-husband.

"I'd be crazy if I ever married another actress, let alone a working one."— movie star Steve McQueen, after his divorce from Neile Adams in 1971 (he'd insisted she give up her promising career when they wed).

In 1973 he wed *The Getaway* costar Ali MacGraw, who put her thriving career on hold till they divorced in 1978 (but it never thrived again).

"When it comes to everything about the weaker sex, I'm hopelessly old-fashioned."— Sean Connery, in the late 1960s (his first wife alleged that he'd hit her; he told Barbara Walters there are "worse things" than striking females).

By 1999 Connery had modernized, at least to the point of declaring, "Why does everybody care so much? It wasn't her pubic hair showing." He was referring to the British press getting its knickers in a twist over Julia Roberts showing up at the London premiere of her film *Notting Hill* with unshaven armpits.

"I'm old-fashioned, so I think the man should pay."— British actress Coral Browne, third wife of Vincent Price, whom she often complained was a cheapskate.

The bisexual couple were devoted to each other, but she kept secret her millions of dollars, which only surfaced after her death. Price's biographer and openly gay daughter Victoria called it a devastating blow to her father. Browne had told one interviewer, "I live in America, darling, but not in luxury....I suppose at my age one must scrimp and make the odd sacrifice here and there."

"Sarah Michelle Gellar Falls Head Over Heels For David Boreanaz!!"— tabloid headline.

Gellar, star of TV's *Buffy the Vampire Slayer*, called the stories "a complete fallacy. In fact, everyone on the *Buffy* set was laughing about the very idea of David and me as a couple....[The article] claimed David and I were together at a Christmas party, and how we were seen eating at health food restaurants. Well, if I ever saw David put any food in his mouth that wasn't fried in a fast-food joint, I'd drop dead."

★   ★   ★

"Here Antonio is, getting into this car with his new girlfriend."— *Hard Copy*, on Antonio Sabato Jr. and his "girlfriend."

The actor explained, "I got filmed going out of a restaurant by *Hard Copy*. I went out with my sister to dinner."

★   ★   ★

"Romantic Matt Dillon Sends Swedish Model 300 Roses...."
— tabloid headline.

The actor retorted, "That's just a total lie. I don't even know who that person is. There's not one ounce of truth in that."

★   ★   ★

"I try not to read those supermarket papers. They say I'm dating girls I haven't even met...like [I'm] on the verge of getting married to one of them....I'm not in any hurry. I'd prefer to marry just once. I think that is possible, even in this business."—Matt Damon.

Time will tell whether the actor becomes another "Matt Trimony." Humphrey Bogart found out, "If you're an actor and you've got any curiosity at all, you're going to have at least two wives." Lucille Ball said, "In any other profession, I'd have had one husband. But the temptations are varied and very hard for actors to resist....I had a husband [Desi Arnaz] who chased too hard after his idea of success—the green kind as well as the kind with long legs."

★   ★   ★

"Our only problem is the prying press!"
— Benjamin Bratt, Julia Roberts' finacé, who after he wed someone else instead, admitted he'd often wondered and worried if Julia was faithful to him.

★ ★ ★

"Giving up your career can be a very romantic thing
if you're not coerced and you're not forfeiting a great,
stellar career. I was happy to spend more time with
my husband...I'd been frustrated as a blonde—'the blonde
character.' I did have ideas in my head, and commitments.
    I was a founder of one of the first Hollywood
groups to oppose the Nazis. If I'd remained an actress, I would
probably have been blacklisted after the war and in the '50s.
    The right-wingers were angry with me at the time,
because our country wasn't at war with Hitler, and during the
witch-hunting period they called me and my friends
'premature anti-fascists.' I wasn't available to be blacklisted,
but how well I know of the sufferings it caused....
    Do not believe these revisionists who pretend there was
no blacklisting. There most certainly was, and it was a
crying shame."— Gloria Stuart, 1930s star best known as elder
Rose in *Titanic*. And that's no lie.

★ ★ ★

"I think vee European men know a leetle more about
making a girl feel like a romantic young lady. For me, I don't
find appealing the modern girls who play hockey or swim the
English Channel."— Bela Lugosi, of *Dracula* fame.
One of the Hungarian's wives, Lillian, thirty years his junior, also bought the romantic image: "Here I was a romantic young girl just out of her teens married to a sophisticated European, and what do you think he wanted me to do? He asked me to massage the bottoms of his feet with the bowl of his pipes! Soon it got to be every night and every morning....There were many times when he would call to me, 'Lillian! I vill get up now.' That was his way of letting me know that it was my fault that he hadn't gotten up, because I wasn't there to massage his feet."

During their marriage, Bela had a mistress—a quaint European custom. And when he performed on stage, Lillian had to sit immediately offstage to keep his cigar going so he could dash off and take a puff whenever he felt the urge. Yet she put up with it for years, only leaving him a few years before his death (reportedly, Lugosi beat all of his wives, though in his final drug-plagued years he was much weaker).

★　　★　　★

Myth: India's Taj Mahal is "the most romantic building on earth."

Sometimes it's called the most romantic, sometimes the most beautiful, sometimes both. It is undeniably beautiful. But though Shah Jahan built it for his beloved wife Mumtaz, she was not his only wife…so much for a grand, exclusive love. Also, the petite Mumtaz was a Muslim fanatic who ordered the executions of hundreds of Indian Christians, a fact seldom mentioned in tourist literature or documentaries on Jahan, Mumtaz and her splendid white-marble mausoleum.

★　　★　　★

"The only two things I ever demand of anyone is that they never hit me and they never lie to me. The relationship is over the second that happens."— James Woods, in 1997, upon his engagement to a much younger woman.

A former wife accused him of wife-beating. (In 1999 he announced he would be wedding his fiancée soon.)

★　　★　　★

"It's going to be perfect….For a rock star, Tommy Lee is very romantic."—newlywed Pamela Anderson Lee.

Years later, after Lee was released from prison for beating her up, Pamela reconciled with him, also informing the public that she wouldn't be getting pregnant again because "Tommy has been fixed. Actually, he has been neutered or spayed. What do you call it?" No comment.

★　　★　　★

AN IDEAL HUSBAND?

"Sure, I've slapped Tina….And there have been times when I punched her without thinking. But I never beat her."
— Ike Turner in his memoirs.

―――――――――

"At this stage of the game, they don't do much else but eat, sleep and poo. I don't have much to do with any of that."
— "Mr. Madonna" Guy Ritchie, on why he leaves the room whenever their baby son needs feeding or a new diaper.

―――――――――

"I couldn't see tying myself down with a middle-aged woman with four children, even though the woman was my wife and the children were my own."
— (middle-aged) writer Joseph Heller.

―――――――――

"During Jim Brown's trial on domestic-abuse charges, his wife claimed that she had given him permission to smash up her car with a shovel."
— *Esquire* magazine.

―――――――――

"I think that all ladies should be treated like ladies."
— Newt Gingrich, referring to women.
Gingrich phoned his wife during her mother's eighty-fourth birthday party to inform her he was having an affair with a thirty-three-year-old congressional aide and wanted a divorce. It also happened to be Mother's Day….As for his first wife, the moralizing Gingrich had informed her he wanted a divorce while she was hospitalized for cancer treatment in 1981.

―――――――――

"Maria [Shriver Schwarzenegger] is very capable… she's independent."
— Arnold Schwarzenegger.
The Austrian-American, whose father was a member of the Nazi party, has political aspirations. By then he likely won't repeat that, like his father, he forbids his wife to wear pants and thinks women should never wear pants, in public or in private.

―――――――――

"My wife's over sixty and she still doesn't need glasses. She drinks right out of the bottle."
— Henny "Take my wife, please" Youngman.

———————————

"Marry an orphan— you'll never have to spend boring holidays with the in-laws…at most an occasional visit to the cemetery."
— George Carlin.

———————————

"The most grim view of marriage is from the entertainment business. Everyone has a story. Peter O'Toole told me that I should find a woman I hate, give her my house, and skip the rest of it."
— Ben Affleck.

———————————

"She needs strong direction. She's such an intimidating individual, the only way to direct her would be to grab her by the balls, so to speak."
— *Snatch* director Guy Ritchie on eventually directing wife Madonna.

———————————

"Sandra [Dee] might have the bigger career…but mine is more important, because I'm the husband. So now she's had to become a little night owl, and it's a little more booze and sleeping pills than she's used to. But she'll get used to it, is all."
— Bobby Darin, nightclub singer.

———————————

Very competitive with Frank Sinatra, Darin (born Walden Cassotto) heard that Sinatra in his early days had made up stories about himself to make his life seem more exciting for the gossip columnists. Darin told his reporter friend John Miller— who played along—"You've got to make me exciting. Why don't you do a story where I punch the waiter who brought me a hamburger that wasn't cooked right."

———————————

"Cher's career has outlasted anything I ever imagined. I figured she'd keep twinkling till she started wrinkling. But I guess women can get their faces ironed out or something. Doesn't seem fair, really."
— Cher's ex-husband Sonny Bono.

In 1995 Cher told London's *The Observer* the recent advice she had gotten from her ten-times-married mother: "'Sweetheart, settle down and marry a rich man.' I said, 'Mom, I *am* a rich man.'"

———————

"Behind every successful man is a surprised woman."
— Maryon Pearson, wife of a former Canadian prime minister.

———————

"If someone is very special to you, is it really that important if every now and then he takes off and has a liaison with someone else? I mean, is it really catastrophic?"
— Susan Sarandon, who is partnered with younger man Tim Robbins.

———————

"I don't think men are romantic, whatever they crave for in bed. Robert and I married— he was becoming famous with *Hogan's Heroes*, he needed a wife, I could stand a husband, there was pressure….It's worked out. Most of the time we're like friends who live together but try to leave each other alone."
— Natalie Cantor Clary, daughter of Eddie Cantor and wife of Robert Clary (Merv Griffin introduced them).

In 1994 Clary was arrested in the men's room at the same Beverly Hills park George Michael would be arrested in four years later. (The BHPD are said to be as john-conscious as traffic-conscious.)

———————

"Burt Reynolds hated my success. Then he hated me. Hit me. Bad. I departed. End of marriage, end of story."
— Judy Carne, who achieved fame first, on *Rowan & Martin's Laugh-In.*

———————

"I left Sean Connery after he bashed my face in with his fists."
— Australian actress Diane Cilento.

———————

"Diane is an extremely strong, protective woman… she likes being rich. What she needs is a wife. She's not easy for a husband to put up with. I'm no wife, and Diane tends to take charge, like a husband."
— Egon von Furstenberg, Diane's former, openly bisexual husband (in 2001 Diane von Furstenberg married Barry Diller).

———————

"I'll probably stop at seven."
— Mel Gibson, father of seven,
all by the same wife.
Gibson's parents had ten or
eleven kids (depending on the
source), and his father was once
described as "the Australian Jerry
Falwell"—he allegedly moved his
family from the "too liberal, too
ethnic" USA to Australia when
Mel was a boy.

———————————

"Sex in marriage is for the
honeymoon or having
kids….Marriage does tend to
cure you of sexual longings—
for each other."
— Spencer Tracy, as quoted
by columnist and former Jack
Warner assistant Richard
Gully (who declared that the
alcoholic Tracy was all but
impotent, at least by the time
he met "platonic girlfriend
Katharine Hepburn").

———————————

"Romance is real difficult to
maintain within a marriage. If
you care about that way of thinking. Most men are content with
the positives of marriage, above
all the cooking and housekeeping, which are otherwise difficult
and boring and expensive….If
you insist on a romantic marriage, live apart or at least have
separate bedrooms. Otherwise,
welcome to reality."
— long-time husband
Alan Hale Jr., aka "Skipper" on
Gilligan's Island.

———————————

"To love oneself is the beginning
of a lifelong romance."
— Oscar Wilde, gay or bisexual
husband and father of two,
and author of the play
An Ideal Husband.

———————————

"It's a gorgeous, romantic, perfectly beautiful wedding…
what a perfect start for a marriage."
— mother of the bride Joan Collins.

But the proof of any marriage is in time, not the ceremony beforehand. Collins' daughter Tara, thirty-six, separated from her French composer husband two and a half years after the wedding and fifteen months after the birth of their first child.

★   ★   ★

"Roseanne is a romantic at heart….She might be tough
on the set, but at home she's soft and laid-back."
— newlywed Tom Arnold.

After their divorce, Arnold noted, "You know how they say men like to have sex and women like to make love. But with Roseanne, she was all over me, really demanding….Sometimes I felt personally attacked, like I was the lone plate of linguini at a dieters' convention."

★   ★   ★

"I am afraid I will never get married, because I am a hopeless
romantic. I am going to end up alone when I am ninety-five,
surrounded by nineteen cats."—Jennifer Love Hewitt, in 2000.
Tune in later and find out if she ever does.

★   ★   ★

"Romance is not dead in Hollywood!"
— actress Susan Strasberg.

In 1995 she admitted, "I did say that, but it was ages ago, and I was in love with Richard Burton. Who basically, he was in love with sex….I mean, there've been lots of romantic movies out of Hollywood. Especially once upon a time. But as to romance, I don't think it's really ever had a chance. The bottom line there is money, and pinching girls' bottoms—or worse.

"In Hollywood, most of the men still don't know that 'harass' isn't two words."

★   ★   ★

Personal Claims

"I completely disapprove of drugs, and would never do them
under any circumstances," said Oscar-winning
actor Jodie Foster.

That was shortly before she was arrested for drug possession, and thus
earned the contempt of Anthony Perkins, who was also arrested for
drug possession but stated that he hadn't gotten on his high horse to
become "a self-appointed anti-drugs spokesperson."

"I firmly believe in a healthy, organic lifestyle, and not just
being vegetarian," pronounced actor River Phoenix.
"It's much more than that, it's your whole way of life."

However, Phoenix was a drug addict, and died in 1993 at age twenty-
three.

"I'm not druggin anymore."

So said John Belushi shortly before he died from a drug overdose.

⋆ ⋆ ⋆

"I'm not the least bit concerned about my weight....
Being a dancer, I don't have to count calories,"
said lovely actress/dancer Vera-Ellen, best known for
White Christmas and *On the Town*.

In fact, she had an eating disorder, and from film to film her weight
diminished, and she retired from movies in 1956 at the age of thirty. By
the time of her death in 1981 she had become anorexic and a recluse.

"You are what you eat," said nutritionist Gayelord Hauser, and the phrase made him rich and famous. He advocated yogurt, buckwheat and blackstrap molasses. Italian food, said Hauser, was the worst for you.

In the 1960s, former neighbor Truman Capote disclosed, "Gayelord lived in a castle on a hill [in Italy], and whenever I saw him eating, it was usually pasta."

★   ★   ★

"Rumors crop up," sighed movie actor Wendell Corey, "But I do not drink, except socially."

Alas, he must have been extremely social, for he died in his early fifties from an alcohol-induced liver ailment.

★   ★   ★

"The only pills I take are vitamin pills. And you can quote me!" huffed Judy Garland.

But the superstar's addictions were common knowledge in show business and led to her death at forty-seven in 1969.

★   ★   ★

"You can luck out in the movies, but a classy TV series ain't nothing to be ashamed of," explained Oscar-nominated Howard Rollins, who became a regular on Carroll O'Connor's *In the Heat of the Night.* "I'm gonna go the distance. I'm in *Heat* from here to its finish."

But Rollins had a cocaine problem and was arrested several times on drug-related charges, as well as for driving under the influence and for publicly wearing drag in the non-receptive Deep South.

P.S. Carroll O'Connor's own son died from drugs, which his father blamed primarily on the drug dealer.

"If I died of drugs, I'd be so sad. I mean, it would be so sad. I always think it is. A life cut short by drugs. [Dying] against your will. That's why I quit hard drugs." — Brad Davis.

On the other hand, people don't have to take drugs against their will. But Davis died, rather, of AIDS (1949-1991), which the star of *Midnight Express* likely got via promiscuous sex.

★   ★   ★

"Medics, worries, pills…someday I may die of any one of them, or some infernal combination."— Isadora Duncan, who instead died in a freak accident in 1927 when her long scarf became entangled in the rear axle of her open car, breaking her neck.

★   ★   ★

"I cannot ever imagine doing a thing like that," said movie star Charles Boyer upon the apparent suicide of Marilyn Monroe in 1962.

Unfortunately, three years later his only child, Michael, fatally shot himself at age twenty-two. And in 1978 Boyer's beloved wife Pat, a British actress he'd wed in 1934, died of cancer. Two days later, Boyer committed suicide via a drug overdose (like Marilyn). (1900 – 1978)

★   ★   ★

"Aside from a few misgivings, I'm deeply grateful for my life," said character actress Clara Blandick in a rare 1950s interview. By then the woman behind Auntie Em in *The Wizard of Oz* (1939) was hardly working, due to Tinseltown ageism and the rise of television.

On top of that, her eyesight was diminishing and her arthritis was more and more painful. So in 1962 she overdosed on sleeping pills, then fastened a plastic bag around her head for insurance—having just had her hair done for the final occasion. (1881 – 1962)

★   ★   ★

"I think a lot of actors, being possibly more open to their emotions, have thought about suicide. But to do it, that's going too far," felt Oscar-winning actor Gig Young.

He later went even farther, committing suicide after murdering his wife.

"I'd never want to commit suicide, though I've often wanted to kill someone else!" admitted author Truman Capote. "The true reason why many people commit suicide is because they are cowards who prefer to murder themselves rather than murder their tormentor. As for me, if desire had ever been transferred into action, I'd be right up there with Jack the Ripper."

But in 1984 the fifty-nine-year-old bought a one-way ticket to Los Angeles, where he installed himself in the home of Joanne Carson (Johnny's ex) and drank and pilled himself to death, reportedly not allowing her to call a doctor to save him. (1924 – 1984)

"So what? I believe in God, not fortune tellers," Porfirio Rubirosa angrily told the press about a prediction that he would die young. "God has blessed me with good looks, great sexual prowess, marriages to the richest women in the world and friendships with the most beautiful ones, and if I drive very fast, it is because I appreciate this life that God has given me....I expect to live to be old enough to regret everything!"

The notorious Dominican Republic playboy did die prematurely, in a 1965 car crash—his speeding Ferrari hit a tree in Paris' Bois de Boulogne. Rubirosa, said to be so testically endowed that it was uncomfortable for him to sit down, had been married to both Barbara Hutton and Doris Duke.

"Writing makes life more exciting."— Louis Joseph Vance,
author of the Lone Wolf stories about a gentleman crook.

That's no lie. But Vance could never have guessed how "exciting" his end would be. He died apparently of spontaneous combustion while quietly sitting in his Manhattan apartment in 1933. His head and upper torso "looked as if they had been pushed into a blazing furnace," while his lower torso was scarcely burned. Nor did anything else in the room burn except his chair, which was completely consumed but for its frame.

★　　★　　★

"His death has truly saddened my heart."—MGM mogul Louis
B. Mayer, on the death of the studio's wunderkind,
Irving Thalberg (1899-1936).

Mayer often said he felt toward his top producer like a father toward a son. But the #1 at Metro—nicknamed by many Louis B. Merde—was antagonistic to his chief rival, a more youthful, more tasteful and more movie-loving filmmaker whose more liberal, sophisticated tastes conflicted with those of the stodgy Mayer. After Thalberg's death, Mayer began phasing out the studio's big female stars—Garbo, Crawford and Irving's widow Norma Shearer—for he disliked strong or Continental women, preferring sexy or demure "all-American girls."

★　　★　　★

"People actually say to me now that I look exactly the same.
It must be the chlorine."—'40s and '50s MGM star Esther
Williams, in 1999, on looking "forever twenty-five."

★　　★　　★

"I grew older without a fight."— Burt Reynolds, in his memoirs.

Of course, in Hollywood without a fight can still mean with toupee and a little help from a plastic surgeon. Reynolds complained that ex-wife Loni Anderson "got better and younger looking every couple of months. She treated cellulite as if the Surgeon General had issued a warning against it. Veins, sags, blemishes were all anathema to her....Do you know what sort of self-confidence that requires from a man? If we'd stayed together, I would've needed a walker about the time she began cheerleader tryouts."

UPPITY WOMEN

"My friends, there are no friends." — designer Gabrielle "Coco" Chanel.

"I have always found women difficult. I don't really understand them. To begin with, few women tell the truth. I always say what I think and feel."
— honorary male Barbara Cartland.

"I have discovered the dance. I have discovered the art which has been lost for 2,000 years."
— Isadora Duncan.

"Nothing that costs only a dollar is worth having."
— Elizabeth Arden.

"The rich and famous should be judged differently. [Beverly Hills] couldn't live with the little people's tax money."
— Zsa Zsa Gabor, after slapping a Beverly Hills cop.

"Taxes are for the little people."
— hotelier Leona Helmsley, prior to being charged and jailed for tax evasion.

"An actress should not have to worry…did they or didn't they pay the taxes. Isn't that what husbands and producers, and those men we pay, do?"
— Sophia Loren, jailed in Italy for tax evasion.

"I'm bringing a woman's point of view to novels, which is rather revolutionary."
— some-time actress Joan Collins.

"My father dealt in stocks and shares, and my mother also had a lot of time on her hands."
— actress Hermione Gingold, in her memoirs.

"So few grown women like their lives."
— publisher Katharine Graham.

"Woman's virtue is man's greatest invention."
— thespian Cornelia Otis Skinner.

"Time is more pressing than ever, you know, and flirting is just the small talk of sex. Thank goodness it's dying out."
— actress Susan Strasberg.

"All married couples should learn the art of battle….Good battle is objective and honest—never vicious or cruel. Good battle is healthy and constructive, and brings to a marriage the principle of equal partnership."
— advice columnist Ann Landers.

"Anger repressed can poison a relationship as surely as the cruelest words."
— advice columnist Dr. Joyce Brothers.

"A man in love is incomplete until he has married. Then he is finished."
— marital expert Zsa Zsa Gabor.

"I earn and pay my own way as a great many women do today. Why should unmarried women be discriminated against —unmarried men are not."
— Dinah Shore.

"In commercial law, the person duped was too often a woman. In a section on land tenure, one 1968 textbook explains that 'land, like women, was meant to be possessed.'"
— future Supreme Court Justice Ruth Bader Ginsberg, in 1974.

"Any intelligent woman who reads the marriage contract, and then goes into it, deserves all the consequences."
— Isadora Duncan.

"Parents of young children should realize that few people, and maybe no one, will find their children as enchanting as they do."
— Barbara Walters.

"I didn't want to be a boy, ever, but I was outraged that his height and intelligence were graces for him and gaucheries for me."
— lesbian writer Jane Rule.

"Maleness remains a recessive genetic trait like color-blindness and hemophilia, with which it is linked. The suspicion that… the Y chromosome is an accidental mutation boding no good for humanity is supported by the recent discovery by geneticists that congenital killers and criminals are possessed of not one but two Y chromosomes, bearing a double dose, as it were, of genetically undesirable maleness."
— librarian/writer Elizabeth Gould Davis, in 1971.

———————

"I keep my campaign promises, but I never promised to wear stockings."
— Connecticut Governor Ella Grasso.

———————

"I'm tired of all this nonsense about beauty being only skin-deep. That's deep enough. What do you want—an adorable pancreas?"
— playwright Jean Kerr.

———————

"Nothing ages a woman like living in the country."
— Colette.

———————

"Men are like the earth and we are the moon; we turn always one side to them, and they think there is no other…."
— South African writer Olive Schreiner.

———————

"When civilizations substituted God for Goddess, they also substituted authoritarian for humane values."
— anthropologist Dr. Margaret Mead.

———————

"But the establishment is made up of little men, very frightened."
— Congresswoman Bella Abzug.

———————

"What is man but a minutely set, ingenious machine for turning, with infinite artfulness, the red wine of Shiraz into urine?"
— Danish writer Isak Dinesen.

———————

"To young women discovering life, I say, after you agonize, organize!" — Prime Minister Sirimavo Bandaranaike of Ceylon (now Sri Lanka), the first elected female head of state.

———————

"I think plastic surgery is kind of sad....It's foisted upon women by male ideas of what's physically attractive."
— but then Jane Fonda went and had her breasts enlarged anyway.

★   ★   ★

"I used to call them laugh lines, not wrinkles. Now, at ninety, I'm happy to call them wrinkles. I'm happy to have wrinkles....In my seventies I said to a friend, 'These are just laugh lines, dear,' and she immediately answered me, 'Come on, dear, what could be that funny?'"—Gloria Stuart (*Titanic*).

★   ★   ★

"Anybody who goes to a psychiatrist ought to have his head examined."—playwright Lillian Hellman; she later considered visiting one to talk about aging, but decided he was too expensive.

★   ★   ★

"I am very opposed to federal financing of public television."
— author William Bennett, who then sold TV rights to *The Book of Virtues* to PBS for a sizeable sum.

★   ★   ★

"I'm not exactly as poor as a churchmouse,"
intoned Cary Grant, "but I'm not rich the way some people like to say I am!"
Nonetheless, the actor renowned as one of Hollywood's biggest tightwads left an estate valued at a reported $20 million. Ex-wife Dyan Cannon said he would recycle the buttons from his old shirts and tried to ration her visits to the dry cleaners. Before that, he and fellow cheapskate Clark Gable would meet the day after Christmas to swap any monogrammed presents they hadn't wanted, later trying to exchange the rest at local stores.

★   ★   ★

"I've heard of some of the cheap-jokes. Some are rather funny. But I'm really not that cheap...I think it's due to my having a Scottish name," explained Fred MacMurray.

His *My Three Sons* costar William Frawley (Fred Mertz of *I Love Lucy*) once bellowed, "I'm a tight sonofabitch, but Fred's in a class by himself!" According to author Paul Rosenfield (*The Club Rules*), MacMurray was "probably the richest man in Hollywood." His frequent movie director Mitchell Leisen offered, "With Fred, charity begins and stays at home."

★   ★   ★

**"When you have to spend money, you have to spend money,"
the Australian press quoted newspaper magnate Rupert
Murdoch. Presumably he meant spending to buy items like
TV Guide, 20th Century-Fox and the Los Angeles Dodgers.
As opposed to more mundane items.**

In 1999 columnist Jack Martin noted that the billionaire was walking through the Beverly Hills Hotel when a leather sole "came adrift" from one of his "unsightly, worn-out shoes." A local shoe store was suggested, but Murdoch dismissed it as "far too expensive." So a hotel employee saved the day, or the sole, by binding it to its uppers with rubber bands.

★   ★   ★

**"My newspapers always enforce a high moral tone….
My editorial policy does not condone living in sin."
— newspaper mogul William Randolph Hearst, subject of the
classic film à clef *Citizen Kane*.**

Hypocrisy, thy name was Hearst. His editorials and columnists, like Louella Parsons (who reputedly got her position to keep her quiet about a murder), often tried to destroy careers—and sometimes succeeded—by pointing out which married star was cheating or what two stars were cohabiting, like Gable and Lombard. Yet all along, the married Hearst, a father and pillar of the community, kept a mistress, actress Marion Davies, with whom he lived in the height of luxury (Depression or not) at San Simeon ("Xanadu") and elsewhere.

P.S. Parsons became so influential that some lecherous producers would promise ambitious starlets, "You show me yours, and I'll show you Louella Parsons."

★   ★   ★

> "...it's an epidemic of immorality, adultery,...every sort of self-indulgent behavior...anything for a buck."
> — radio shrew Laura Schlessinger, author of *How Could You Do That?! The Abdication of Character, Courage, and Conscience* (if not alliteration).

That was before anyone knew of the self-righteous host's nude photos, taken by the man with whom she was carrying on an adulterous affair and which weren't exposed until 1998. In her '98 book *The Ten Commandments* Schlessinger whined, "I have been shocked by the rampant cyber-adultery on the Internet," about people who hadn't even cheated in real life. Anything for a buck.

★   ★   ★

> "I believe in all-American, good, decent moral values."
> — director Frank Capra.

The immodest Hollywood veteran, who titled his memoirs *The Name Above the Title* also believed in the un-American value of anti-Semitism.

★   ★   ★

> "I don't hold with bigotry, and anyone at all who can afford it is welcome to stay in my hotels."
> —Conrad Hilton, founder of the hotel chain.

Hilton's comment alluded to an era when hotels could be "restricted," keeping out other nationalities, colors and religions. However, the innkeeper refused to attend one of Eva Gabor's weddings because she was marrying a Jewish man. (It's been said that the Gabors hide that they're half-Jewish.) Hilton, a practicing Catholic, fathered the only child (Francesca, Zsa Zsa's daughter) born of the umpteen marriages of the three Gabor sisters.

★   ★   ★

> "Some of my best friends are homosexuals."
> — then-actor Ronald Reagan.

Upon being elected governor of California in 1966, one of his first acts was to fire two of his staffers simply for being gay (which is still legal in some forty states, though not California). When he ran for president he pressured his ballet dancer son Ron (about whom there'd been rumors) to give up his career; Junior also got married, although he remains a non-father.

P.S. At least Senior was consistent about ecology. Running for president in 1979, he told radio listeners that most air pollution wasn't due to cars or smokestacks, but plants and trees.

"Overpopulation is simply not a real issue."
— Dan Quayle, whom comedian Steve Bhaerman described as "the only politician in history to pick a fight with a fictional character and lose" (TV's *Murphy Brown*).

According to scientists Robert Hazen and Maxine Singer of the Carnegie Institution of Washington's Geophysical Laboratory, "At present (1997) growth rates, the human population will double to about twelve billion by 2025, and double again by mid-century....The 22nd century would see the population soar past half a trillion—a density of people comparable to that of metropolitan Los Angeles on every available square mile of Earth's land, including Siberia, the Sahara Desert, and Antarctica."

"Jane and I support zero-population-growth."
— Ted Turner, in 1998, on one of his pet pro-environmental causes.

But to support such a goal, a couple must not have more than two children. Jane Fonda had two, and Turner five.

"Forget it, she's way too old."—Rod Stewart, reportedly dismissing a woman, thirty-three, one of his bodyguards brought to his nightclub table as a potential dance partner.

Stewart is fifty-four....Known for his preference for much younger women, perhaps he should pen a tune titled *Do Ya Think I'm Sexist?*

"I think doing this, this seriously, may be the best thing I've done for myself in a long time."— singer "Mama" Cass Elliott, in 1968, on dieting that eventually took her from 285 to 175 pounds.

After leaving The Mamas and the Papas, Elliott was offered a near-record fee to make her solo bow in Las Vegas. Within months, she'd lost that amount of weight, but the dieting and stage fright took their toll: within twenty minutes, she fled the stage and escaped to her dressing room, canceling the rest of her much-hyped run. She was out of the limelight until a 1969 comeback, and died in 1971 at age thirty-one—but not via the widespread ham sandwich story (see elsewhere in book).

★   ★   ★

Myth: Celebs grow thick-skinned and even learn to enjoy being mentioned by such as Joan Rivers or Mr. Blackwell.
Thin or thick skin seems something most people are born with. As former secretary Ethel Merman put it, "I felt this way before I ever hit Broadway." Professional reviews are bad enough, but celebs usually cringe when ridiculed in public; most don't sue, for that would appear to be being a bad sport. Of course some women enjoy the attention from being named to Mr. Blackwell's annual worst-dressed list, but many are hurt by the insult to their fashion sense. Critiques of an actress' face, body, looks and style cut much deeper than critiques of her emoting on screen.

Elizabeth Taylor declared of Joan Rivers' famous fat jokes about her, "I couldn't be bothered paying any attention to anything she says about me." But insiders noted how hurt she was. And Jenny McCarthy (*Diamonds*, directed by husband John Asher) is still incensed by remarks Joan made about her years back that made her mother cry. Referring to upcoming awards shows, McCarthy states, "The next time I see Joan and she says, 'You look great—talk to me,' I'm gonna say, 'Thanks, you look like shit,' on live TV." Rivers' response? She feels that someone who does ads for candies while sitting on a toilet shouldn't care too much what people say about her.

★   ★   ★

"Always remember others may hate you, but those who hate you don't win unless you hate them. And then you destroy yourself."—President Richard Nixon, who composed the infamous White House enemies' list before his fall.

★   ★   ★

"She's such an icon to so many of us…we grew up on her, we worshipped her….I'd love to work with her, or just to meet her."—**Sandra Bernhard, on Barbra Streisand.**

Though still a fan, by 1998 Bernhard had much less desire for personal contact. She wrote: "I met her one time at the Academy Players screening of something. She was wearing a big hat….I was standing three steps below her, thank God. If I had been taller, she probably would have pulled out a gun and shot me. I was totally nervous, but I worked up the balls to say, 'Uh, hi, Barbra.' Not a word. She just looked down at me from her perch. She froze me the fuck out!"

P.S. Streisand was on Nixon's enemies' list, though not for her lack of manners.

"I never stopped loving him."
— **Cher, in 1998, on the late Sonny Bono.**

Later in the year, she sued his estate for $1.66 million in unpaid alimony.

"I'm so lucky to have met this person. I've never met anyone so supportive."— **Drew Barrymore, in 1994, on her marrying a bar owner.**

Two months later, she'd filed for divorce, referring to the man as "the biggest schmuck I've ever met in all my years of existence." The marriage, she excused as "a green card situation."

"I'm not quite sure whether I am [an alcoholic] or not."
— **Richard Burton, at the time an alcoholic by any definition.**

"I don't drink as much as people think….Drinking is good for not having clogged arteries to your heart or [not having] strokes. They're just finding this out….I'm no lush."
— **Dean Martin, in the late '60s.**

In the 1970s his license plate read DRUNKY, and in the '80s he admitted he'd rather drink than sing. In the mid-'50s he'd advised a reporter that rock 'n roll was "disgusting" but "Thank heaven it is on the way out."

"We'll be very happy....We're in love."—producer Robert (*Love Story*) Evans, on his fifth marriage, to young actress Catherine (*Dynasty*) Oxenberg; the marriage lasted twelve days: she claimed she'd been brainwashed into it after attending a spiritual retreat, he attributed it to "irrational behavior caused by my stroke."

★　★　★

"I just got off tour."—Whitney Houston's excuse, on arriving late at a White House dinner honoring South African leader Nelson Mandela.
She *had* just gotten off tour...four days earlier.

★　★　★

"It hasn't put a strain on our marriage."—Whitney Houston, on Bobby Brown's arrests for lewd behavior, drunk driving, etc., and their frequent—and frequently public—fights.
Though he has allegedly hit her, she denies it. After receiving a two-inch gash on her face and being rushed to the hospital, she explained, "As I fell, I must have hit a plate or something," about the supposed tumble on her yacht. She has declared about their tumultuous relationship, "Contrary to belief, I do the hitting, he doesn't....When we're fighting, it's like that's love for us. We're fighting for our love." Whatever.

★　★　★

"The secret is that it takes a lot of makeup to make me look like the kind of woman who doesn't wear makeup."
— Salma Hayek, who advertises for Revlon.

★　★　★

"I'm not stupid."—Melanie Griffith, who starred in a movie with a World War II theme.
She expressed surprise that six million Jews had been murdered in the Holocaust, explaining, "I don't know why I didn't know. Maybe I missed school that day." Ms. Griffith, who went to Washington, D.C., to lobby for the National Endowment for the Arts, was listening to Senators debating the arts' future when she fell asleep.

**"I am known as a man of enormous good taste
and personal discretion."—Alfred Hitchcock.**

"Hitch" had a blonde fixation, and his final major blonde was Tippi Hedren, whom he'd made a star in *The Birds*—during the making of which she endured dangerous conditions (including almost having one eye pecked out by an avian costar) that no star today would dream of putting up with. Hedren starred for a second and final time in Hitch's *Marnie*. His advances were increasing, but she kept resisting. The director was most excited about the film's rape scene. He explained to screenwriter Evan Hunter, "When he sticks it in her, I want that camera right on her face." Hunter protested, and was eventually released from *Marnie*. People speculated that the rape scene was Hitchcock's revenge or wish fulfillment, and the invasive camera his substitute. Female screenwriter Jay Presson Allen, hired to replace Hunter, informed him that the rape scene was Hitch's whole reason for making the 1964 movie. Despite costarring Sean Connery, it flopped. Hedren had been under exclusive contract to Hitchcock, and made no more major films. Her daughter Melanie Griffith (Melanie was Tippi's character's name in *The Birds*) did, with a fraction of her beautiful mother's glamour or allure, become a multi-film movie star.

P.S. After one final clash, Hitchcock reportedly never spoke to Hedren again. Why? Biographer John Russell Taylor quoted the rotund director, "She did something that no one is ever allowed to do. She referred to my weight."

"I love and treasure women."—George C. Scott, who was
however a wife-beater and abused, among others, Ava Gardner and
Colleen Dewhurst; in later years he was still coming on to women a
third his age, some of whom threatened suit for sexual harassment.

**"I'd rather not talk about it. It wasn't that eventful."
— Ava Gardner, on her marriage to Mickey Rooney, a
bigger star than she at the time.**

In his memoirs, Rooney recalled returning home after a fight with

Gardner: "Ava had taken a kitchen knife to every piece of furniture in the house. There was stuffing everywhere, and the living room looked like the set of a horror movie."

"Marrying Ava…I feel like a champ!"
— musician Artie Shaw, on his prize.
Many years and marriages later, Shaw mused, "Love is an agreement between two people to overestimate each other. I grew up in a broken marriage; my mother and father proved every day that marriage doesn't work."

"I like it. I listen to [disco] all the time…it's the new thing."
— Ethel Merman, Broadway diva who in 1979 released a unique album of her hits done to a disco beat; privately, she declared, "What the hell do they call it music [for]? This is guano for your ears, for cryin' out loud!"
P.S. The album flopped but is now a collector's item.

"Ooh, the rock 'n roll sends me….The Beatles sent me a big fan letter….Yeah, I think they'd like my new record—and how!"—stage and screen legend Mae West, seventy-something, who in 1966 released a rock 'n roll album titled *Way Out West*. Her subsequent "electric" Christmas album included the single *Put the Loot in the Boot, Santa*, and in 1973 the octogenarian capped her rock career with the album *Great Balls of Fire*.
P.S. The Beatles letter never surfaced.

"Live and let live…it's rock."—David Bowie, in the early '70s.
In 1976 he told a Swedish journalist, "I believe Britain could benefit from a fascist leader. After all, fascism is really nationalism." The comment was widely deplored in Britain.

"…salacious suggestions."—what Michael Jackson called editor Jacqueline Onassis' suggestions that he be honest about his private life in his autobiography *Moonwalk* (he wasn't).

★ ★ ★

"I'm a romantic. I want to be swept off my feet.
Which with my weight, it ain't easy to do."
— hefty comic Totie Fields.

But Fields was also a clear-eyed realist: "So a wife can fake an orgasm, so what? It's called politeness and saving his face. But husbands, they can fake a whole relationship!"

★ ★ ★

"My husband Steve has excellent taste."
— novelist Judith Krantz.

As a TV producer, Steve Krantz was partly responsible for *Hazel*, *Dennis the Menace* and *Bewitched*. On the big screen, the X-rated animated *Fritz the Cat*. In early 2000 Krantz did twelve paintings for "an autobiographical account of his life through art called *From Bris to Viagra*." The press release further explained that Krantz "decided to take a brush in hand to tell the story of his life from circumcision...to Viagra seventy-five years later." (At least it was a brush....)

★ ★ ★

"I sort of jerked my way through World War II."
— former movie star Victor Mature.

He was too modest, for he served in the Coast Guard and gave up three years from his thriving career for the war effort, seldom speaking about it afterward—unlike some who did far less but boasted far more.

★ ★ ★

"My readers...I think the world of them."
— novelist Jackie Susann, on TV.

In private, the author of *Valley of the Dolls* told her editor, "I write for women who read me in the goddamn subways on the way home from work....They want to press their noses against the windows of other people's houses and get a look at the parties they'll never be invited to, the dresses they'll never get to wear, the lives they'll never live, the guys they'll never fuck.

"But here's the catch: All the people they envy in my books, the ones who are glamorous or beautiful or rich or talented, they have to come to a bad end, see, because that way the people who read me can get off the subway and go home feeling better about their own crappy lives…."

It's called show business.

"Everybody loves me because I go out there…I meet the people, from the publisher to the guys who deliver my books to the bookstores….I meet them, we make friends, and…they end up loving me."— Jackie Susann, **author of** *Once Is Not Enough*, **her third #1 best-seller (a record).**
Simon & Schuster published her second best-seller, *The Love Machine*, that company's top-selling novel till then. But the print diva's demands were too huge, and on publication of *Once Is Not Enough*, her former publisher sent her a single rose with a note reading, "For us, once was enough."

"All I know is, my mother always says I was an adorable infant. I can only take her word for it."— Liberace, **when asked if he'd always had a sunny disposition.**
But mother Frances didn't always compliment the big baby, who was born weighing over thirteen pounds (on May 16, 1919). He was to have been one of twins, but the other was stillborn and, according to a biographer, "tiny and shriveled, an apparent victim of Lee's greed in the womb." When Frances got very angry with her third-born (of four), she reminded him of his "inherent insatiability and selfishness."

"He does what he does, and I do what I do, and we each do it very well….But I know he admires what I do too."
—Liberace, **on musical colleague Leonard Bernstein.**
Though Bernstein had been married and was a father, he, unlike Liberace, did finally come out of the closet. He and the campy pianist

were by no means friends and very seldom met. However, at one dinner party given by a mutual friend, Liberace was regaling the guests with a story about his latest concert triumph, concluding, "I had the audience glued to their seats." Lenny reportedly cracked, "How clever of you to come up with that solution."

"To die abed, in slumber—the short, smooth bridge between the little sleep and the great one."—Jean Baptiste Lully (1632-1687), Italian-born French composer, perhaps expressing his preferred mode of demise.

Sadly, in those days even conducting could be dangerous, and Lully died of blood poisoning: the conductor had struck his foot hard with a sharp, pointed cane used to pound out the beat, leading to gangrene, then death.

★　★　★

"I don't remember. I was too drunk."—singer Jim Morrison, arrested for indecent exposure on stage in Miami in 1969, when asked whether he had or had not exposed himself.

Morrison was eventually found guilty of exposure—but not public drunkenness. Not quite a deep thinker, he once philosophized, "I think the highest points and the lowest points are the important ones. All the points in between are, well, in between."

★　★　★

"My looks?...I don't think about them."—Elvis Presley, when asked how it felt being "a handsome male sex symbol."

But he did remember to have his hair dyed regularly. So often and thoroughly that by forty it had reportedly turned entirely white. He also increasingly worried about his girth. During his "Aloha From Hawaii" concert in 1973, while singing *Suspicious Minds* he interpolated the words, "I hope this suit don't rip up, baby." Being a big star has its pressures. Baby.

★　★　★

"The projects were a block away from my house, and that's where my friends were from. I grew up on the streets."
— white rapper Vanilla Ice, inventing a more
"soulful" background for himself.

The singer born Robert Van Winkle grew up in an affluent suburban neighborhood in Dallas, Texas. His posture was defensive because his *Ice Ice Baby* (1990) was the first rap song to achieve #1 on the mainstream, or pop, charts. But along with the apologetics came plenty of premature attitude. "Elvis had his time, [but] I'm Vanilla Ice, and it's my turn now." It was a brief one—Van was a one-hit wonder. In 1997, in Austin, Texas, he didn't even show up for his own sold-out comeback concert.

"Miss Ross is not black. Not in her mind, and not in the mind of anyone who works for her."—a representative for Diana Ross, at a meeting with Revlon executives.

The meeting was about the possibility of Ross launching her own line of cosmetics. One Revlon spokesman said to Diana that he was "certain [she] could do quite a bit for the black women's market of cosmetics." According to the book *Rock Stars Do the Dumbest Things*, the diva then jumped up and stormed out of the negotiations. Several minutes later, her spokesperson entered the room and reportedly made the above statement.

A few decades back, Ryan O'Neal was widely quoted—after the breakup of his romance with Ross and her declining to costar with him in *The Bodyguard*—as saying that Diana didn't "want to be black." The film was made much later, with Kevin Costner and Whitney Houston.

"The bottle's out of my life for good."—Whitney Houston's husband Bobby Brown, in 1995.

At the time, he declared that he had abused Houston because she made him feel bad "every time she went off with another woman." Presumably platonically, as per her denials. When Brown made the above comment, it was after leaving rehab—in a Miami bar where he ordered champagne and had a few beers. He was later back in rehab.

"I do tend to think the raunchy aspect of movies has sort of gotten out of hand. When it comes to entertainment I'm kinda conservative."—Bob Crane, star of *Hogan's Heroes*.

When Crane was murdered in Arizona in 1978 police found extensive photographic equipment in his room. Also photo albums, definitely X-rated. Turned out Crane, who made a career out of his average-joe image, liked to take photos (via a delayed timer) and make videos of his myriad sexual encounters with women. Police theorized that the murderer may have been a jealous husband.

"The thing I really most want not to happen is to end up an old, ugly has-been. You gotta stay young, and not just in this business. It's a way of life in this day and age."
— Rick Nelson.

The former Ricky Nelson's fame peaked during the fourteen-year-old sitcom *The Adventures of Ozzie & Harriet*, starring his parents and older brother. He became a teen idol briefly rivaling Elvis, and for a while a movie actor. As an adult singer he had to tour the nation, performing in fairs, restaurants, etc. His much-publicized marriage went sour, Rick became a reclusive drug addict, and he worried about losing the looks and sex appeal that had made him a millionaire by age twenty-one. Eventually he refused to leave his house without putting on makeup first. Ever trying for a musical comeback, he died in a plane crash in Texas in 1985, at forty-four, a million dollars in debt.

So, sadly, he never ended up "an old, ugly has-been." He ended up a young, still good-looking has-been.

"I'm against killing…there's too much of that in movies now."
— Audie Murphy, in 1970.

Murphy was the most decorated American soldier in World War II, earning twenty-eight medals and killing 240 Germans. As the son of

Texas cotton sharecroppers, he'd often shoot a hare for dinner, among other things. And in 1970, after beating up a man in a barroom brawl Murphy was acquitted of attempted murder charges. Most of his movies were westerns, or *a* western: "The scripts were the same, only the horses were changed," he joked. Ironically, the war haunted him the rest of his life; his soldierly photo on the cover of *Life* had led directly to his Hollywood career. He admitted, "I can sit at a bar and somebody slams the door—my reflexes go into action and I am ready to kill."

In 1971, attempting a screen comeback and badly in debt, he died in a plane crash, at the age of forty-six.

"I love him, and I only want the best for us."—Mayo Methot, in 1944, on her estranged husband Humphrey Bogart.

The blonde actress with the drinking habit and the strong streak of jealousy wed Bogart in 1938, becoming his third wife. When he made *Casablanca* (1942), Methot was wildly jealous of leading lady Ingrid Bergman. By then her looks had gone and she was washed up as a performer. The "Battling Bogarts" often took potshots at each other, hurled liquor bottles—empty or not—and at one point Mayo slashed her wrists to try and get her wandering husband's sympathy. After one battle, the star went to a nightclub to escape his wife; the doorman noticed that Mr. Bogart's back was bloody: Methot had stabbed him with a kitchen knife and Bogey hadn't even noticed!

Humphrey gave Mayo one last chance when she promised to give up drinking, though he was in love with the far younger Lauren Bacall. But Mayo couldn't give it up, the old violence resurfaced, and he left her for good. He wed Bacall in 1945, and Methot soon left Hollywood for her native Oregon. She drifted and drank, and was found dead, alone, in a motel room six years later.

"I've been a fan of writers all my life. I thought when I became a writer, it would be, 'Hello, Gore, hello, Truman.' I can't understand his jealousy."— novelist Jacqueline Susann, on Truman Capote, who'd said on national TV that she resembled a truck driver in drag.

Susann failed to say that she'd provoked his put-down by nastily mimicking his babyish voice on a recent radio program and, in an *L.A. Times* interview, "implied that I am a homosexual (big news!) and a lazybones jealous of her productivity." The provocation was all the more hypocritical since the gay-baiting Jackie was herself reportedly bisexual, which she could hide behind her husband-manager.

As for Gore Vidal, he sniffed, "She doesn't write, she types," a line used earlier by Capote about writer Jack Kerouac. (Too true: writers can be just as bitchy as actors.).

★   ★   ★

"I suppose it's rather flattering, if they do it well…and it depends on what they're saying while they're doing it."
— Cary Grant, on Cary Grant imitators.

Privately, Grant admitted he had no use for mimickers. "They're sloppy and an embarrassment," he told friends. Also, because he was relatively easy to imitate, it sometimes caused problems for him. The book *Cruel City* reproduced the following exchange which occurred when the actor was in his Manhattan hotel suite:

"May I speak to Mr. Grant? Tell him I'm a young actress who would like some advice."

"This is Mr. Grant. What can I do for you?"

"You can't fool me. I understand very well that you're not Cary Grant. Tell him from me that I think he's an awful snob who won't come to the phone."

"My dear young lady, this is Cary Grant." But maybe not the younger Cary Grant voice the actress was used to hearing on screen.

"Sure, you sound a little like him. That's why he employed you, huh? I knew damn well that he'd think he's too good to speak to somebody like me!"

★   ★   ★

Myth: Actors with friendlier, more positive images have it easier when meeting the public than those who play villains or "bitches."

It's true that in the old days, a lot of fan hatred was transferred from the villainous character to the actor who enacted him or her so convincingly. Today's audiences are usually more sophisticated. Also, more intimidating actors, from Bette Davis to Eddie Murphy, are less likely to be approached than, say, Kim Basinger (sans Alec Baldwin!) or mellow Keanu Reeves. And more fans are apt to make contact with a female celebrity (imagine interrupting Jack Nicholson in a conversation or at lunch....)

"Experts say that fans turn violent, not out of hatred, but because their romantic fantasies are unable to be fulfilled. A false bond is created, fostered by an 'I see her every week. How can she not know me?' attitude," says Marianne Ruuth, former president of the Hollywood Foreign Press Association (the Golden Globes people). "Celebrities who seem sweet and approachable are especially vulnerable to this psychosis because their unavailability becomes more frustrating, more intense.

"The girl-next-door, the character created and championed by Theresa Saldana and Rebecca Schaeffer, is in much greater danger than the portrayer of the eternal bitch."

Saldana was repeatedly stabbed by a male fan, and Schaeffer was shot to death by a male fan.

★   ★   ★

"I definitely like having a man around the house, even if he's an actor....I'll just wait for the next man to come along."
— Ann Sothern, in 1951, after the end of her second marriage in 1949 to actor Robert Sterling.
Sothern, (1909–2001) never remarried.

★   ★   ★

"*Stand By Your Man*,"
— Tammy Wynette, 1969.
Of course it was a song, not necessarily a personal philosophy. The queen of country singers was born Virginia Pugh and married five times. *Man* was her lone crossover hit, but one of her country hits was *D-I-V-O-R-C-E.*

★   ★   ★

"Former Julliard School of Acting classmates Val Kilmer and Kevin Spacey always shake hands when they meet....

The formerly close pals hope to do a movie together and are searching for the right script."—*Women's Weekly* column item.

More like they shake fists when, and if, they meet. Columnist Arlene Walsh advised, "Don't invite Kilmer and Spacey to the same party. They haven't spoken since" Julliard. At that time, Spacey was "poverty-stricken" and Kilmer's wealthy father loaned him the $18,000 tuition fee, knowing he and his son were "best friends." But "years later, Val ran into Kevin and asked about repaying the loan. Apparently, Kevin paid a paltry sum and wrote a long letter that Val said was all lies." End of friendship—or sponsorship

"No big deal."—Pat Boone, post-Y2K.

According to a January 2000 column by Jack Martin, fundamentalist Boone was preparing for Armageddon or Apocalypse or whatever. He "stocked up on enough chow to feed a small army, liquidated his Wall Street holdings, and removed most of his cash from the bank." After it didn't happen, Boone reportedly donated the food, got back into the stock market, and redeposited his money at the bank: "No big deal."

"I'm not a big optimist, but yeah, I think my future's pretty rosy."—David Strickland (*Suddenly Susan*), in 1998.

Later that year, there was a drug-related arrest. In 1999 he tragically effected his own apocalypse by taking his life in a Las Vegas motel room, at age twenty-nine.

"If John [Lennon] had stayed in England, this would not have happened."—former Beatle George Harrison, in the 1980s.

But in 1999 the British-based Harrison was nearly stabbed to death by a lunatic intruder. While recovering from the attack, Harrison announced he would hire two elite former British commandos as body-guards. The weekly cost of such protection was about $1,500. On the other hand, George dwelt in a 120-room mansion.

"She was that, she was the girl next door."
— Eddie Fisher, in the '60s, on former wife Debbie Reynolds.
In 1999 when his tell-all book came out (some said it was tell-all-and-then-add, others called it *Fink and Grow Rich*), he explained: "Debbie was indeed the girl next door—if you live next door to a self-centered, insecure, untruthful phony."

P.S. Fisher left Reynolds for Liz Taylor. Today Liz and Debbie are on friendly terms, Eddie and his exes are definitely not.

"I don't like them."—Elton John, on throwing tantrums.
Butcha do, Elton, ya do throw them. He threw a turn-of-the-century one at Winnipeg Airport when it took Canadian customs nearly two hours to process his five-person entourage. The slowness may have been due to Elton's (distant) drug-related past. Elton made himself heard, and the city's mayor, Glen Murray, was called in to deal with the concert superstar. "When Elton discovered we were both gay, and that I do a lot of AIDS work (E.J. has his own AIDS charity foundation), it helped calm him down." Mayor Murray took the opportunity to make Sir Elton an honorary citizen of Winnipeg. (Sometimes tantrums do pay off.)

"Yes, of course I am. Of course."
— Angela Lansbury, on being pro-gay.
And she is, but in a 1992 *TV Guide* article the impression was given that her marital history didn't start until *after* her brief marriage to gay actor Richard Cromwell (not unusual for *TVG*, which did a tribute article to late *Perry Mason* star Raymond Burr without mentioning his male life partner of over thirty years!). More unusually, in a 1992 interview with *The Advocate*, Angela claimed not to know the meaning of the word "homophobic," which had to be explained to her.

"She's a strong character, very intense, but that's what it takes, so God bless."— Blondie's Deborah Harry, on Courtney Love.

EMBARRASSED?

"I try to bring a sense of honesty to all my work."
— Nick Nolte.
The honest actor did so immerse himself in his role as a tramp in *Down and Out in Beverly Hills* that his costars Bette Midler and Richard Dreyfuss couldn't stand his realistic aroma. But at age twenty-two Nolte was sentenced to five years' probation for selling fake draft cards.

_____

"I always had confidence, also dignity, including when I was a bartender."
— Bruce Willis.
Known as the class clown, Bruce once streaked through town on a bet. A friend tipped off a photographer, who captured the future big star on film.

_____

"I'm a virgin." — Gary Coleman (*Diff'rent Strokes*) at thirty-two. A "confirmed bachelor" too?

_____

"Irresistible *Magnum P.I.* Hunk Tom Selleck!!"
— *Star* tabloid. Irresistible to whom? Pre-series, Selleck twice appeared on *The Dating Game*. Neither woman picked him.

"People seem to love me....I hope what I'm doing to Regis isn't cruel." — Kathie Lee Gifford on her imminent departure from *Live! With Regis and Kathie Lee*.
The retitled *Live! With Regis* (how can they tell?) soared in the ratings after la Gifford left, and later remained 17% higher than the year before.

_____

"Peter Lawford, Well-Loved Father, Actor and Former Kennedy Insider, Laid to Rest by Grieving Loved Ones."
— newspaper headline in 1984.
In 1988 Lawford's remains had to be removed from his marble crypt at Westwood Village Cemetery— where Marilyn is—because, according to his fourth wife and widow, "The [four] Kennedy children from his previous wife wouldn't pay the burial bill of $10,000." (Elizabeth Taylor had reportedly paid his funeral expenses.) Peter's ashes were then turned over to his widow and the *National Enquirer* paid to have them scattered over the Pacific. The entire episode was said to have "mortified" the Kennedy clan as a whole.

"You know, as you get older, money just means less to you."
— Barbra Streisand.
Yet soon after earning some $10 million for her New Year's Eve gig in Las Vegas, the thrifty chanteuse was seen at Starbucks in Malibu presenting a coupon for a free cup of coffee.

————————

"It's just all lies, man."
— Eddie Murphy on the *National Enquirer*'s coverage of his close encounter with a transvestite prostitute in West Hollywood on May 2, 1997. The actor had claimed the coverage "caused" him to seek medical help for "severe emotional and physical distress." But on July 31st Murphy dropped his $5 million lawsuit against the *Enquirer* and wound up paying all the tabloid's legal costs in defending itself. Wondered columnist Harold Fairbanks, "Gosh, does this mean the story was true?"

————————

Frank Sinatra and Sammy Davis, Jr. made like best friends in mourning at Peter Lawford's funeral, which was highly publicized (he'd been JFK's brother-in-law and possibly the go-between for JFK and Marilyn Monroe).
But before the 1984 funeral, Frank and Sammy were no longer close to Peter. According to friend and entertainer Skip E. Lowe, "When [Lawford] lay dying at Cedars-Sinai Hospital, his once closest friends Sammy Davis, Jr. and Frank Sinatra didn't come by for a single visit or even send a message. Peter waited in vain for a phone call or the merest hint that his pals might give a damn. Their silence broke his heart."

————————

David Kaczynski did the right thing and turned in his brother Ted, who was the Unabomber. He then sold the movie rights to Avnet/Kerner, who will make the film with Disney.

————————

"I love Halloween. Giving candy to all those little kids. Does my heart good, and I meant that sincerely."
— Bob Hope.
It was later revealed Hope gave away not candy but photos of himself.

————————

"She's an incredibly resourceful refinery—she knows how to refine elements and make them completely understandable and saleable to the public....God bless her too."
— Debbie Harry, on Madonna, whom she admits she influenced.
In an *Esquire* interview, Harry noted, "I can't say that I even believe in God, but I certainly like the slogan, so God bless [Madonna and Courtney]."

"Naomi and I are close. We're not that close, but we're friends. It's cool."—comedienne Sandra Bernhard, on Naomi Campbell.
But in Bernhard's latest one-woman-show, she dissed her former friend, then advised the press, "My piece is multi-layered....It's about culture. It's about media. It's about manipulations....At the end of the day, I'm sure that Naomi's thrilled that I'm still talking about her. That anybody's still talking about her."

Which puts one in mind of the adage: Love your friends, love them well. But to your friends no secrets tell. For if your friend becomes your foe, your secrets everyone shall know.

"Good motto…I like that."
— Frank Sinatra, on What, Me Worry?
But ex-wife Mia Farrow later revealed that he would change his underwear as often as ten times a day because he felt "unclean."

"I uphold traditional values…."—Ronald Reagan.
But when he wed Nancy Davis in 1952, they had their first child well under nine months later. (Papa, don't preach.)

"Television is the natural enemy of the motion picture business, and I for one intend to completely boycott it."
— movie fixture Joan Crawford, in the early 1950s; she even refused to present an Oscar on the first Academy Awards telecast.
By the '60s she'd changed her tune and was an avid awards presenter,

particularly when she got a chance to compete with or upstage long-time rival Bette Davis, who was one of the first movie stars to embrace TV. Another movie actor who initially fought the small screen, but then worked for it when his big screen career faltered, was Ronald Reagan.

"Actors do an awfully good job, in performing their craft and entertaining the public and lifting their minds from their problems."— Ronald Reagan, who eventually had enough time on his hands to become president of the Screen Actors Guild.

Nancy Kulp, who played Jane Hathaway on *The Beverly Hillbillies* and later ran for Congress, stated, "More than any one person, Mr. Reagan, when he was president of SAG, lost actors the residuals for reruns to which we're entitled. He sold out to the other side…[and] I think he was already planning to abandon our business for politics and corporate interests."

One example: all of the actors portraying the von Trapp children in *The Sound of Music* sang on the soundtrack album of the movie, which became the most popular movie album of all time. Not one of them earned a penny from it. Of those singing on the album, only Julie Andrews made any money from it. In showbiz, the star gets beautifully paid, the non-stars often minimally. It's a take-it-or-leave-it situation, with countless competitors.

As Shirley MacLaine once observed, "Hollywood always had a streak of totalitarianism in just about everything it did."

"Voters quickly forget what a man says."—Richard Nixon.
Not when it's into a tape recorder.

**"It's wonderful being Superman….The kids love it, and I love it."
— George Reeves, in the mid-1950s.**

The kids loved it. Till they stopped being kids. But the *Superman* TV series locked the actor into a stereotype. Previously a movie actor, after 1958 he got very few offers of work—how many superheroes can you play? To make a living, he had to participate in exhibition wrestling. Humiliated and depressed—and not getting any younger in a youth-oriented field—he may have committed suicide…or he may have been murdered, as at least one book biography has proposed.

★ ★ ★

"In this business, when you achieve success, you got to try and keep a sense of perspective."— Denzel Washington.
The actor, who usually portrays heroes and role models, has, like any human, lost some—or a lot of—his perspective to success. Once, when he boarded an airplane, he was peeved to find there was someone else sitting next to him. He announced to the flight attendant, "I thought I was going to sit alone." The man next to him retorted, "You are alone! I don't know who you are, I don't care, and I don't plan to talk to you!" Denzel reportedly "pouted" for the rest of the flight.

★ ★ ★

Myth: We should always feel sorry for celebrities—they're so vulnerable.

Vicki Samson wrote in *Frontiers* magazine: "OK, let me get this straight: They spend their lives doing just about everything imaginable to achieve fame. Once they've gotten attention, they'll pull whatever cockamamie stunt they and their publicists can drum up to get even more. And once they're finally stars, they whine about their lack of privacy. Excuse me, but if it's really so taxing, why don't they just go work at Wal-Mart or something? It's not like anyone forced you to be a star, honey.

"This all started with the death of Princess Di-paparazzi chase connection….Tom Cruise even wailed to the cops over his cell phone from—what else?—his Sport Utility Vehicle when a couple of shutterbugs wanted a snapshot of [him]. Sorry if I'm not exactly overflowing with empathy. Hasn't he ever heard of a limo?

"Let's face it, with her kindergarten training, Di certainly could have come to Boston and become an au pair."

★ ★ ★

"I'm not this diva…."—Barbra Streisand, insisting in 2000.

Not all divas exhibit diva behavior all the time—and divos do it too. The following may or may not be true, but is according to the book *Movie Stars Do the Dumbest Things*:

"Streisand flew to Washington, D.C., to attend Bill Clinton's inauguration in 1993. When she arrived at her hotel, she asked if her suite was the largest. The staff told her that there was one other suite which was slightly larger. The star demanded the larger suite, but was told that it was occupied by Hillary Clinton's parents. 'I don't care,' Streisand screeched. 'Get them out or I will stay in another hotel!' Barbra stayed at another hotel."

"I'm an ordinary person."—Barbra Streisand, defending herself against press exaggerations of her behavior.

Just before a dinner party in Malibu, Barbra broke one of her Fu Manchu fingernails. So she hired a helicopter to fly her to her Beverly Hills nail specialist for an emergency repair. Total cost: $900.

Yet, when Madonna was a promising newcomer and wangled a lunch date with Babs, they went "Dutch." The future Material Girl impressed the superstar by ordering, and paying for, a whole fish.

And in '99, Streisand was observed at a local Starbucks using a coupon for a free cup of coffee. (So stars shouldn't save money too?)

**"Honey, when in Rome I do as the Romans do."
— Streisand, singing a lyric in the '60s.**

Decades later, Barbra was in Greece and did as the Greeks do, hurling an empty dinner plate at the wall. Alas, a sharp piece boomeranged back at her, cutting a seven-inch gash in her foot. The accidental tourist wound up on crutches.

"Photographers and most journalists are a scummy lot, but at least ours are English—they maintain a tiny degree of decorum and respect."— Rex Harrison (*My Fair Lady, Cleopatra*), in the 1970s.

That was then, and most paparazzi aren't Italians or New Yorkers.

Author Paul Gallico felt, "No one can be as calculatedly rude as the British, which amazes Americans, who do not understand studied insult and can only offer abuse as a substitute." Author Anthony Burgess believed, "You're a more violent people, but our violence is embedded in our system [including royalty]…and comes out in never-to-be forgotten words."

A man identified on TV only as "Princess Diana's hairdresser" revealed on the first anniversary of her death, "She felt regularly raped [by photographers]….She would tell me how a grown man on a bicycle would pull up next to her car and then call her ugly names just so he could get pictures of her crying."

★ ★ ★

"I'm easy to work with, when I do have to work with someone."—Graham Greene, a leading 20th century novelist.

When *Playboy* magazine considered excerpting Greene's latest book, *Travels With My Aunt*, they found the title "too prissy." Greene's American publisher, Viking, also wanted to change the (British) title and sent the author a list of alternate titles. He cabled back from Europe: "Easier to change publisher than title. Graham Greene."

P.S. Greene once uncharacteristically exploded when an American at a dinner party professed that the Nobel Prize was given out impartially. Like any human organization, it has its biases. Surprisingly, Graham Greene never got the Nobel Prize for literature, but it was because one member of the Swedish Academy, who disliked the writer's mixture of Anglo Catholicism and liberal views, blackballed him each year.

★ ★ ★

"Great work bears reinterpretation."—filmmaker Patricia Rozema, on her *Mansfield Park*, very freely adapted from Jane Austen's work.

Casting director Stanley Soble wrote that "reinterpreting and updating are excuses for attempted box office insurance and…egomaniacal imagination run auteur-rampant….Also for gratuitous feminine nudity which still won't bring in the sort of male spectators who avoid movies based on classics like the plague."

"My name is Sacheen Littlefeather and I'm the president of the National Native American Affirmative Image Committee."—the woman who accepted Marlon Brando's *Godfather* Oscar for him.

It turned out her name was Maria Cruz and she was the former Miss American Vampire of 1970.

★ ★ ★

"This is great. This is very encouraging…it may lead to bigger and better things."— Oscar-winner Eileen Heckart (*Butterflies Are Free*, 1972)

The day after she won her supporting Academy Award, Heckart was at the unemployment office collecting a check.

★ ★ ★

"That was the Kennedy tragedy for the year…most years, there seems to be one."—*Sydney Morning Herald*, 1999.

But the same year that Jackie Kennedy Onassis' son John Kennedy, Jr. died in a plane crash, her younger sister Lee Radziwill lost her son Anthony, forty, to cancer.

★ ★ ★

"After children, I love animals best." — actress Maureen O'Sullivan, the movies' Jane (from *Tarzan*) and mother of Mia Farrow.

Apparently not all animals, for she recalled, "Cheetah, that bastard (the chimp in the Tarzan films), bit me whenever he could. The apes were all homosexuals, eager to wrap their paws around Johnny Weissmuller's thighs. They were jealous of me, and I loathed them."

★ ★ ★

"She ain't skinny, she's my sister."—attributed to Richard Carpenter, about sibling Karen Carpenter, who died of anorexia.

The comment has appeared in various periodicals and one music anthology. Richard Carpenter insists he never said it.

★ ★ ★

NAÏVE, OR WHAT?

"The public never felt AIDS was a gay disease."
— Sally Jessy Raphael, talk show host.
The public believes what they are told by the media, and though the overwhelming majority of people on planet Earth with AIDS, especially in Third World countries, are heterosexual, AIDS was until recently depicted as "a gay disease."

"I don't know a gay from a hole in the ground. In my part of the country, we don't have 'em."
— Lillian Carter (1898-1983), Pres. Jimmy Carter's mother, who was from Georgia.
There are also no gay people on Mars, because there are no people there.

"When you get played in elevators, you know you've made it."
— singer/songwriter Barry Manilow in 1993.
But people in elevators don't get to choose what they listen to. (Manilow also proclaimed that he considered "myself the hippest man on the planet."
Not Mars, surely.)

"I think you have to die young to stay very famous."
— Jane Russell in 2001, comparing herself to her late costar Marilyn Monroe (1926-62).
Actually, to stay very famous one has to do either of two things, neither of which Russell did: keep working and/or keep appearing in hit movies.

"I hate being fat, desperately. I really want to lose weight. I weigh myself every morning and I hate it, hate it. I feel guilty all the time." — Drew Carey in the *New York Post*.
But not guilty enough. Where there's a will, there's a way (as opposed to a weigh).

"As a singer, I do one basic thing. I project. That means that I belt the lyrics over the footlights like a baseball coach belting fly balls to an outfield....But it's always been hard to imitate me. Have you ever seen a good Merman burlesque?"
— Ethel Merman, Broadway belter and superstar, in her first set of memoirs.

Not only is she one of the most imitated of singers, but a good Merman imitation is one of the easiest to recognize.

"The thought of being President frightens me and I do not think I want the job."
— Ronald Reagan in 1973. Years later, Walter Mondale, running against Pres. Reagan, observed, "You've got to be careful quoting Ronald Reagan, because when you quote him accurately it's called mudslinging."

"As I got more comfortable in my skin and feminism became part of my core being, I suddenly realized it could have been a feminist movie. Here was this woman who rode rocket ships into space to save planets and conquer evil."
— Jane Fonda, sixty-three, on the sexy cult film *Barbarella* which she made at thirty-one. It's called rationalizing.

"I think Madonna called Cher a cunt once, but I'm sure she meant it in the nicest possible way."
— Liz Rosenberg, publicist to both Cher and Madonna.

Referring to Madonna's success, Cher once said—in the nicest possible way, of course— "[She] should be a little more magnanimous and a little less of a cunt."

In 2001 Madonna sent a Buddhist book to author Andrew Morton with a note reading, "This will help you and make you a better person." Morton was writing a tell-all book about Madonna.

"It cemented a friendship that has lasted thirty years."
— Julie Andrews in 1995 on making *The Sound of Music* and supposedly remaining pals with the actors who played the von Trapp children. It was naïve not to think that one of those ex-von Trapps would eventually reveal the lack of a relationship, or "friendship," as Charmian Carr did in her 2000 memoirs *Forever Liesl*. Carr noted that she'd tried to keep in touch with Andrews, but to no avail.

"I was insane for thirty-one years." — Anne Heche to Barbara Walters for the book-buying public's benefit, in September of 2001. Thirty-two-year-old, bisexual Heche, whose drug problems broke up her relationship with Ellen DeGeneres, was plugging her brand-new book, *Call Me Crazy*. Anne now claims that she is officially "heterosexual" again. P.S. Contradiction and naïveté seem to run in the Heche family. Anne's father was a secretly gay Baptist minister who died of AIDS. Anne's sister, estranged from her famous sibling, wrote a book about their family titled *Anonymity*. Anne's mother also stopped speaking to her when she moved in with Ellen; at an awards show, Anne publicly revealed that her mom had had a lesbian affair.

———————

"I put a very high premium on honesty....As to whether I'm a lipstick lesbian or a butch femme, who gives a fuck? I'm an actress, I alter."
— Anne Heche, altering actress, during her time with Ellen. The naïve ones are people who believe almost anything an

actress or actor says. The words "candid" and "celebrity" are usually mutually exclusive.

———————

"Some people have better-looking butts, I guess."
— Rick Schroeder on his bare-behind shot on *NYPD Blue*. The actor's twenty-nine-year-old butt got the benefit of half an hour of body makeup and the best camera angles and most flattering lighting. An actor usually covers his ass before filming such a scene.

———————

"I always, always used contraception."
— Brazilian model Luciana Morad, whose child via Mick Jagger caused the breakup of Mick and supermodel Jerry Hall. Morad also told the press that Mick is "a very loving father," even though he's never seen his offspring by her.

———————

"If I wasn't in a relationship [with actress Christina Applegate] and he [Tom Cruise] wasn't married and he wanted to have sex with me, I would have sex with him."
— actor Jonathon Schaech in 2000 to Britain's *Hello* magazine. Schaech first confessed his

crush on Cruise to Rosie O'Donnell, admitting that his, unlike hers, *is* sexual. But when asked how he would label his sexuality, the actor replied, "I wouldn't." Others would.

———————

"My mom was the last person to find out I was gay. My father, everyone else, already knew."
— Chastity Bono.
"I can't imagine that Cher

didn't know!…I've known Chastity since she was young, and this girl was a total tomboy. I just assumed she was gay from when she was five. I can't imagine Cher could be in that kind of denial. But I guess she should talk to my dad."
— Jason Gould, openly gay son of Barbra Streisand and Elliot Gould.

———————

"The people who manufacture my clothing line work in better conditions than most people in…Third World countries."
— Kathie Lee Gifford, about her presumably adult employees.

★   ★   ★

"People only say I remind them of Liz Taylor because I'm not skinny."—Christina Ricci.

The comparisons are due more to the two actors' dark hair and pale coloring, also to the young Ricci's air of world-weary sexuality. But Christina, who first became a child star in *The Addams Family*, had a most un-Liz-like habit: stubbing out cigarettes on her arm. She explained, "You get this rush. You can actually faint from the pain. It's kind of calming." So's a deep breath!

★   ★   ★

"[I'm] fed up to the teeth with years of mediocre [movies] and directors ogling my tits."— Sharon Stone, before she made *Basic Instinct* and let the world ogle her everything.

Two years before *B.I.*, in 1990, Stone was involved in a major car accident and got a severe concussion. Her biggest complaint was, "I sat on the street for three hours. Nobody recognized me." Three days later she decided to see a doctor.

Years after, Stone claimed that kicking the caffeine habit cures cancer: "When I stopped drinking coffee, ten days later I had no more tumors in any of my lymph glands."

★   ★   ★

"I really wanted to sue the pants off her, but she doesn't wear any."—the son of Beverly Hills jeweler Harry Winston, whom Sharon Stone had sued for $12 million.

Why did the blonde sue the famous jewelry company that lent her a $400,000 diamond necklace for her *Sliver* (1993) publicity tour? Because after it was over, Winston wanted it back. Stone claimed she thought the jewelry was hers to keep, in return for her wearing and thus publicizing it. Eventually, she had to return the precious stones, but Winston had to make a donation (via an out-of-court settlement, terms undisclosed) to Sharon's favorite charity.

P.S. In recent years, Stone has become involved with fighting AIDS, but some columnists have hinted that the completely dedicated Elizabeth Taylor is less than enchanted with Stone and allegedly prefers not to appear with her at fundraisers.

⋆　⋆　⋆

"I was Queen Nefertiti in a previous life."—Ann Miller.

⋆　⋆　⋆

"One of my past reincarnations was Nefertiti of Egypt."
— Natalie Schafer, a.k.a Mrs. Howell on *Gilligan's Island.*

Now, one cannot prove or disprove reincarnation. But notice how many people living at the same time claim to have been Nefertiti or Cleopatra or Napoleon?

⋆　⋆　⋆

"I'm gonna live forever—at least ninety!"
— *Beverly Hills Cop* producer Don Simpson, in 1994.

Because he was drug-addicted, Simpson got himself a personal drug-expert doctor. In 1996, Simpson died at age fifty-two—months after his doctor, who turned out to have been a fellow addict.

⋆　⋆　⋆

"…and we live longer than men. We're very lucky."
— Jane Fonda.

However, actor-writer Carrie Fisher feels, "Well, it's longer for women, but only at the bad end. I wish we got our seven extra years (of lifespan) up front, or in the middle somewhere (because) we look worse faster."

⋆　⋆　⋆

"He doesn't age. He's like one of those male pin-ups they
have in the gay magazines."
— Puerto Rican actor Raul Julia, on Mel Gibson.

Gibson has stopped not aging. As Australian Nobel Prize-winning writer Patrick White put it, "First a star twinkles, then she wrinkles." With the actors generally wrinkling far more above and between the eyebrows than actresses—Gibson being a good example.

"I don't want to surgically move my fanny up to
my shoulders. I just don't want to do it (plastic surgery).
It seems unnatural to me. I love the acting business…
but I have to draw the line at blood sacrifice."
— fifty-three-year-old Tyne Daly, of TV's *Judging Amy*.

Plastic surgery isn't much more "unnatural" than cutting or dyeing one's hair, just more drastic—and more necessary for people who want to look young after a certain age. As for whether Daly has had any, if one sees her close up, she has no bags beneath her eyes. Which for someone her age would be quite remarkable….

P.S. Not everyone goes the whole hog, pardon the expression. Some just have a nip here or a tuck there; eyebag and eyelid surgery are the most common operations on actors.

"I'm too old to talk about my dating routine,
as if I even had one."— Joan Rivers.

"At my age, I'm flattered people even think I have a sex life,
never mind speculating about what kind."
— former New York mayor Ed Koch.

But elderly is as elderly does, and not every
senior citizen requires a date or a lover to feel, shall we say,
the flush of spring. *Titanic* star Gloria Stuart, ninety, wrote
in her memoirs about one of her secrets for staying young:
"I am devoted to masturbation. I had and have no guilt
whatsoever when it comes to pleasuring myself."
(Which proves one's never too old to loin.)

"It's so embarrassing [in America].
The reporters will ask anything, even about sex and
affairs and infidelities…there are no limits."
— Joan Collins, in the 1960s.

But in the '80s and '90s, Collins was writing her own books, telling about sex, affairs, etc. And not just about herself—she revealed that her younger sister (novelist Jackie Collins) had been deflowered by Marlon Brando.

"I hate interviews….Journalists can get so damn personal!"
— Meg Ryan.

They can try, but as Oscar Wilde once said, "Questions are never indiscreet, but answers sometimes are."

Costars and Cohorts

**Myth: Fans aren't really that "fanatic"
about their favorite stars.**

Russian ballet star Alexander Godunov said, "Marilyn Monroe was my dream lover…and not only when I was alone." Impressionist Charles Pierce felt that "Ramon Novarro was as real to me as anyone in my romantic life. Not a very good actor, but one of the most appealing and vivid men that ever lived."

And in 1999 Audrey Jean Knauer of Louisville, Kentucky, stated in her will that "under no circumstances is my mother Helen to inherit anything from me." Rather, Knauer left some $300,000 to her favorite star, Charles Bronson.

★   ★   ★

**"Dana's cool….She's a cool girl."—Gary Coleman,
on his former *Diff'rent Strokes* costar Dana Plato.**

But after her premature death from drugs in 1999, Coleman's attitude had cooled. "My thoughts were more for her son and the press issue and whether it would affect my ability to get employment." The diminutive ex-actor, estranged from his parents, had recently filed for bankruptcy, and continued, "I have lifestyle requirements. Photos, meetings, lunches, dinners, facial care, tooth care. It requires an exorbitant amount of money." But minimal grief.

★   ★   ★

**"Yes, I would defend him. And I would win."
— author and Harvard University law professor Alan
Dershowitz, on whether he would defend Adolf Hitler
(he successfully defended Claus von Bulow).**

"I write songs for the Eagles."
— **Patti Davis, daughter of Ronald and Nancy (Davis) Reagan.**
Singular, not plural. In the 1970s Eagles guitar and vocalist Bernie Leadon dated Davis. He persuaded the band to include her song *I Give You Peace* on their album *One of These Nights*. The group was furious when the ambitious Patti made the above comment to the press.

*　*　*

"Marvin [Gaye] was great to work with."—Diana Ross, in 1973, about a record she'd made the year before with him.
Ross had been pregnant at the time, but the singer lit up a joint in front of her. She complained. He retorted, "I'm sorry, baby, but I got to have my dope or I can't sing." Screamed Diana, "What kind of crap is this?" before throwing grapes at producer Berry Gordy and walking out. The singers recorded their parts separately.

*　*　*

"Your deep faith in God and adherence to traditional values are an inspiration to all of us."
— **then-president Reagan, in a telegram to Michael Jackson.**

139

*　*　*

"Michael is pretty stable. I think it's his raising."
—**mother Katherine Jackson.**

*　*　*

"You're displaying some pretty bad judgment."
— **Elvis Presley's personal physician, Dr. "Nick," who'd prescribed the twenty-five or so pills Elvis would ingest daily, after the doc took away his pills and Presley reacted by shooting at him.**
In 1970 Elvis had met with President Nixon and informed him he'd been studying the drug culture for a decade. The singer hugged the prez and gave him a pistol. Nixon gave him an honorary Narcotics Bureau badge, unaware that Presley's war on drugs was being waged at home.

P.S. Elvis also feared that the Beatles might have "communistic" tendencies, because of their longer haircuts. More likely, he was jealous, for the Fab Four knocked the Pelvis off the charts for years to come.

"I think I am the reincarnation of Patsy Cline. You may think Patsy Cline died in a plane crash in 1963, but she's living right here in my merry body, I tell ya."—k.d. lang, in 1987.

In 1982, lang had asked, "Who's Patsy Cline?" when told to act like her at a musical show in Canada. In 1992, lang said of Cline, "She's kind of moved on. I'm sure she's picked some young singer to pick on now."

★   ★   ★

"I like Beethoven, especially the poems."
— Beatle Ringo Starr.

★   ★   ★

"Oh, they're playing *Song Sung Blue*."—Neil Diamond, out in London after a gig, listening to background music.

"No," a friend corrected him, "they're playing Mozart." Diamond had forgotten that he'd "borrowed" the tune to his hit song from Mozart's Piano Concerto #21.

P.S. When Diamond played Australia he wore a t-shirt reading, "I'm not Neil Diamond—I just look like him."

P.P.S. Mozart, at age two, heard a pig squeal, and cried, "G-sharp!" Somebody went to a piano and struck a G-sharp. The child was correct.

★   ★   ★

"Well, the key to it is research, really. We always do a lot of research."—British writer/director Mike Leigh, on the key to the "authenticity" of some of his films, in an interview about his latest, *Topsy-Turvy*.

Research means little if it isn't applied to the final product, and *Topsy-Turvy* was about Victorian composers Gilbert & Sullivan. Leigh left out one major "detail" in his overly mainstreamed movie: Sir Arthur Sullivan (1842-1900) was gay. Wrote historian Martin Greif, "Sullivan's homosexuality, though widely known to his contemporaries, was practiced discreetly. He played by the rules that permitted the upper classes their 'vices' so long as there was no threat of public scandal.

"That Sullivan, unlike his straight partner, was knighted shows how well, and how prudently, he played the game. Hypocritical? Perhaps. But the Irish Oscar Wilde might not have died quite so young had he understood the English character as well as Sullivan."

Hypocrisy and lack of integrity are not limited to Hollywood.

★   ★   ★

"I was as candid as I could be."
— former movie star Esther Williams, regarding her memoirs, in
which she stated boyfriend Jeff Chandler was a transvestite.

A number of people who knew actor Chandler (1918-1961) question the revelation, which could have been, if true, very much hidden. Why hadn't Williams said it before (before she had a book to sell)? She joked about a "statute of limitations." What she did not address in the book—for, she did marry him—were the widespread rumors that actor Fernando Lamas was bisexual....

★   ★   ★

"There isn't that much money in the world."
— Scottish rocker Rod Stewart's response when
girlfriend Britt Ekland sued him for $12.5 million after their
split (more disbelief was to come: after he broke with
Kelly Emberg, she sued him for $25 million).

★   ★   ★

"Her looks emphatically outstrip her talent."—Laurence
Olivier, on ex-wife Vivien Leigh, who won two Best Actress Oscars.

★   ★   ★

"She's unprofessional and not a very talented actress," said
Michael Douglas in 1998, referring to costar Gwyneth
Paltrow's comments that maybe their film *A Perfect Murder*
flopped because Douglas was too old to be her love interest.
He added, "Miss Paltrow isn't as well-known for her acting as
she is for the men she's been involved with," referring
primarily to her long affair with Brad Pitt.

Douglas spoke too soon. In early 1999 Paltrow hit it big with *Shakespeare in Love*—featuring a male costar of her own generation—and the year's Academy Award for Best Actress.

P.S. Jodie Foster had sued after she was dropped from a project that was to team her with Douglas as her father. But he didn't want to play his age, so the female star was dropped, replaced by a less powerful and demanding actress.

* * *

"I love her. She's my long-lost sister," prematurely affirmed Rosanna Arquette, star of *Desperately Seeking Susan*, about costar Madonna, whose big-time screen bow the film was (which reviewers said she stole).

But during filming, tempers flared when a scene of Rosanna's was rewritten to highlight the ambitious blonde. The sisterly feeling didn't return, and post-*Susan* the two are no more than ex-costars, chilly ones at that.

* * *

"This is more than friendship, and it's going to endure," proffered comedienne Sandra Bernhard about Madonna, who announced that she didn't mind if people thought they were lovers. "Nothing can come between us because we're friends, not competitors," felt Bernhard.

What came between Sandra and Madonna was Bernhard's lesbian girl-friend, Cuban model turned entrepreneur Ingrid Casares. Madonna took her up and dropped Bernhard (she also appropriated the song *Fever*, which Sandy had done in her nightclub act for years, and used it on her latest album). Bernhard was furious and began an anti-Madonna campaign which has yet to abate, while Madonna and Ingrid have remained friends (some say more than friends, although the pop tart has asserted that she's not lesbian—say bi, bi, baby?).

* * *

"I met them all at about the same time. It was so lucky, like, as totally fated....These three people will always be integral to my life," said Madonna of husband Sean Penn, costar and perhaps lover Warren Beatty, and friend and perhaps lover Sandra Bernhard in the mid-1980s.

Less than a decade later, she was through with all three.

* * *

**"Bob [Hope] and I are great pals. The best of friends.
If I seem to worship the ground he walks on, it's because
it's prime real estate," noted Bing Crosby.**

The frequent costars afforded each other extra publicity by publicly parading as friends, ribbing each other on stage and even in their separate movies, etc. In reality, they were financially competitive (Hope even richer than Crosby) and didn't socialize much, if at all. "Whenever they met," said *Road*-movies costar Dorothy Lamour, "it was usually for the cameras or other publicity….They were never enemies, but pals? No, no." Hope's nephew Peter Malatesta revealed, "They're each too cold and domineering to be very close to anyone they can't either screw or control."

★　★　★

**"Adam West and I are friends, not just costars.
We get along just super," declared Burt Ward, aka Robin the
Boy Wonder, of his *Batman* costar in the 1960s.**

Some three decades later, Ward wrote, "What that kind of actor [West] really wants…is to be onscreen every second of every day with no distractions, such as commercials or other actors—just limitless closeups of his face. This is the person who envisions conquering everyone and forcing them to fix their attention on him, and to worship him like a god—the ultimate screen hog.

"We all know what happens to hogs. They get slaughtered."

★　★　★

**"Diana [Ross] is more than my best friend," chirped Michael
Jackson. " I love her. I really and truly love her."**

Like a sister? Jackson and Ross were great for each other, publicity-wise. At first, he basked in her bigger star-glow. Later, as her star descended, his megastar shine reflected on her. But both were quite competitive, and after she married a Norwegian tycoon and moved out of Michael's sphere of influence, the real friction began. He refused her social invitations, and she pulled out of hosting a TV special about him. The final split occurred after his child-molestation scandal broke; Michael was hurt that Diana—a mother of five—didn't publicly stand by her man-boy friend.

"[I'm] unable to attend…for reasons my
mother would have understood."
— Liza Minnelli, in 1998, on why she would not participate in a
two-week tribute to her mother Judy Garland at Carnegie Hall.

Reportedly, the true reason was the ongoing feud between Liza and her half-sister Lorna Luft, who was hosting the event. In 1999 Liza did her own, Luft-less show in New York, paying tribute to her father, Vincente Minnelli. It was titled *Minnelli On Minnelli*. So there.

★ ★ ★

"Are you getting this?!"—Demi Moore, yelling at three
cameramen she'd hired to film her first baby's birth, just as its head
was coming out. Moore later complained about paparazzi taking
pictures of her kids, although daughter Rumer appeared in her movie
Striptease, in which mommy appeared topless.

Once, at a Baltimore hotel, Moore took her kids to the pool area. One hopped into the jacuzzi, where children weren't allowed. When a hotel staffer pointed this out, Moore gave him the bird, began screaming obscenities at him in front of her kids, and later had him fired. Five months later, when one of Demi's staff was heard cussing in front of her daughter, she was immediately dismissed.

Demi Moore's own mother Virginia informed the tabloids that she and her daughter had done drugs together. The star was furious. After Virginia was arrested for drunk driving, Demi declined to bail her out.

"I don't like to take my clothes off," demure Demi declared. She had a secondary role as Michael Caine's daughter in *Blame It On Rio*. The attractive young blonde newcomer who played her pal, in love with Caine, took everything off. Moore took nothing off, but later made up for it by going topless in six movies, appearing in a revealing spread in *Oui* magazine, and posing nude for the cover of *Vanity Fair* twice.

★ ★ ★

"Nudity should be barred from actors over twenty-five,
and anyone fat or unsightly….Americans are mostly too shy
for it, and…I think [UK] actors like Alan [Bates] and
Glenda Jackson must have a strong exhibitionist streak."
— Oliver Reed, in 1972.

However, the British actor (nephew of director Sir Carol Reed) had already appeared fully nude opposite Alan Bates in *Women in Love* (1969), at age thirty-one.

P.S. Eventually, Hollywood actors were no more shy about taking it off than their UK counterparts. At least not the female ones.

★　★　★

"He won't do drugs. He won't take his pants off without underwear. And he will not be unmanly and let some girl, you know, dominate him."—Elvis Presley, enumerating what his screen characters would not do.

Of course actors act, and it's not necessarily hypocritical to do in life what, acting, one wouldn't do on screen. Unless one pretends one is one's image. But when Elvis met Barbra Streisand in her dressing room, he said, "Hi," then dropped to one knee and began painting her fingernails. Presley decided not to costar with Streisand in her *A Star Is Born* remake, afraid she might dominate him as she often did her leading men. In real life, girlfriend Linda Thompson once saved Elvis from drowning after he passed out, face-first, into a bowl of soup.

★　★　★

"No, I don't think so," replied Madonna in 1989 when *Rolling Stone* asked if she had a child, would she raise it Catholic?

"Catholicism is not a soothing religion. It's a painful religion." She added, "I can't describe the way I pray. It has nothing to do with religion."

In 1996 Madonna named her newborn daughter Lourdes Maria.

★　★　★

"[I] try to be the best mother I can possibly be," gushed Kathie Lee Gifford.

According to *The I Hate Kathie Lee Gifford Book*, she told son Cody, "I won't talk about you on the show if it's not okay with you. But then Mommy's going to have to find a new job and you might not be able to go to Disneyland anymore."

UNCONGENIAL COLLEAGUES

"You look disgustin!"
— Danny Bonaduce to *Partridge Family* costar Susan Dey, when he saw her in a bikini. Supposedly, the 5'7", eighty-nine-pound actress was so shocked, she finally began to battle her eating disorders. However, by the late '90s Dey was said to be so gaunt and "worn out" that former costar Shirley Jones passed her on a Beverly Hills street without recognizing her (Jones played Dey's mother on the sitcom).

_____

"He's a tyrant, and I don't like him!"
— Frances Bavier ("Aunt Bee"), on her costar and employer, Andy Griffith.

_____

"She grabbed that lip and just ripped it right off."
— John Cusack, complaining about Julia Roberts' kissing technique while filming *America's Sweethearts*.

_____

"Actually, my mother got along with Whoopi beautifully, because my mother's a dyke."
— Ted Danson (*Cheers*) on costar-pal Whoopi Goldberg at a 1993 Friars roast.

_____

"I feel just like Oprah, except my man married me and I let other people read what they want."
— Lovita
(*The Steve Harvey Show*).

_____

"She projects the passion of a Good Humor ice cream: frozen, on a stick, and all vanilla."
— Spencer Tracy on actress Nancy Davis, later Nancy Reagan.

_____

"I made over seventy movies and that [*Shadow on the Wall*, 1950] was not one of the best. I remember Nancy Davis as quite soft and pudgy and she looked like she'd had a nose job. Although she was pleasant enough, she seemed rather devious to me. I can't tell you exactly why…it's just a feeling I had. Maybe it was because she was so ambitious….She was a tough lady…who definitely knew where she wanted to go.

"I came to MGM as a star making $100,000 a year and Nancy was just a little contract player who didn't make much of an impression on anyone at the studio. I never would have known her had we not been in the same film, and even then she didn't impress me much."
— Ann Sothern in 1989.

———

"I'll hit him when I see him. I'll punch him right in the nose, and I hope I have these rings on."
— Lucille Ball in the second issue of *People* magazine, referring to her anger at Marlon Brando for having starred in an X-rated movie, *Last Tango in Paris* (1972).

———

"I never knew him well, but he was the kind of man who didn't interest me, as Gable or as Rhett Butler. Neither of them had a lot of sensitivity."
— Olivia De Havilland on her *Gone With the Wind* costar Clark Gable.

———

"She is humorless and uncomfortable being a woman."
— Arthur Laurents, playwright and screenwriter, on Katharine Hepburn, with whom he worked and played tennis (she played at championship level).

———

"She keeps putting so much makeup on during the day that by nightfall she looks like she's in drag."
— actress/screenwriter Carrie Fisher on Joan Collins; Fisher wrote a TV movie costarring Collins, Carrie's mother Debbie Reynolds, Elizabeth Taylor and Shirley MacLaine.

———

"We had an earthquake here in L.A. over the weekend. They said it's the first time Kathie Lee Gifford's CD actually flew off the shelf."
— Jay Leno.

———

"I think Dolly Parton's a celibate in slut's clothing."
— writer/director Colin Higgins (*Nine to Five*).

———

"I'm old enough, I can say it. I always thought it rather odd how the female is required to shave off or pluck away her hair not growing directly under a hat. Legs, armpits, eyebrows, what have you. It's ultimately pointless. If men don't like to see it, don't look! I tell you what I find pretty repulsive: whenever I've seen Peter Sellers—marvelous talent, mind you—topless, for want of a better word. Hair on his shoulders and back…a virtual forest. For the camera, couldn't he have at least shaved? Are men that lazy? That one-sided? I suppose only what the male decrees or wants, counts."
— Estelle Winwood, who lived to 101 (both appeared in *Murder By Death*).

———————————

"I worked in two Cary Grant movies. He wanted to have an affair, I resisted…when you get into the business, you're warned that business and sex don't mix. I've known other closeted stars, men like Rock Hudson, far more easygoing than Grant. With Grant, everything was sealed off or a lie. His forbidden past. Such insecurity. And such cheapness. Probably the cheapest man in Hollywood. Amazing."
— Dick Sargent, best known as Darrin #2 from *Bewitched*. Cary Grant's *North by Northwest* costar Eva Marie Saint has revealed that he would charge twenty-five cents to give autographs, claiming the money went to charity. Did Grant really donate the money, asked *TV Guide*? "I don't know if I believe that one."

———————————

"My boat's bigger than yours!"
— what director Francis Ford Coppola reportedly yelled from his yacht in the late '70s at producer Sir Lew Grade aboard his. Grade yelled back, "Yes, but I own mine!"

———————————

"I felt it was kind of a snub…of all the other people who did care and had sweated blood for the movie. So I kept calling him….The message I got on my machine, like, the day before was, 'It just ain't me, bro.' Apparently, getting $4 million to do a juice ad that only airs in Japan is him; going to the Oscars is not."
— *Titanic* director James Cameron on no-show Leonardo DiCaprio, whom Cameron said "looked like a spoiled punk."

———————————

"He has $100 million in guarantees, plus what he's winning on the tour. He never has to worry again in life. He could have told General Motors, 'I've got an obligation to a union I belong to, let's work something out.' But he didn't, deciding to make big bucks on the short term.

"We have members and their families in financial troubles, losing their homes, not working over principles. How much money does Tiger Woods need?"
— Screen Actors Guild member Kent McCord (*Adam 12*) on the golfer who crossed a picket line to make a commercial in 2000.

———————————

"Anyone who believes that Tom Cruise and Penelope Cruz have 'found each other' must be from another planet. They share the same publicist. They costarred in the soon-to-be-seen *Vanilla Sky*. Even when Nicole Kidman was told about them, she said she didn't put much credence in it."
—Hollywood columnist Arlene Walsh.

———————————

"He looks like a female llama who has just been startled in her bath." — British head of state Winston Churchill on French head of state Charles DeGaulle.

———————————

**"I'm honored to be chosen Mother of the Year,"
declared Joan Crawford on radio, "and will try to serve as
an example for mothers everywhere."**

The glamorous, ever-poised movie star who was Mommie Dearest behind closed doors did indeed win a Mother of the Year award. Which shouldn't be surprising, since Hollywood-engineered publicity has seldom had much to do with reality. Besides, at that time, millions of fans believed it was just short of saintly for Joan to adopt four unwanted children and provide them with the good life.

★　★　★

**"Robert and I are as happy as anyone could possibly be!"
said Diana Ross on the birth of her first child. "we want to
have more children…soon. We want a big family!"**

But Diana's first wasn't husband Robert Silberstein's child. The real father was Berry Gordy, founder and head of Motown Records. Ross and Silberstein subsequently had two daughters of their own, and Diana later had two sons via her second, Norwegian husband.

★　★　★

**"My mother is a movie star but she's also an
honest, devout, extremely religious person,"
said Loretta Young's daughter Judy.**

Later, in the book that estranged mother and daughter, Judy Lewis revealed that she was the love child of Clark Gable and the devoutly Catholic star nicknamed Attila the Nun. As a child, Judy's prominent ears were surgically pinned back so that there would be less resemblance to her real father.

★　★　★

**"My mother Frances is a sweetheart, the queen of my life, and
I even built a real throne for her, to show her how extremely
special she is," declared dutiful son Liberace.**

In his heyday, "Lee" was often criticized for the degree of his mother-love. Publicly, he always idolized her. One biography posthumously noted, "All the Liberaces suffered the whiplash of their mother's anger. She dominated them as youngsters, and she continued to dominate them as adults. On occasion I saw her poke them with her cane to get their attention. Lee lavished public affection on her while avoiding her in private. Frances could be a…merciless nag. She frowned on cigarettes and would snatch them from Lee's mouth as if he were a little kid instead of a sixty-year-old superstar."

★ ★ ★

"My parents are the most talented people I've ever known."
— Joely Fisher, daughter of Connie Stevens and
Eddie Fisher and costar of *Ellen*.

Chalk it up to filial pride.

★ ★ ★

"My father taught me everything I know about acting."
— Brian Keith, movie (*The Parent Trap*) and
TV (*Family Affair*) actor.

Possibly, however, the rugged Brian was physically and professionally nothing like his mousy father, character actor Robert Keith.

★ ★ ★

"My father was a movie star, but I think more significantly, from an acting point of view, he was a very big star of the stage….For a long time I felt I was living in his shadow."
—Anthony Perkins.

Osgood Perkins, a film character actor, was a sometime stage star. Tony named one of his two sons after him, but thanks to *Psycho* was far more famous than his father ever was.

★ ★ ★

"My father is one of the most richest men in Brazil. He is the biggest exporter of bananas—he is a fruits tycoon!" enthused "Brazilian Bombshell" Carmen Miranda in Hollywood.

When he emigrated from Portugal, where Carmen was born, her father was a barber. In the New World, Senhor da Cunha (Carmen took her mother's name) apparently entered the wholesale fruit business, but never became the millionaire his flamboyant daughter claimed.

★ ★ ★

"I don't believe my father ever hurt anyone, really,"
said Woody Harrelson, formerly of *Cheers*.

But the man is in jail for murder.

★ ★ ★

"My dad was a fine classical musician and conductor, and a
very good father....We were a typical all-American family,"
offered Liberace in the early 1950s, when his TV show
reached more homes than *I Love Lucy*.

With Liberace, little was as he said. His father was never a conductor,
but played the French horn with the Milwaukee symphony. While Lee
was in his teens, his dad left his family to "shack up"—as Lee later told
companion Scott Thorson—with a fellow (female) musician. "I never
forgave my father for that," said Liberace, one of four children. He didn't
speak to the man again until he was old and ailing, and refused to pay
his medical bills—which he let brother George do.

★ ★ ★

"It hurts me to give my little girl away. But the price of this
wedding—it's deluxe and just the way Liza wants it—might
hurt just as much!" quipped director Vincente Minnelli on the
occasion of Liza's second marriage, to Jack Haley, Jr., son of
the actor who played the Tin Man in
The Wizard of Oz opposite Liza's mother Judy Garland.

The wedding invitations announced that Vincente was cohosting with
Liza's friend Sammy Davis, Jr. According to author Paul Rosenfield
(twenty years with the *Los Angeles Times*), Sammy paid for the entire wedding. (Of course the director had another secret: friend Ann Miller
admitted recently for an A&E Biography of Garland that Minnelli was
bisexual, but that was censored out of the final TV version.)

★ ★ ★

"I am proud of my son. His success is really
phenomenal to me." So said actor Jack Cassidy at the time
of eldest son David's TV success in both *The Partridge
Family* and as a pop singer.

However, in the 1990s, long after Cassidy, Sr. had died in a fire, the former teen idol admitted, "The more famous I became, the more my father resented me."

*   *   *

"In spite of Hollywood and everything, I've had a pretty normal life," declared Sandra Dee (née Alexandra Zuck), the junior Doris Day of the 1950s and '60s.

Decades later, in conjunction with publication of her son's book, she admitted on national TV that her stepfather had sexually molested her. (Her mother had pushed her into and through show business until Dee prematurely walked away from her stardom.)

*   *   *

"I loved being on *Father Knows Best*, and I did have a happy childhood, I did."

It was much later that former actress Lauren Chapin, who played Robert Young's younger daughter, "Kitten," revealed that her real-life father had sexually molested her. Also that her boyfriend had hooked her on heroin and urged her into prostitution.

*   *   *

"You might look on me as a ladies' man. But not a kiddies' man. I don't see myself in the role of father."

Thus spake Cary Grant in the 1950s while married to wife #3. In the '60s he had his first child with #4, actress Dyan Cannon (who has gone from movies to *Ally McBeal*). By then Grant was in his sixties, and the press marveled at his late fatherhood—few dared question why the much-married, very closeted gay or bisexual actor had waited so long.

*   *   *

"My private life is boring. That's why I don't talk about it. It wouldn't interest anyone…It's so mundane," emphasized actor James Daly of TV's *Medical Center* (and father of TV stars Tyne—*Cagney & Lacey*—and Timothy—*Wings*).

In fact, inquiring minds would have been fascinated by Daly's relationship with live-in partner Randal Jones, an ex-model. When Daly died in 1978 at sixty, his and Randal's condo in Marina Del Rey was reportedly invaded by James' three daughters, who forcibly evicted Jones. He then filed the first gay palimony suit, for $5 million, against the estate and "the three furies." He'd lived with Daly for years, and the suit was settled quietly out of court. To this day, Tyne Daly won't discuss her late father's sexual orientation (nor did the gay magazine *The Advocate* bring the subject up in a late-'90s interview!).

* * *

"He's a real lady-killer. All the ladies wanted to make it with Mr. Brady," said Barry Williams, aka Greg Brady, about his TV dad Robert Reed, while promoting his memoirs. In *Growing Up Brady*, Williams fictitiously described Reed as "boffing secretaries."

Show biz habit is to closet fellow celebrities—unless, and even sometimes when, they're openly gay. Robert Reed was gay and closeted. He'd had a wife and daughter, but rather than living with a male mate, he sought anonymous quickies in his car with dark-tinted windows near his Pasadena home. Reed died of AIDS in 1992, soon after publication of his costar's memoirs. Florence Henderson, aka Mrs. Brady, later admitted, "I knew [he was gay], and he knew that I knew."

P.S. When Elizabeth "Samantha" Montgomery of *Bewitched* was asked if she'd known Darrin #2, Dick Sargent, was gay, she answered, "From the minute I met him." The TV couple were the 1992 grand marshalls of the Los Angeles gay pride parade.

* * *

"I fell in love with all my leading ladies. Oh, except Monica Vitti. No one could love Monica Vitti."
— Dirk Bogarde, who did not reveal that he was gay.

"It was reported that Barry Manilow was taking a year off to write a Broadway musical....Taking a year off from what?"
— *Late Night* host Conan O'Brien, in 1996.

Where's that musical?

* * *

"Michael Jackson's album was only called *Bad* because there wasn't enough room on the sleeve for *Pathetic*."—Prince.

★   ★   ★

"Just another black guy looking for his fifteen minutes of fame."—Charlton "Guns don't kill people" Heston, about Ice-T in *Esquire*, 1997.

★   ★   ★

"Chanel has never influenced fashion one bit."
— rival designer Pierre Cardin.
On the other hand, or sleeve, designer Elsa Schiaparelli observed, "That damn bitch sold the same jacket for thirty-five years!"

★   ★   ★

"Kurt Cobain was...a worthless shred of human debris."
— Rush Limbaugh, 1994.
If so, it takes one to know one. If it weren't for their propagandist bent, Limbaugh's books could be called semi-fiction.

★   ★   ★

"Good career move."—Gore Vidal, on rival Truman Capote's death in 1984 (if it were, Vidal would have copied it).
Tru once observed of a rival's best-seller, "It's a real page-turner, all right, but not all pages get read."

★   ★   ★

"A tart...an embittered man."— Charlton Heston, the allegedly unembittered former movie star, on Gore Vidal, in 1997 in *Esquire*.

★   ★   ★

"My brother is a proudly cynical man, despite his success....The only way he'd ever commit suicide is if he ever allowed himself to trust the rope."
— Tom Conway, who died first, an alcoholic ex-actor, on George Sanders, who did take his life, with pills.

★   ★   ★

"Mr. [Arthur] Laurents jumped at the chance to do a musical about my life....Well, for a while I thought why a musical? Wasn't my life dramatic enough without songs?"
— stripper Gypsy Rose Lee.

Screenwriter Laurents (*The Way We Were*, *The Turning Point*) was not interested in writing the book for the musical *Gypsy*. "He knew that Lee made up a new life story every time someone asked," according to show-biz columnist Harold Fairbanks. Rather, *Gypsy* was basically about Lee's mother: "Laurents found out that Lee's mother, Rose, was a lesbian who had once pushed a hotel manager out a window and killed him. 'How can you resist doing a musical based on a woman like that?' Laurents says."

(Rose's grandson, born of Lee and director Otto Preminger, confirms, "My grandmother was indeed lesbian," though not in the Broadway musical or the film version, which both omit—also—the alleged murder.)

★   ★   ★

"I am one thousand percent for Tom Eagleton, and I have no intention of dropping him from the ticket."— Senator George McGovern, shortly before dropping Eagleton—who had been to a psychiatrist—from his 1972 presidential ticket.

★   ★   ★

"Yeah, I told the producer I was thirty-five. Whoever heard of a middle-aged gladiator?"
— Woody Strode, who played Draba in *Spartacus.*

Strode knew Draba had a fight scene with star Kirk Douglas, who was thirty-two. So Strode claimed he was thirty-five rather than forty-five. He got the role and later found out Douglas, actually forty-two, had also shaved off a decade from his actual age.

★   ★   ★

"The only difference between Vanessa and me is six years of age and an inch of height."—Lynn Redgrave, who years later made efforts to put a lot of philosophical distance between herself and her big sister, who, among other things, opposed Israel's existence and America's participation in the Gulf War.

"Girls swoon over what Shakespeare wrote...I
mean, lines like, 'Shall I compare thee to a summer day?'"
— Gwyneth Paltrow, *Shakespeare in Love.*

In fact, Shakespeare wrote that sonnet to a young man.

*   *   *

"I admire and encourage young talent, I always have."
— Lucille Ball.

But eventually she had *Mame* costar Madeline Kahn fired. The younger, talented comedic actress was replaced by older, plainer Jane Connell (from the Broadway musical) as Agnes Gooch.

*   *   *

"In real life I'm allergic to gadgets. They just don't work for
me, not even those plastic cards for hotel room doors."
— Desmond Llewelyn, in *Computer Life* magazine,
revealing the truth behind his screen image as Q, the gadgets expert
in the James Bond movies.

*   *   *

"I'm too raw for TV...I'm not crazy about being compared
with other actresses, and 'specially not with Mabel [King].
I got nothing against her, but just 'cause we're both round,
dark and was on [TV sitcom] *What's Happenin'!* that don't
mean we had one blessed solitary other thing in common."
— stand-up comic Shirley Hemphill.

Ironically, both women died in 1999.

*   *   *

Lie by omission: *TV Guide's* year-end obituary
round up for 1999 included "survived by" for most of those
involved in contractual opposite-sex marriages and even the
opposite-sex "mate" of a *panda*, but no same-sex survivors,
including that of *The Waltons'* Ellen Corby, who'd been with
her partner going on half a century.

*   *   *

"I think Mick Jagger would be astounded and amazed if he realized to how many people he is not a sex symbol but a mother image."—David Bowie.

Truman Capote once avowed, "[Jagger] is about as sexy as a pissing toad." But a "mother image"?

★ ★ ★

"Very soon."

— David Copperfield, in 1998, on when he would wed German supermodel Claudia Schiffer.

"Marriage is the inevitable end to this kind of love."
— Claudia Schiffer, in 1997.

But in 1999 the very publicized pair broke off their six-year engagement.

★ ★ ★

"The second time's supposed to be forever."
— Michael Jackson, on contractually marrying Debbie Rowe, who'd worked for his plastic surgeon.

After less than three years, she filed for divorce. The action was not titled Rowe vs. Weird.

★ ★ ★

"Have you ever noticed how all newspaper composite pictures of wanted criminals resemble Jesse Jackson?"
— Rush Limbaugh, in *Newsday* in 1990.

And how all newspaper composite pictures of wanted white criminals resemble you-know-who?

★ ★ ★

"Puffy is a visionary and a great talent."—Donald Trump, self-appointed musical expert, on Sean "Puffy" Combs.

Trump made this statement after Combs was arrested for beating up a record executive and before his arrest for illegal gun possession at a Manhattan nightclub. Whatever possessed Trump? Whatever possessed Jennifer Lopez?

★ ★ ★

"Robert Downey, Jr. will become a star…known for his daring choices of roles."—movie historian Tony Thomas.

Downey, star of *Chaplin*, *Less Than Zero* and *Home for the Holidays*, is unfortunately now better known for his drug-related arrests and prison time. Clarinetist Kenny G stated on TV, "As a taxpayer, if I am going to pay for needles, I'd like to see the drug-users doing something for the society. Come and clean the streets, wash the cars, you know, do something. Not that I'd want Robert Downey, Jr. in my garage or anything like that."

★　★　★

"It used to be sex and drugs and rock 'n roll. Nowadays, with all these undisciplined young bucks and [actresses] like Mackenzie Phillips [of *One Day at a Time*], it's getting to be sex and drugs and TV."
— Vic Tayback, aka Mel of Mel's Diner on the sitcom *Alice*.

Exaggeration. Television actor Christopher George of *Mission: Impossible* opined, "We're too busy to get into much trouble…the pace of working in TV is grueling….Psychologically, we're in a very different situation than movie actors. They have it much easier on their sets, more of a money cushion, less of a by-Friday-or-else schedule…and they work on the one project for a few months at the most. Then they get a few months' rest, or too many months' rest, which is unemployment, until—or if—their next project."

★　★　★

"I offer an option to people who are tired of the usual television fare…more intellectual and stimulating….I'm introducing the stars of tomorrow."
— variety host Ed Sullivan.

Talk show pioneer Virginia Graham felt, "The trouble with Ed Sullivan, bless him, is the same as the trouble with television overall— these shows don't merely take people's minds off their problems, they take our minds off our minds." Many people then (the mid-'60s) and now feel that too much TV causes "cavities" in the mind. Architect Frank Lloyd Wright was quoted as saying both "Television is bubblegum for the mind" and "…bubblegum for the eyes."

"Gandhi has been assassinated. In my humble opinion a bloody good thing but far too late."
— Noel Coward, in his 1948 diary.

"Well, new people and styles, fresh faces and sounds, come along….Pat Boone was one who didn't take well to being displaced by the Beatles. But then he became this angry pillar of righteousness, indignation and all-around condemnations. He became a joke in the business, not just an aging anachronism. A crusading bigot…I've heard his main exposure now is on one of those crank American religious cable channels."
— Lionel Bart, composer of *Oliver!*

"It's great to be with Bill Buckley, because you don't have to think. He takes a position and you automatically take the opposite and you know you're right."
— super-economist John Kenneth Galbraith.

"An asshole." — Associated Press reporter and author Bob Thomas, on "National Rifle Association mouthpiece" Charlton Heston.

"In his three-hour lie [*JFK*, 1991], Stone falsifies so much he may be an intellectual psychopath."
— commentator George Will, on writer/director Oliver Stone.

"My boy, when I want to play with a prick, I'll play with my own." — W.C. Fields, after MGM tyrant Louis B. Mayer suggested a round of golf.

"That's got every fire hydrant in America worried."
— Bill Clinton, about Dan Quayle's goal to be a "pit bull" in helping Republicans retain the White House; Quayle didn't achieve his goale (sic).

"If I'd lost to Donny Osmond, I would be living in Tibet so nobody would recognize me."
— Danny Bonaduce (*The Partridge Family*), on a charity boxing match against Osmond.

"Michael Jackson is not a star. He's got no business being on stage. He's too fat, he wears underwear on the outside, and he's been accused of abusing children." — Nash Kato of Urge Overkill, in 1993.
(Too fat??)

———————————

"I've always thought Marilyn [Monroe] looked fabulous, but I'd kill myself if I was ever that fat." — Elizabeth Hurley, Hugh Grant's longtime model/actress girlfriend, in *Allure* magazine.
(That fat??)

———————————

"...John Malkovich, the bald, cross-eyed actor with a voice like an unbroken dial tone.... There's one insurmountable fatal flaw in this alarmingly and hysterically overhyped wreckage: who in his own right mind would want to spend one day, one hour, or one minute in the brain of John Malkovich?"
— critic Rex Reed, on the movie *Being John Malkovich*.

———————————

"I think that the acceptance of Andy Warhol as some sort of a so-called artist is a farce and reflects badly on us, or those who decided to elevate him....He created next to nothing—he virtually photographed Campbell soup cans or took [others'] photos of Marilyn and Mao and then colored them in with pastels. He had no depth, nothing to say, he was passive and superficial... he was like a politician, but without the promises."
— *Vogue* photographer Horst.

———————————

"Dan Quayle is more stupid than Ronald Reagan put together."
— cartoonist and *Simpsons* creator Matt Groening, in 1993.

———————————

"I could easily see Mel Gibson getting elected. He'd be a cinch. Faded looks, a semi-convincing smile masking anger and pettiness,...born in the USA but grew up in Australia so he's a foreign policy expert, right? Catholic but a huge family, big family man, hates all the right minorities but doesn't diss the wrong one, and a recovered alcoholic—or is that a liability? Anyway, if he hadn't gotten into directing, Mel could become our second Republican actor president. But he does direct, so I guess he'd settle for mayor of Malibu."
— producer Allan Carr (*Grease, Where the Boys Are 1984*).

"O, for the fit of Rostand's Cyrano to evoke the vastness of that nose as it cleaves the giant screen from east to west, bisects it from north to south. It zigzags across our horizon like a bolt of fleshy lightning; it towers like a ziggurat made of meat. The hair is now something like the wig of a fop in Restoration comedy; the speaking voice continues to sound like Rice Krispies if they could talk."
— critic John Simon, on producer/star Barbra Streisand in *A Star is Born* (1976).

———————

"Herzog is a miserable, hateful, malevolent, avaricious, money-hungry, nasty, sadistic, treacherous, cowardly creep. His 'talent' consists of nothing but tormenting helpless creatures and, if necessary, torturing them to death....I absolutely despise this murderer Herzog.... Huge red ants should piss into his lying eyes, gobble up his balls, penetrate his asshole, and eat his guts!"
— Polish-German actor Klaus Kinski, who didn't get along with his director, Werner Herzog, on *Aguirre: The Wrath of God* (1972), made in the Amazon jungle.

———————

"Jodie Foster. I hate everything she stands for and everyone gathered around her to help her stand for it. It's a big fat fuckin' lie. Let's not be who we are. Let's hide behind our art. Let's oppress everybody who is exactly like us. In her fuckin' Armani with her tits hangin' out. And constantly rewarded and rewarded. And by who? The power structure that she totally speaks for."
— Roseanne.

———————

Besides, most of Ed Sullivan's performers weren't future stars, but novelties like Topo Gigio the Italian mouse and ventriloquist Señor Wences, or so-so talents. Sullivan's tastes were often outmoded. He featured young talents like Elvis, Streisand and the Beatles more for ratings than his own pleasure, and censored Presley's swaying hips. After presenting the Rolling Stones he said, "I promise you they'll never be back on my show. I was shocked when I saw them."

★ ★ ★

"How can I tell you how convinced I am? But trust me, this girl will be the biggest thing in pictures...bigger than Garbo. She has everything...everyone will love her, and for me she will make a goldmine."—producer Samuel Goldwyn, on his 1933 discovery, Russian actress Anna Sten.

Only the public didn't love her. Goldwyn got the message after she starred in four costly flops.

★ ★ ★

"He's going to be a big fat star. I spoke metaphorically of course."—Joan Crawford, on Jack Palance, her leading man in *Sudden Fear* (1952).

But Palance's face was considered too scary for romantic leads. He wasn't Crawford's first (or second or...) choice to play the younger husband who tried to murder her. She wanted new star Marlon Brando, who didn't even reply to her offer, and after she pressed him responded that he didn't feel up to any mother-son projects at the moment.

P.S. Palance went on to become an Oscar-winning supporting actor.

★ ★ ★

"*Mork and Mindy* is harmless enough entertainment, occasionally very funny...rarely inspired...aimed a bit too directly at under-teens....Costar Pam Dawber is refreshing, lovely and has true comedy timing...and a big future. Robin Williams is harder to take in large doses...he is too much the oddball to be cast [in movies] easily or often."
—Wayne Warga, *Entertainment Tonight* writer.

★ ★ ★

"The latest battle of the girl singers pits Cyndi Lauper against Madonna....Lauper is the more obvious talent, but her rainbow-colors hair distracts from her singing and composing....My money's on Lauper, who has energy plus [while] Madonna is another in a long line of Marilyn wannabes [with] far less sex appeal than Blondie's Debbie Harry...really just another over-sexed, over-bleached blond girl singer."
— showbiz historian David Shipman.

★　★　★

"I might be writing a workout book [that] would be the, like, male equivalent to Jane Fonda's popular book."
— John Travolta, 1984.

(Like, writing?) Travolta may have been buffed when he did *Staying Alive*, the sequel to *Saturday Night Fever* (directed by Sylvester Stallone, which explains a lot). But unlike Fonda, seventeen years his senior, he didn't stay lean and in great shape. Besides flying, food is John's other (public) hobby. In late '99, on location, he enjoyed the services—paid for by the movie company—of a chef d'haute cuisine who ground $50 worth of filet mignon into hamburger that the star refused because "it wasn't rare enough." A second burger deluxe was sent back because "there was something wrong with the mayonnaise." Happily, the third time was the calorific charm. A crew member offered, "The guy just eats and eats. He's like one of those geese who gets force-fed to make foie gras."

★　★　★

"Martha Stewart is a role model for the '90s."
— TV director George Schaefer.

A symbol of the American '90s, yes. But a role model? A model of success, perhaps—at fifty-eight she took her company public and reaped some $1.2 billion. But on her climb to the top, Stewart has alienated numerous former friends and employees. One Philadelphia cooking school owner feels, "Martha is not respected in any food community I know of. It looks like she's ripped off recipes from too many people!" Including, allegedly, recipes for orange-almond cake and raisin-cherry pound cake "almost identical to" those in Julia Child's *Mastering the Art of French Cooking.* Stewart denies all charges of plagiarism.

Like many corporate heads, among them Walt Disney, Stewart may have taken credit for some of her employees' work. She got a big advance for her book *Menus For Entertaining*, though an ex-staffer alleged, "It was compiled largely by employees." Martha states that "95% of the articles" in her magazine are her ideas; she is said to pop into the office "once or twice a week."

Her ex-partner in a small catering business quit after less than a year: "She was resentful that I wasn't willing to work 128 hours a week." One paper noted that Stewart "grew up in a large family that struggled to make ends meet in Jersey City, N.J.," but became "one of the world's biggest cheapskates," despite her wealth. "She once charged a major company $1,000 after she invited executives to her house for three tuna sandwiches, a pitcher of iced tea, and dessert," according to "an insider." Maybe it was very tasty tuna, tea, and dessert?

Ironically, the "perfect" homemaker's profitable homemaking cost her part of her home: in 1987, husband Andy was reportedly "so fed up" with the domestic diva that "he simply jotted down a goodbye note and walked away."

Under Stewart's high school yearbook photo was this apt quote: "I do what I please and I do it with ease."

★　　★　　★

"I'm what you could call the old man in this outfit…not old, really, but one look at me and the other guys get to feeling young and spry….I'm not exactly known as Mr. Excitement."
— TV star Joey Bishop (ne Joseph Gottlieb),
member of the Rat Pack.

But ironically, Bishop is the sole survivor of the fabled group, which also counted Frank Sinatra, Dean Martin, Peter Lawford, and Sammy Davis, Jr. Not a believer in "big public goodbyes," Bishop reportedly didn't attend any of the Rat Pack funerals, which is said to have angered Sinatra's family.

P.S. Daughter Nancy Sinatra missed Frank's dying moments because she stayed home to watch the final *Seinfeld* episode. She later conceded, "I could have taped it."

P.P.S. Bishop, born 1918, wasn't the oldest Rat: Sinatra was born 1915, Martin in 1917, Lawford in 1923 and Davis, Jr. in 1925.

★   ★   ★

"I know him. Slightly....Sensible man, very rich."
— Winston Churchill, on Lord Berners.

W.C. was not the best judge of character. He admired fascist Mussolini (as did some Hollywood moguls of the era) and loathed the saintly Mahatma Gandhi, who wanted India to be ruled by Indians rather than British. In 1935, on Berners' English estate where he housed white doves dyed in several colors, he built a 141-feet-high tower. At its entrance the Lord placed a sign reading, "Members of the Public Committing Suicide From This Tower Do So At Their Own Risk."

★   ★   ★

"It's hard for me to go places, in public."
— Leonardo DiCaprio in 1998.

Later that year, Troy Donahue, himself a box office heartthrob in his own day, commented, "You know, Leo can get from A to B without being recognized if he really, really wants to....I think a lot of this stuff about 'He can't move around and he can't do this' is just hype." Speaking of hype and glory, a 1999 series of photos of Leo, back in lean shape after filming *The Beach* and hoping to stay that way, showed him, unawares, doing chin-ups at a Hollywood park. As he proceeded, he put forth a titanic effort, but on his last attempt had to be physically aided by a shirtless, attractive and very built "buffed pal," as the caption put it.

★   ★   ★

"My son-in-law, you know, he is a prince."
— Jolie Gabor, mother.

She wasn't indicating how much she liked him, but referring to the German—Frederick von Anhalt—who became Zsa Zsa's last husband and via whom she began calling herself "princess." Actually, the man purchased the title, but *Hollywood Squares* gladly and unquestioningly billed the Hungarian personality as "Princess Zsa Zsa." Vy not? One of Hollywood's leading restaurateurs was "Prince" Mike Romanoff, who explained, "I'm so conservative and royalist, I might as well be one of them."

Jolie herself tried to get into the nobility act when she unsuccessfully attempted to have her younger husband (like mother, like Zsa Zsa) listed in Palm Springs' *Little Gold Book*—a local society Who's Who—as a count. One socialite remarked, "Things like that go over very, very poorly in the desert."

✴   ✴   ✴

"It was the fairy tale love story and wedding of the century."
— playwright George Kelly (*Craig's Wife*), on his niece Grace's marriage to Prince Rainier of Monaco in 1956.

Like everyone else, Kelly (himself a deeply closeted gay man) upheld the traditional view of the supposedly spontaneous love story between the prince and the actress, who was no virgin despite her image (it was said Grace "told enough white lies to ice a cake," and virtually all her biographers agree she slept with many men in Hollywood). Aristotle Onassis, the major shareholder in the Monte Carlo casino, had requested Rainier to wed a name actress, preferably blonde, to boost Monaco tourism and thus the casino's takings. Marilyn Monroe was considered, only briefly, for her image was too sexy and she didn't even pretend to be a virgin. And the Kellys were nothing if not ambitious, particularly her father, who finally agreed to Rainier's then-outrageous demand of a $2 million dowry. Pa Kelly had called the portly Monegasque a "broken-down prince who's head of a country that nobody ever heard of." Thanks to the wedding, everyone heard of it....

✴   ✴   ✴

"She's very, very happy...a lovely lady. I'm very happy for her."
— Cary Grant, in 1964, on his former *To Catch a Thief* costar Grace Kelly, who was said to be disappointed in not being allowed to return to the screen in Hitchcock's *Marnie* that year.

Grant, of all people, was commenting on Her Serene Highness' marital bliss, and also her purported contentment with not acting—ever again. However, insiders felt Rainier was cold toward Grace and that there was mutual disenchantment. Even at the time of their wedding, he was no prize physically....Grace was apparently shocked that she would never be allowed a movie comeback….Eventually her disillusionments led to alcoholism, and she died (1928-1982)—as Princess Diana later would—in a car crash.

⋆   ⋆   ⋆

"Miss *Mork and Mindy*? Too saccharine for my taste…like an '80s June Allyson."—Johnnie Ray, in 1986, on Pam Dawber.
Many of Ray's '50s songs, which sometimes required him to cry on stage, were considered "too saccharine." But Ms. Dawber, after all, was not the innocent Mindy character she played on TV: Dawber and her actor husband Mark Harmon were looking after the youngest son of his sister Kris, former wife of Ricky Nelson. When Kris got out of rehab, the couple sought to gain custody of the boy. But in court the actress was asked if she'd ever used cocaine. She said no. Then the lawyers asked if she'd used it with Robin Williams. Or actor Robert Hays. Or actor Gregory Harrison. She said no, and they asked, if they brought in those men and asked them under oath if they'd done cocaine with Pam Dawber, what would they say? The following morning, Pam and Mark Harmon gave in, and Kris got her son back. She has never since spoken to her brother or his wife.

⋆   ⋆   ⋆

"Frankly, I was shocked and offended. This could never have gone over in my day….I figure it'll make her another fortune."
— Sandra Gould (Mrs. Kravitz on *Bewitched*),
on Whoopi Goldberg's "Book."
Though it earned Goldberg a reported $6 million advance, the book, which included a whole chapter on farting, did terribly. Many critics felt it proved that publishers should stick to putting out books by writers and actors should stick to acting.

⋆   ⋆   ⋆

"He is so deep, man, like, fathoms."— River Phoenix, on his *My Own Private Idaho* costar Keanu Reeves.
A sample Reeves quote: "I cried over beauty, I cried over pain, and the other time I cried because I felt nothing, I couldn't help it. I'm just a cliché of myself."

Perhaps his female counterpart is Alicia Silverstone, who asseverated, "When I get lonely, I want to be alone, I like to indulge in my loneliness so I can figure out that I'm not really lonely." Deep, huh?

P.S. *My Own Private Idaho* was basically gay-themed, but when it was packaged as a videocassette the Phoenix and Reeves characters were misleadingly depicted on the box with girlfriends at their sides. It's called a Hollywood sell.

★　★　★

"Well, when I worked with her, she seemed quite down to earth to me....Her little boy flirted with my little girl, it was really cute."—Michael Crawford (*Phantom of the Opera*), on his *Hello, Dolly!* costar Barbra Streisand.

From her first movie, *Funny Girl*, Babs was rightly or wrongly reported as bossing around her director. In her second, she alienated leading man Walter Matthau, who finally misinformed her that she had less talent than a butterfly's fart. Crawford and Streisand had very few scenes together, and that may have been the reason they got along so swimmingly. But when Streisand fan Roseanne Barr met Barbra decades later, she complained to the press that Babs behaved like "queen of the United States." (The diva behavior must have been catching....)

P.S. Parents often read their own wishes into their children's behavior. At the time of *Dolly!*, Barbra's son Jason was little more than a baby. So much for flirting. He later became an actor and is openly gay.

★　★　★

"Robert [Young] deserves his success on the small screen. I have known him quite a long time...we did some lovely pictures together, and he is the hard-working, conscientious model of a fine actor."—Joan Crawford in the late '50s.

But beneath the polished exterior, Young, like so many other actors, felt very insecure. After *Father Knows Best*—which followed dozens of movies—he admitted, "When I became an actor, I constantly felt I wasn't worthy, that I had no right to be a star....I hid a black terror behind a cheerful face. Naturally, I tried to find a way out. Alcoholism was the inevitable result." In his 80s he tried to commit suicide.

Marlon Brando has stated, "I can walk into a room where there are one hundred people. If there is one person in that room who doesn't like me, I know it and have to get out."

★ ★ ★

"God makes stars, but the public has to make them popular."—Joan Crawford, who boasted about never declining a fan's request.

The ultimate movie star, Crawford supposedly had a special outfit for answering fan mail. She sometimes took loyal female fans and pressed them into service (unpaid) as secretaries, helping her sort her mountains of fan mail. In 1940 Joan gushed, "Did you know there were 25,000 baby girls christened with the name Joan this year? Half were called after me, and the others were named for Joan of Arc. Isn't that wonderful?"

But back in the late '50s, when Crawford deemed herself semi-retired as an actress, she was approached by a pre-pubescent fan for an autograph. According to an eyewitness, she smiled coolly and advised, "Go away, little girl. I don't need you any more."

★ ★ ★

"They both started here [in Britain], and they're within a few years of each other in age. But Miss Taylor grew up [in the U.S.], and has far more difficulty remaining svelte. Joan [Collins] has a much easier time of it, I dare say."
— UK actor/producer Derek Nimmo, in 1996.

Liz may be metabolically challenged, but Joan has been known to binge on occasion, particularly on chocolate cake. Not to mention the dismal fact that as one ages, one must eat less in order to weigh the same. As Joan put it, "A waist is a terrible thing to mind."

★ ★ ★

"She is a wonderful hostess and a superb cook."
— Roddy McDowall, on dear friend Edith Head,
the eight-time Oscar-winning designer.

It was once said that McDowall had had a reality-bypass operation. Closeted and a closeter, he upheld every traditional myth and image pertaining to "golden age" Hollywood. Head may have been a wonderful host, but as for her cooking, who could ever be sure? She boasted about her Mexican food, yet most of it—even though she took credit for it, a habit also practiced at work—was created by others, usually Mexican cooks at the Farmer's Market, who catered many of her parties.

⋆　⋆　⋆

"I gave him the benefit of the doubt…. Maybe those reports were exaggerated."
— Raul Julia, in 1988, on his costar Mel Gibson's drinking.

Julia and Gibson appeared in, ironically, *Tequila Sunrise* (1988). But Gibson's drinking before then is a matter of public record. His movie *The Bounty* got more publicity for his off-set beer-guzzling than its content—it was a costly flop. The benders and barroom brawls weren't brand-new, but Mel's superstar status was, and so was the spotlight on his behind-the-scenes behavior. His first big break in America was *The River*, and he behaved himself, but during his next Hollywood-financed picture, *Mrs. Soffel* (1984), Gibson got into a car accident and was arrested for drunk driving.

He tried to dry out, but the habit continued during his next effort, the third installment in the Mad Max series, *Mad Max: Beyond Thunderdome* (1985). Proving that good looks and financial success do not necessarily a happy, secure human being make.

⋆　⋆　⋆

"I'm so proud of Docky Wocky! Nobody works harder when he's working."
—columnist Louella Parsons, on her alcoholic M.D. husband.

"He was the disgrace of Hollywood," explained Paramount publicist Charlie Earle about that studio's official doctor, who kept his well-paid post via his powerful wife. "'Docky' was also house doctor to the town's top bordello, and he was the first to know when an actress got pregnant. He would feed the information to Lolly and she'd announce it in her column, often before the mother-to-be knew herself….The man's hygiene was disgraceful. He'd pee anywhere, and often, he drank so much.

"Rarely did he come to work mornings, nursing a hangover from the night before….He often accompanied Lolly to parties, and as often as not he'd be on the floor, passed out. No one ever said anything, no one dared. This woman could stifle or even terminate an actor's career unless he [or she] were a huge star, like Ingrid Bergman….When Lolly would walk over Docky, she'd typically look down, shake her head, and announce rather cheerfully to those assembled, 'Poor Docky's had a beer!' She was exceedingly generous to the old fool. Unlike to many of the victims of her column."

P.S. Parsons had a knack for saying the wrong thing at the right time. For instance, interviewing Ingrid Bergman on radio after her extra-marital affair with director Roberto Rossellini, Louella whined, "But tell me, Ingrid, what everyone wants to know, is whatever got into you?"

★　★　★

"I found this girl in a fjord."
— producer Samuel Goldwyn, on his discovery Sigrid Gurie, whom the press labeled "the Norwegian Garbo."

Gurie was another Goldwyn star-to-be who didn't become one, back in the 1930s. More to the point here, the so-called "Siren of the Fjords" was born and raised in Brooklyn.

★　★　★

"Boris Karloff hadn't really done much before *Frankenstein*. He was a bit player in a couple of pictures."— Elsa Lanchester, costar in the sequel *The Bride of Frankenstein* (1935).

Lanchester was no film historian. Karloff, born William Henry Pratt, was (according to his daughter) in eighty movies before *Frankenstein*.

★　★　★

"I discovered Cary Grant…he was just walkin' around the Paramount lot. I took one look and said, 'Put 'im in muh next picture.'…He'd only done a few bit parts in B-pictures before that."— Mae West.

More than most stars, West lived—at least publicly—in a fantasy world. Pre-Mae, Grant had costarred in several A-movies, some of them starring such West rivals as Marlene Dietrich, Sylvia Sidney and Tallulah Bankhead. But for most of his life—until Mae died—Grant didn't contradict the "Western" version.

"I have put all my heart into this song…
my own most personal creation. It is what I think I
will be most remembered for….I have even gotten fan letters
about it from big stars like Diana Ross and Cary Grant."
— Morris Albert, singer/composer of *Feelings*, in 1976.

His heart wasn't all the handsome Brazilian (Morris Albert Kaisermann) put into the huge hit that topped the international charts for some eight months in the mid-'70s. A Federal District Court in New York City ruled in 1985 that over 80% of *Feelings* had been plagiarized from *Pour Toi (For You)*, a 1956 French song by Louis Gaste, who received a $500,000 settlement. Morris' post-*Feelings* followup, *Sweet Loving Mary*, topped at #93 in 1976, and he eventually returned to São Paulo.

P.S. A fan letter from Miss Ross? Not too likely. Cary Grant, however, was a big fan of Elvis Presley and came out of screen retirement to appear briefly in the documentary *Elvis: That's the Way It Is* (1970).

★   ★   ★

"I was merely born. Long ago. But Mrs. [Dorothy] Parker is a
born writer…I believe she would write if she had to pay
them."—Robert Benchley, writer and wit, now also remembered as
father of Peter Benchley, author of the novel *Jaws*.

Very few writers in the limelight would write solely for the joy of writing. Parker, a poet, writer, scenarist (*The Little Foxes*) and quite a wit herself, once rhapsodized that "The two most beautiful words in the English language are 'check enclosed.'"

★   ★   ★

"Younger writers seem to have a mania [for writing].
Almost as if they're trying to prove something…always
writing. Disciplined like robots….I don't mind saying I often
had to be nudged to write. I wasn't a script machine."
— Dorothy Kingsley, coscenarist of *The Valley of the Dolls*.

Age blinds many people to the similarities they share with their juniors. Kingsley was not unique. Writer Paul Rudnick, the man behind *In & Out*, *Addams Family Values* and *Isn't She Great?*, offers: "I'm always sort of appalled at writers who say, 'Yes, I wake up every morning and I go to my little writing room at 9 AM and I work till noon and I take a half hour for a light lunch and then I return and write till six.' Why don't they work in a bank?

"The whole point of writing is procrastination and leisure time and television. Sometimes I'll write very late at night after I've called everyone, watched every possible infomercial, and eaten everything in the house—the only thing left to do is great literature."

*   *   *

"Well, to me, Ellen [DeGeneres] seemed more loose before she came out….Now she seems rather preoccupied. She's still funny, but she didn't seem so uptight then."
— (gay) Broadway director José Quintero.

Former stand-up comic Ellen has explained, "When you start out, the room is full of people who don't know you and don't care. You have to win them over. Then you play to a bigger group of people, and automatically a lot of them think you stink, especially being a girl on stage. 'You're not going to be funny—you're a girl.' That's a huge thing to overcome.

"Then you become popular and people pay good money to see you, and they want you to be very, very good 'cause you're famous and they've paid….Finally you reach a point of wide popularity where people are waiting to see you fail….So you're always having this very tricky relationship with a room full of people, whether it's nine people or nine million or ninety million."

As for seeming "preoccupied" after coming out, it would be understandable, in light of a brave and honest move that can cost one one's income, civil rights and safety. In 1999 tennis legend Martina Navratilova discussed ongoing anti-gay discrimination on *Larry King Live*: "I left [communist] Czechoslovakia so I would be free. I thought this was the land of the free. I didn't think it meant the land of the free as long as you're heterosexual."

*   *   *

> "Mr. [Sherwood] Schwartz has given my career a
> new perspective…you might say a new lease on life."
> —*Brady Bunch* star Robert Reed, on the TV tycoon who
> also created *Gilligan's Island* and other hit shows.

Reed was more into Shakespeare than sitcoms, and had hoped to be a movie actor. When he accepted the dad role on *The Brady Bunch*, he effectively killed his future chances for a film career or a diversity of roles on the big or little screen. Post-*Brady*, the actor and sometime acting coach shunned the sitcom that made him a household name. In 1989 he told an interviewer, "The whole thing was a joke…from the first script I ever saw, I knew [it] was going to be *Gilligan's Island* or worse….Things might have been different if [the series] hadn't gone into rerun-infinity. It is no joke watching your choices shrink and your opportunity to be taken seriously fade, all because of one ill-fated 'yes' to your agent when you were feeling too greedy for your own career's good."

* * *

> "If in ten years she is still walking around and
> allowed to make movies, I will be amazed."
> — *Chinatown* director Roman Polanski, in 1974.

> "She demonstrated certifiable proof of insanity."
> — Jack Nicholson, on his *Chinatown* costar Faye Dunaway.

Ironically, Polanski is no longer allowed to make movies in the U.S., or set foot in it without being arrested, having fled to Europe after being charged with statutory rape. As for the definitely diva-ish Dunaway, she's still working, and still looking great. Her roles may not all be that stellar now, but don't expect this star to Faye Daway.

* * *

> "Lorne was meant to be Ben Cartwright…he was crazy
> about anything western."— Michael Landon,
> on his late *Bonanza* costar Lorne Greene.

But as Greene quipped, "Michael and I don't know from horses. What do two nice Jewish boys know about riding?" The Canadian Greene began as a radio announcer north of the border, replacing Charles Jennings (father of ABC's Peter). To keep better track of the minutes remaining on radio programs, Lorne invented a stopwatch that counted backwards. While pitching his invention to an NBC executive, Greene was "discovered" and launched on his stage/screen/TV career.

P.S. In 1964 Green also had a #1 hit song titled *Ringo*, about a gunslinger.

★   ★   ★

"Yul [Brynner] told me he was born in the Far East.
I pinned him down: where? Outer Mongolia, he told me,
without specifying a town. But he was a Gypsy, and most of
those are in Europe. So who knows?"—George Sanders,
Brynner's costar in *Solomon and Sheba* (1959).

"When I first met Yul Brynner in 1949, he was producing
wrestling shows for one of the [TV] networks [and] his only
accent was straight out of the South Bronx."
— columnist James Bacon (when Brynner starred in
The Ten Commandments (1956), Paramount publicity created a new
background for him).

★   ★   ★

"I could...I could see myself as the Petula Clark of the
'80s....Singing has been a major, the major, portion of my
life."—Tracey Ullman, in 1984, when she made the pop charts
with *They Don't Know*.

Ullman had quite a musical background and had appeared in stage productions of *Grease*, *Elvis* and *The Rocky Horror Show*. In 1984 she was in Paul McCartney's flop movie musical *Give My Regards to Broad Street*. But in 1987 she took up American TV with her own *The Tracey Ullman Show* and left music behind.

★   ★   ★

"I'm the most disrespected singer since Elvis...."
—Billy Ray Cyrus, in 1992.

That year, the country singer's *Achy Breaky Heart* crossed over. But the country pin-up spoke too soon, because unlike Presley he remained a one-hit-wonder (outside of country music, where he still gets some criticism for his un-country-like packaging). On the other hand, though his debut album was a big seller, Cyrus was incorrectly described by much of the media as "an overnight success," when he'd been singing his achy breaky heart out for twelve years.

★ ★ ★

"Will we be the new Culture Club? I think so. That suits me fine….But I don't have to be the new Boy George, do I?"
—Richard Fairbrass, of Right Said Fred, in 1992 when
their song *I'm Too Sexy* hit #1.

Alas, outside of Britain, that was the three-man group's only chart-topper. Culture Club, though not long-lasting, had numerous hits. But Fairbrass did come out as "bisexual" in order to avoid tabloid speculation about his sexual orientation—and the announcement didn't seem to hurt, or help, the group's popularity.

★ ★ ★

"I've worshipped him for years. He's fantastic. I like George's smile too."—singer Ricky Martin, on fellow singer George Michael, in the *New York Daily News* in December, 1999.

How could this not be true? It's only surprising that the much speculated about singer—born Enrique Martin (pronounced Mar-teen) Morales—made the statement. What is he saying? What does he mean? What is he not saying?

P.S. In a 1999 puff-journalism biography of the Puerto Rican singer, Trivia Tidbit #6 informs us that "Ricky wants to be a father someday and have lots of children"—tune in someday and find out; time will tell—and #9 declares: "The quality that Ricky tolerates least of all is hypocrisy." That's show biz!!

Say What?!

"I'll have a double cheeseburger and a chocolate shake."
— Paul Lynde, comic actor and Hollywood center Square,
upon rolling down his window after a police chase on Sunset Boulevard
that ended with the drunk driver's car jumping a curb onto the
front lawn of a Beverly Hills mansion.

"Hail the flaming freebase Richard Pryor Comet, flashing
through the Tinseltown night! Scar tissue, anyone?"—writer
Kenneth Anger, on former drug addict and comic Richard Pryor.

"Thank God there's somebody here to talk to. There are
only old folks in the kitchen."—Madonna, reentering the
living room at a party at Yoko Ono's (Bob Dylan and
David Bowie were in the kitchen).

"For the most part, he's innocent."—Coolio's spokesman Bill
Harris, in 1998, on charges that the rapper had stolen $900 worth
of clothes and assaulted a store clerk in Boeblingen, Germany.

★   ★   ★

"Hollywood, forget it. But outside of Hollywood, Jews don't
rate much influence."—anti-Semitic actor Charles Farrell, ignorant
of the influence of Einstein, Freud and Marx on the 20th century.

SIGNS OF THE TIMES

"Books are for sale.
Please do not read."
— Long Beach, Calif.,
bus terminal bookstore.

———————

"It Is a Federal Offense to
Assault a Postal Employee
[While on Duty]."
— U.S. post office placard.

———————

"Courteous, Efficient
Self-Service." — Ann Arbor,
Mich., cafeteria.

———————

"Daily Special: Hare Pie—
$1.75. For the Kiddies: Bunny
on a Bun—$.75."
— Springdale, Nev., inn.

———————

"Clam Chowder—$3.00. Texas-
size Bowl—$1.50."
— Alaska restaurant.

———————

"Please take lost children
to the Lion House."
— Washington, D.C., zoo.

———————

"In case of emergency:
1) Do not be alarmed,
2) Push the alarm button."
— Pueblo, Colo., elevator.

———————

"To touch means instant death.
Anyone caught will be prosecuted
to the full extent of the law."
— Indiana power station.

———————

"Easy to Lay Yourself."
— Edinburgh, Scotland,
carpet store.

———————

"Have Your Next Affair Here."
— Holiday Inn marquee.

———————

"We want to apologize
for our erotic service."
— *Saturday Review* magazine.

———————

"Father of Eleven Fined
for Not Stopping."
— *Boston Herald*
car accident headline.

———————

"Drive Carefully—We'll Wait."
— New Mexico mortuary sign.

———————

"Have you seen *The Way We Were*? It's your basic boy meets gargoyle story, really charming." –comic Henny Youngman; *WWW* starred Barbra Streisand and Robert Redford.

★   ★   ★

"In her movie debut (*She Devil*), Roseanne Barr loses her husband…you could say it's a case of boy loses grill." — British comedian Peter Cook.

★   ★   ★

"Sexist…Howard Stern is so sexist. He thinks women should be obscene and not heard."—Dorothy Kingsley, screenwriter (*Valley of the Dolls*).

★   ★   ★

"If it comes to a divorce with Jane [Wyman], I think I'll name *Johnny Belinda* corespondent."—actor Ronald Reagan, who disliked having an actress wife who was more successful than him (Wyman won an Oscar for *Belinda*).

★   ★   ★

"[I wish you could be here to] see all these beautiful white people."—Nancy Reagan, to Ronald, in 1980 during a Chicago campaign fundraiser, via an amplified phone hookup.

★   ★   ★

"I remember Ronnie [Reagan] telling all of us not to join TV because it was the enemy of the movies. Next thing, he was on *G.E. Theater* with his contact lenses reading the commercials."—Warner Bros. star Ann Sheridan.

★   ★   ★

"Michael Douglas Settles $60 Million on Satisfied Ex-Wife Diandra."—1999 tabloid headline/understatement.

★   ★   ★

"I told the baron I was sorry but I couldn't accept an expensive gift from a man. His charming wife then asked me, 'How about from a woman?'"
— bisexual Marlene Dietrich, commenting on a 1930s affair.

"My last husband charged calls to his girlfriend in Berlin on my phone, so I refused to pay and had to change the number I'd had for eighteen years. What I really missed after he left was that phone number."
—actress Viveca Lindfors, on director Don Siegel (*Dirty Harry*).

"I'm a firm believer in getting married early in the morning. That way if it doesn't work out you haven't wasted a whole day."—Mickey Rooney.

"We spent the night in the sack, dahlings, just to prove there were still no hard feelings."—Tallulah Bankhead, to the press, on a reunion with her estranged husband (she blamed the breakup on his "no-comings rather than his shortcomings").

"If it's long enough, hard enough, and in far enough, it's indecent."—entertainer Belle Barth's definition of "indecent."

"It needs to be said that the poor are poor because they don't have enough money."—Sir Keith Joseph, British Minister of Health, enlightening the nation in 1970.

"For a star, he's not so spoiled like he could be...but I don't know how committed he is to monogamy...he does tend to dress down a lot. You could say he's a wolf in cheap clothing."—a "rising starlet," quoted in a tabloid on former beau Brad Pitt.

"Wearing the correct dress for any occasion is a matter of good manners."—movie/TV star Loretta Young.

★ ★ ★

"It absolutely puzzles me why so many people seem to say that I'm daffy."—Carol Channing, human kewpie doll.

★ ★ ★

"Padded bras and falsies were all the rage [in the '60s]….Diane [Diana Ross] and I, being beanpoles, used anything we could. Diane added hip pads, and I added my backside as well. In my new curves, I was strutting around Motown…chatting with some people in the lobby when, unbeknownst to me, Lamont Dozier stuck a long straight pin into what was supposed to be my derriere. When it was obvious to everyone that I hadn't felt a thing, they broke out laughing, and for a few seconds I fancied myself a very entertaining conversationalist."
—former Supreme Mary Wilson.

★ ★ ★

Asked what she'd do if an audience member admitted to being hurt by one of her fat jokes: "I'd say, 'Stop eating, okay? Pull away from the table!' You know, I'd like to sit around and inhale food like I'm going to the electric chair, but come on! Have a little self-respect for yourself. Use a little self-control. Pull away from the table and say, 'I'm done.' How hard is that? Is it better for you to look like a school bus? I'd say, 'I'm offended by the fact that you're a house when you should be a person, okay? So we're even!'"—comic Judy Tenuta.

★ ★ ★

"One real turning point in my life, I guess, was when I found out from an old dictionary that 'o.k.' stands for oll korrect, only they spelled all correct wrong, which is so wonderfully human. But instead, they kept the initials

anyway, and it became probably the most popular word in the world. And there's a real lesson and a moral in that."
— blonde sex symbol Jayne Mansfield.

"My foreskin, which my parents managed to save from my circumcision. That way, if anyone wanted to clone me, they wouldn't have any problems. It lies like a crusty Life Saver in a small plastic jar."
— Marilyn Manson, in 1999, informing *Rolling Stone* what he would contribute to a "millennium time capsule."

"Personally, I'm not too worried about Y2K….And I don't need the millennium to convince me to keep all my money stuffed in my mattress."—Rolling Stone Keith Richards.

"Billions of Chinese people are celebrating 9970 or whatever, so it doesn't mean fuck-all to them."—musician Michael Stipe, on the media's millennium madness.

"Millennium, shmillennium. It's a man-made concept, and advertising gimmick…and it's only one calendar, one point of view,…one more way to get us excited, scared and shopping."
— author/musician Paul Bowles.

"I'm going to have to, at some point, drop this stuff and do something that's more of a service….I'm talking about, like, painting in malls or something for a living."
— $20-million-a-movie star Jim Carrey, in 1999, looking forward (in an interview…).

"By the time I was your age, I was fifteen!"—director Michael (*Casablanca*) Curtiz, scolding a child star.

NOT TO WORRY

Fact: If you sneeze too hard, you can crack a rib. If you try to prevent a sneeze, you can burst a blood vessel in your head or neck and die. And an unusually lengthy yawn can break your jawbone.

Fact: Sulfur-based legal preservatives which highlight the colors and crispness of some vegetables found in salad bars can cause life-threatening allergic reactions.

Fact: One out of thirty-three people will lose their job in the coming year. And death rates are substantially higher among the unemployed.

Fact: Plastic mini-blinds manufactured before July, 1995, deteriorate with time and expose dwellers to poisonous lead dust. Inhaling or swallowing a minimal amount can cause brain damage.

Fact: People who use a cell phone while driving increase their chances of being in an accident by 34%. Phone-wise: there are at least eighteen ways to tap an ordinary telephone. P.S. You can be electrocuted while speaking on the phone during a thunderstorm.

Fact: A remote keyless entry device enables you to unlock your car door at a distance by the click of a button. However, somebody with a receiver can pick up the signal sent by your keyless remote, record it, then resend it later to unlock your car.

Fact: The malleable, plastic headphones used on airplanes create a moist, warm climate in the ear canal perfect for breeding bacteria. Using such headphones for one hour increases the bacteria in your ear by seven hundred times. Cameron Tuttle, author of *The Paranoid's Pocket Guide* asks, "Could the static you hear while watching an in-flight movie actually be the sound of bacteria rapidly reproducing inside your ear?"

Fact: All restrooms in commercial airplanes can be unlocked from the outside just by moving a small lever which is in plain sight. Worse: 29% of pilots have become too ill to complete a flight—most had eaten at the airport.

Fact: Rats breed so quickly that two can yield over one million descendants in eighteen months.

Fact: Fifteen percent of fatal traffic accidents in the U.S. are caused by the 1% with revoked or suspended licenses (the rats).

Fact: The chance of contracting an infection while staying in a hospital in the U.S. is one out of fifteen. (Also, more than 30,000 people are seriously injured by exercise equipment each year.)

Fact: The Centers for Disease Control admitted in 1996 that it does not have a big enough budget to research all of the emerging pathogens. One unwelcome addition is a new Salmonella bacteria—*salmonella enteritidis*—which lives inside raw eggs. Consuming raw or undercooked eggs can bring on severe food poisoning, even death. Eggnog, homemade ice cream, hollandaise sauce, smoothies, French toast, Caesar salad,...anything made with raw eggs also puts one at risk.

Fact: On a lighter but possibly costly note, many department stores now release scents into the air which make you feel good and want to buy.

"I don't think anybody should write his autobiography until after he's dead."—producer Samuel Goldwyn.

★   ★   ★

"Someone opened [Eva Gabor's] refrigerator and found only orchids and salami in it, so that's what they named the book. Not a very good title. Not a very good book. She didn't even put me in the book. 'I was afraid to write about you,' she said, 'for fear you would sue me, so instead I wrote about Papa.' So no wonder it was not a terrific success. How could it be good without me in it?"—Jolie Gabor, on her youngest daughter's autobiography.

★   ★   ★

"We were like another version of Lucy and Desi."
— Merv Griffin, comparing himself and the late Eva Gabor to the heterosexual couple.

★   ★   ★

"Well, darling, I thought one more bitch wouldn't matter."
— actress Hermione Gingold, with a canine in tow, joining guests Zsa Zsa Gabor and Pamela Mason, after host Merv Griffin noted, "Hermione, you've never brought a dog on before!"

★   ★   ★

"If you make a movie with a male star, everyone assumes you're fucking. If it's with a female star, everyone assumes you're fighting."—Susan Sarandon.

★   ★   ★

"Andre Agassi is very, very intelligent, very, very sensitive, very evolved more than his linear years."—Barbra Streisand, whose only child is openly gay, on her platonic beau at that time, the non-intellectual and homophobic tennis player Andre Agassi.

★   ★   ★

"Brooke Shields' and Andre Agassi's grounds for divorce may be irreconcilable height. He only comes up to her chest, and apparently he didn't come up there often enough."
— 1999 item from columnist Cindy Adams.

"Fortunately, no reputation in art or letters rests on the verdict of majorities, which always hate new art, new forms. It is the opinion of the few—the thoughtful, the tasteful—which finally triumphs....All great art is eccentric to the conservative multitude. The decoration on the Parthenon was so eccentric that Pheidias was put in prison. The first tulip that blossomed in England was rooted out and burnt for a worthless weed by the conscientious Scotch gardener."—writer Robert Ross, who was also the friend and executor of Oscar Wilde.

"Far too noisy, my dear Mozart. For too many notes."
— Austrian Emperor Josef II, in 1786, after attending the first performance of Mozart's opera *The Marriage of Figaro*.

"We fancy that any real child might be more puzzled than enchanted by this stiff, overwrought story."—1865 *Children's Books* review of Lewis Carroll's *Alice in Wonderland*.

"This is a terrific script. It just needs a complete rewrite."
— director Peter Bogdanovich, to writer Alvin Sargent regarding his script for *Paper Moon*.

"[It has] no legs, no jokes, no chance."—producer Mike Todd (Elizabeth Taylor's third husband), on the new 1943 Broadway musical *Oklahoma!*, which went on to a record run of 2,212 performances.

★　★　★

"You ain't goin' nowhere, son. You ought to go back to driving a truck."—Jim Denny, Grand Ole Opry manager who in 1954 fired Elvis Presley after a single performance.

"Stick to driving trucks, kid."—Rock Hudson, quoting one of several agents who felt he had no movie star potential; he finally got a break via gay agent Henry Willson.

"You're too short ever to be a leading man in pictures…. Stick to radio."—agent Sue Carol, quoting an agent on her client and husband Alan Ladd.

"It's pretty thin, son. I don't think people will follow it." — Henry Fonda, to son Peter on his new movie *Easy Rider*, which became a huge hit.

"A flash in the pan." — 1983 *Billboard* magazine assessment of Madonna.

"Newcomer Marilyn Monroe will never make moviegoers forget Rita Hayworth."—1948 fanzine movie review.

"For Broadway and records, she's a star…for the closeup mediums of television and motion pictures, Miss Streisand will have no more success than Ethel Merman did." — Arthur Godfrey, in 1966.

"They've got their own groups. What are we going to give them that they don't already have?"—Paul McCartney, in 1964, worrying about the Beatles' upcoming American debut.

"We're going to make everybody forget the Beatles."
— Bee Gee Barry Gibb, on his group's screen version of the Fab Four's *Sgt. Pepper's Lonely Hearts Club Band*, 1976 movie megaflop.

⋆　⋆　⋆

"I don't know if any of them are gay. Stop asking me that!"
— gay producer Allan (*Grease*) Carr, on The Village People, who starred in his 1980 movie musical *Can't Stop the Music*.

"This [movie] will do for The Village People what *A Hard Day's Night* did for the Beatles."—Allan Carr.

"*Can't Stop the Music* will be bigger than *Grease*."
— Allan Carr (as with the Bee Gees, The Village People's starring debut was also their disastrous finale).

⋆　⋆　⋆

"Get rid of the pointed-ears guy."
— an NBC-TV executive, to *Star Trek* creator Gene Roddenberry in 1966, on the Mr. Spock character.

⋆　⋆　⋆

"Change the last name, kid…sounds too Jewish."
— anonymous TV executive, to newcomer Jerry Seinfeld.

⋆　⋆　⋆

"They said there hadn't been any blond movie stars besides Alan Ladd."—Robert Redford, on sexist producers who equated yellow hair only with actresses.

⋆　⋆　⋆

"Preempt Doris Day? Are you out of your mind?"
— CBS president Robert Wood, in 1970, declining the opportunity to broadcast Monday Night Football.

⋆　⋆　⋆

THEY SPOKE TOO SOON

"The surest way to be alone is to get married." — feminist Gloria Steinem in a 1990 book.
Ten years later, she married.

———————

"Don't you dare go out with that half-breed again." — director Cecil B. DeMille in 1937 to actress Evelyn Keyes, on hearing that she was dating Mexican-Irish actor Anthony Quinn.
Months later, Quinn married DeMille's daughter Katherine.

———————

"The last man I'm going to marry is a man in show business. They're selfish, unreliable and make lousy husbands....I'm going to take a good long look before I get married. I'm not going to jump into it. Certainly not to a show-biz character." — Sandra Dee to *Parade* magazine in 1960.
Months later, after barely knowing him—they costarred in a movie—the blonde movie star wed singer/actor Bobby Darin.

———————

"I will never do another TV series. It couldn't top *I Love Lucy* and I'd be foolish to try. In this business, you have to know when to get off." — Lucille Ball in 1960.

She did two more series in a row, until 1974, then returned in a short-lived, disastrous series in 1986.

———————

In 1959 Elvis Presley publicly stated that one of the last things he would ever do would be to kiss a Mexican woman.
The following year, in *Flaming Star*, Mexican movie star Dolores Del Rio played his mother. Fox felt that costarring them would help diminish some of the under-standable hostility caused by the uneducated singer's comment.

———————

"No. No comment. I don't talk about my son or...um, his career." — Frances Milstead, mother of drag actor Divine, in the 1970s.
In 1981, after a nine-year separation, Harris Glenn Milstead and his parents made up. In 2001 Frances published a book, *My Son Divine*.

———————

"If I had a son and he was watching some guy making music on TV, and he came downstairs with makeup on and his mother's shoes and said, 'I want to be like Boy George,' I'd beat the shit out of him." — Eddie Murphy in *Cosmopolitan* magazine in the '80s. In the '90s it became public knowledge that he's not exactly repulsed by cross-dressers....

———————

"Least likely to succeed." — the verdict on thespic roommates Dustin Hoffman and Gene Hackman while they tenured at the Pasadena Playhouse.

———————

"The Clinton deficit-reduction plan will cost jobs, not create them." — Senator Pete Domenici in June, 1993; actually, over ten million jobs were created during President Clinton's first term.

———————

"That's what I'm going to do— kick Jay's ass." — talk show host Arsenio Hall in 1992, prophesying his show's triumph over Jay Leno's.

———————

"I care about being with my husband. I take my marriage seriously." — TV actress Shannen Doherty in January, 1994, four months after wedding actor Ashley Hamilton and three months before filing for divorce. (Ashley, son of George Hamilton, once claimed his father had been a boxer in college. Asked which college, he replied, "Uh...the College of the Performing Tan.")

———————

"Don't pay any attention to any of the drivel you hear about me and Jack Kennedy. It doesn't mean a thing." — Jackie Bouvier in 1952 (she was engaged to a John Husted but a year later married John Kennedy).

———————

"It's too early for a Polish pope." — Polish cardinal Karol Wojtyla in October, 1978, two days before being elected Pope.

———————

"To marry a senator and settle down in Georgetown." — seventeen-year-old Hillary Rodham's career goals as noted in a December, 1964, spoof interview with the future First Lady and senator in her high school newspaper.

———————

"I'm fifty now, and I am sure I won't be doing *The Tonight Show* in ten years. I doubt if I'll be doing it at fifty-five."
— Johnny Carson, who did it until he was sixty-six.

★   ★   ★

"The fact is that I don't like publicity."—Donald Trump, in 1987; he has put his name on a bicycle race, an airline, a casino, a Manhattan tower,...

★   ★   ★

"You bet I will pull through!"—tycoon J.P. Morgan, in 1913, on coming out of a coma...minutes later he died.

★   ★   ★

"You will never amount to very much."—a Münich school teacher, in 1889, to ten-year-old pupil Albert Einstein.

★   ★   ★

"I'm going to live to be a hundred."—health expert/author Jerome Rodale, in 1971; he died the next day at fifty-one.

★   ★   ★

"I have just one father. I want to make peace with him."
— singer Marvin Gaye, 1984, shortly before a fatal fight with his father, who shot him.

★   ★   ★

"I've got [Pres. George] Bush by the balls."
—Panamanian leader Manuel Noriega, in 1988; two years later, Noriega was in prison.

★   ★   ★

"Mr. Darwin's theory of evolution will never be proven."
— Church of England pamphlet, 1870s.

★   ★   ★

"Louis Pasteur's theory of germs is ridiculous and fiction."
— Pierre Pachet, French physiology professor, in 1872.

★   ★   ★

"What use could this company make of an electric toy?"
— William Orton, Western Union president, declining
in the 1870s the opportunity to buy the patent for Alexander
Graham Bell's telephone.

★   ★   ★

"Everything that can be invented, has been invented."
— Charles Duell, U.S. Patent Office commissioner, in 1899.

★   ★   ★

"Man will not fly for fifty years."
— airplane pioneer Wilbur Wright, 1901.

★   ★   ★

"The aeroplane will never fly."
— Lord Haldane, British minister of war, 1907.

★   ★   ★

"[Air mail] is an impractical sort of fad, and has no place in
the serious job of postal transportation."—Paul Henderson,
Second Assistant U.S. Postmaster General, 1922.

★   ★   ★

"I think there is a world market for about five computers."
— Thomas Watson, IBM chairman, 1943.

★   ★   ★

"But what good is it for?"—anonymous IBM engineer, in 1968,
on the recently invented microchip.

★   ★   ★

"What's it good for?"—Gordon Moore, Intel chairman and
cofounder, in the early '70s, on the concept of personal computers.

★   ★   ★

193

"There is no reason for any individual to have
a computer in their home."
—Ken Olsen, president of Digital Equipment in 1977.

★   ★   ★

"Computers in the future may weigh no more than 1.5 tons."
— *Popular Mechanics*, 1949.

★   ★   ★

"640K ought to be good enough for anybody."
— Bill Gates, Microsoft president, on the sufficiency
of computer memory in 1981.

★   ★   ★

"I am prepared to be a full-time chairman of Apple.
I am not walking away from Apple. I have no plans to go
anywhere else."—Apple Computer chair John Sculley, 1993, four
months before quitting to take another job.

★   ★   ★

"For the majority of people, the use of tobacco
has beneficial effect."—Los Angeles surgeon Ian MacDonald,
in 1963, quoted in *Newsweek*.

★   ★   ★

"The worst drug today is not smack or pot. It's refined sugar.
Sugar kills!"—actor/sun-worshipper George Hamilton.

★   ★   ★

"If you don't mind smelling like a peanut for two or three
days, peanut butter is darn good shaving cream."
— Senator Barry Goldwater.

★   ★   ★

"My favorite sandwich is peanut butter, bologna,
cheddar cheese, lettuce and mayonnaise on toasted bread with
lots of catsup on the side. Another favorite is toasted peanut

butter, cheese and bacon, or, if I'm in a hurry, just peanut butter and jelly."—presidential candidate (in 1968, against Nixon) Hubert Humphrey.

★　★　★

"It is not fatness. It is development."—former sex symbol Anita Ekberg, on her excess poundage..

★　★　★

"A lot of my peer group think I'm an eccentric bisexual, like I may even have an ammonia-filled tentacle or something somewhere on my body. That's okay."
— chemically-challenged actor Robert Downey, Jr.

★　★　★

"Charlie Chaplin used his ass better than any other actor. In all of his films, his ass is practically the protagonist. For a comic, the ass has incredible importance."—anatomically imaginative double-Oscar-winner Roberto Benigni.

★　★　★

"I concentrated on my private parts, trying to will my penis and testicles to grow. I even spoke to them. But my mind failed me. I was humiliated."
— double-Oscar-winner Marlon Brando.

★　★　★

"You'll enjoy a jock full of nuts special at lunchtime."
— Morey Amsterdam, mispronouncing his TV sponsor Chock Full of Nuts.

★　★　★

"I'm better-looking than people have any idea."
— Dennis Rodman.

★　★　★

"I don't think I'm that overweight, though, do you?"
—Alfred Hitchcock.

"Ooh, I hate looking at myself on the screen! I look awful!"
— Ursula Andress, in the 1960s.

* * *

"Talent is my life."—Madonna.

* * *

"I just get real uncomfortable if a guy near me
is dressed up, you know, in drag."—Eddie Murphy
(referring to dragged-up costar Arsenio Hall).

* * *

"I don't think I'll be remembered for nude scenes."
— Sharon Stone.

* * *

"I try to be God-like."—Michael Jackson.

* * *

"He is the least weird man I've ever known."
— Elizabeth Taylor, on Michael Jackson.

* * *

"We can fly, you know. We just don't know how to think the
right thoughts and levitate ourselves off the ground."
— Michael Jackson, who dearly wanted to play
Peter Pan on screen too.

* * *

"I catnap now and then…but I think while I nap, so it's not a
waste of time."—living expert Martha Stewart.

* * *

"I think my subject matter—living—has made such
an impact because it affects all of us so deeply….Living is
something we do take seriously."—Martha Stewart.

* * *

"People should turn to politicians for advice on life…. We know about more than just the business of politics, or business."— advice-challenged former vice president Dan Quayle.

★   ★   ★

"You know, I once played Grover Cleveland in the movies." — Ronald Reagan, in 1981, about House Speaker Tip O'Neill's desk, which once belonged to President Cleveland. Reagan had enacted Grover Cleveland Alexander, the baseball player.

★   ★   ★

"Who the hell wants to hear actors talk?" — Warner Bros. founder Harry Warner, in 1927, months before Warner Bros. pioneered "talkies."

★   ★   ★

"Television won't be able to hold on to any market it captures after the first six months. People will soon get tired of staring at a plywood box every night."—20th Century-Fox mogul Darryl F. Zanuck, in 1946.

★   ★   ★

"We expect within two or three years to have virtual parity with the NFL."—real estate expert Donald Trump, about his moving into sports via the New Jersey Generals of the upstart U.S. Football League. The USFL went under three years later, in 1986.

★   ★   ★

"I'll stick to building ships."—George Steinbrenner, in 1973, declaring his non-interference policy after buying the New York Yankees.

★   ★   ★

"I have more faith in my wife than to bump off her competition."—Jeff Gillooly, then-husband of skater Tonya Harding in 1994, weeks before pleading guilty to assaulting rival skater Nancy Kerrigan.

"I don't need bodyguards."—union scion Jimmy Hoffa, in 1975, several months before being abducted and murdered.

"I have no enemies. Why should I fear?"—President William McKinley, days before his assassination in 1901.

"We are not about to send American boys nine or ten thousand miles away from home to do what Asian boys ought to be doing for themselves."—President Lyndon Johnson, in 1964, about Vietnam.

"We are not interested in the possibilities of defeat. They do not exist."—Queen Victoria, in 1900, about the Boer War in South Africa, which Britain later lost.

"It is inconceivable that the Viet Cong could ever defeat the armed forces of South Vietnam."—General William Westmoreland, in 1964.

"We will drive them into the sea."—Egyptian ruler Gamal Abdul Nasser, speaking of Israel in 1968.

"No woman will in my time be prime minister."
— Margaret Thatcher, ten years before she became Britain's prime minister in 1979.

"With your voice, nobody is going to let you broadcast."
—CBS honcho Don Hewitt, in 1958, to Barbara Walters.

★   ★   ★

"Castro won't last a year."—deposed Cuban leader Fulgencio Batista, in 1957.

"I have no political ambition for myself or for my children."
— Kennedy patriarch Joseph P., in 1936.

★   ★   ★

"The vice presidency is not much of a job."— multi-millionaire
Nelson Rockefeller, in 1974, weeks before accepting the #2 post.

★   ★   ★

"…the fire of an election no longer burns in me."
— Arkansas governor Bill Clinton, in 1990, explaining his lack of
interest in running for office in the future.

★   ★   ★

"I don't want to be prime minister again.
It's pretty tough going."—Indira Gandhi, in 1974, not
long before running again and winning.

★   ★   ★

"I promise that truth shall be the policy of the Nixon
administration."—Vice President Spiro Agnew, in 1968.

★   ★   ★

"I applaud President Nixon's comprehensive statement
which clearly demonstrates again that the president was not
involved with the Watergate matter."—George Bush,
in 1974, months before Nixon was forced to resign.

★   ★   ★

"I want to be an old-fashioned lawyer, an honest
lawyer who can't be bought by crooks."
— Richard Nixon, to his mother in 1925.

★   ★   ★

"I have often been accused of putting my foot in my mouth,
but I will never put my hand in your pockets."
—VP Spiro Agnew, in 1969; he eventually had to resign for accepting political kickbacks.

"Read my lips: No new taxes."—President George Bush, in 1988, eighteen months before raising taxes.

★   ★   ★

"I'm telling you, I didn't write it."—novelist Joe Klein, in 1996, denying to the *Washington Post* that he'd written the Clinton roman à clef *Primary Colors*.

"For God's sake, definitely I didn't write it."
— Klein, in '96, denying to the *New York Times*.

"It's not me! I didn't do it. This is silly."—Klein, '96, denying to CBS News; five months later he admitted authorship.

★   ★   ★

"*Gone With the Wind* is going to be the biggest flop in Hollywood history."— Gary Cooper, in 1937, after declining to star in the screen version of the best-selling novel.

★   ★   ★

"The girl doesn't, it seems to me, have a special perception or feeling which would lift that book above the curiosity level."
— publisher's rejection letter, in 1952, declining
the diary of Anne Frank.

★   ★   ★

"If you read that they offered me $6 million to write a book, what else can I tell you? These publishers know what they're doing."—Whoopi Goldberg, whose *Book* was a costly flop.

★   ★   ★

"My James Bond novels are really for a very specialized, limited market. I am not courting the great unwashed public and do not expect them to fancy anything I write."
— 007's creator, Ian Fleming
(most of Bond's success followed Fleming's death).

★   ★   ★

"The book I have completed, *Answered Prayers*, just might be considered the second-greatest novel of the 20th century.... It certainly would rank among the top five on any objective critic's list."—Proust fan Truman Capote, who apparently completed only a few chapters of his magnum opus.

★　★　★

"They say it might break all records…and, well, that's something I think I can live with!"—Ronald Reagan, on his imminent memoirs, which were not a big hit.

★　★　★

"I wouldn't dream of writing a book about myself— what a ludicrous suggestion!"—Katharine Hepburn, in the 1970s; she later wrote two.

★　★　★

"My sister is the writer in the family…I don't think she'd like it if I put pen to paper, except to write about my life." — Jackie Collins' sister Joan, now herself a novelist.

★　★　★

"I was just a pup when I started swimming…and diving. I once saw a sign that said 'No Diving Unless Pool Is Full.' Well, the most people there [were] six or seven, so I never did dive that day."—Johnny Weissmuller, Olympic swimming champ turned movie Tarzan.

★　★　★

"There is [sic] not enough troops in the army to force the Southern people to break down segregation and admit the Negro race into our theaters, into our swimming pools, and into our churches." — Senator Strom Thurmond, in 1948—still serving fifty-four years later.

★　★　★

"Mistreatment of Jews in Germany may be considered virtually eliminated."—U.S. Secretary of State Cordell Hull, in 1933, during Hitler's first year in power.

* * *

"Germany has no desire to attack any country in Europe."
— Former U.K. Prime Minister David Lloyd George, 1936.

* * *

"I have no more territorial ambitions in Europe."
— Hitler, in 1938, after invading several countries and three months before invading Poland, thus starting World War II.

* * *

"The United States will not be a threat to us for decades."
— Adolf Hitler, 1940.

* * *

"It has been assumed, in my opinion erroneously, that Japan covets these islands."—General Douglas MacArthur, in 1939, on rumors that Japan would invade the Philippines.

* * *

"There is no Soviet domination of Eastern Europe, and there never will be under a Ford administration."
— President Gerald Ford, 1976.

* * *

"Approximately 80% of our air pollution stems from hydrocarbons released by vegetation, so let's not go overboard in setting and enforcing tough emission standards from man-made sources."—Ronald Reagan, conservation inexpert, 1979.

* * *

"On the whole, women think of love and men of gold braid or something of that nature. Beyond that, people think only of happiness—which doesn't exist."—Charles de Gaulle.

"You know, the difficulty with a president when he makes a statement is that everybody checks to see whether it is true."
— Richard Nixon.

*   *   *

"The President of today is just the postage stamp of tomorrow."—Gracie Allen.

*   *   *

"People talk too much politics and not enough nutrition, in my opinion....We should scrutinize our food suppliers as carefully as we do the men we put into office."
— nutritionist/author Adelle Davis.

*   *   *

"Culture is what your butcher would have if he were a surgeon."—writer Mary Pettibone Poole.

*   *   *

"I wasn't surprised that Elizabeth Dole tried running for president. She was trying to get out of the house, away from the horrors of Viagra. They never actually tell you about the other side, about the person who is on the receiving end."—Bette Midler, 1999, on the wife of Viagra spokesstud Robert Dole.

*   *   *

"When Republicans say they're for less government, it means more government in your bedroom and more files on you if you disagree with them."
—former California Governor Jerry Brown.

*   *   *

"Hmm, yes, well. One saw the consequences."—former UK PM Edward Heath, on former UK PM Margaret Thatcher, after being reminded that she needed only five hours of sleep a night.

*   *   *

"Too stupid."—then-Prime Minister Harold Wilson's (1964-1970) excuse for not inviting Prince Charles to dinner at 10 Downing Street on his eighteenth birthday.

★   ★   ★

"I can't really remember the names of the clubs that we went to."—basketball player Shaquille O'Neal, when asked if he'd visited the Parthenon while in Athens (Greece, that is).

★   ★   ★

"No, no. What if they were not as good as me? What would I do with those imbeciles?"—ballet dancer Rudolf Nureyev, to Morley Safer, on why he didn't want to be a father.

★   ★   ★

"It's really great being Magic Johnson the basketball player for eight months and then just plain Earvin Johnson for the other three."—"Magic" Johnson.

★   ★   ★

"If you can't keep quiet, shut up!"
— movie director Gregory Ratoff, to his crew.

★   ★   ★

"We have a marriage, like a father and son."
— boxing promoter Don King, on himself and Julio Cesar Chavez.

★   ★   ★

"You just cannot drive a Royce-Rolls (sic) in Beverly Hills anymore, because they have it in for you."
— personality Zsa Zsa Gabor.

★   ★   ★

"I was very ill and afraid for my sanity, but that was before I changed my name."—The Artist Formerly Known as Prince.

★   ★   ★

"The worst thing a man can do is go bald. Never let yourself go bald."—political aspirant Donald Trump.

★　★　★

"I don't like Mexican pictures. All the actors in them look too goddamn Mexican."—movie mogul Jack Warner.

★　★　★

"Mr. Nixon was the 37th president of the United States. He had been preceded by thirty-six others." — 38th U.S. President Gerald Ford.

★　★　★

"The last time I checked, the Constitution said 'of the people, by the people, and for the people.' That's what the Declaration of Independence said."—President Clinton, 1996 (in fact, the phrase comes from the Gettysburg Address).

★　★　★

"Straight men need to be emasculated. I'm sorry. They all need to be slapped around. Women have been kept down for too long. Every straight guy should have a man's tongue in his mouth at least once."—Madonna, not explaining why she thinks male tongue "emasculates."

★　★　★

"If he were here, I'd ask him if I could lick his eyeballs." — Christian Slater, on his idol Jack Nicholson.

★　★　★

"It is not true that Andrew Lloyd Webber and I are no longer speaking. I saw his last show. At least, I hope it was his last show."—Tim Rice, Webber's former partner (*Evita*).

★　★　★

DID YA KNOW?

Fact: Approximately 3.7 million Americans claim to have been abducted by aliens from outer space. Most described it as a pleasant experience. (Perhaps because they were asleep at the time?)

———————

Fact: A man is twice as likely to fall out of a hospital bed as a woman.

———————

Fact: Just over one-third of hunting deaths and injuries are self-inflicted.

———————

Fact: Heading a soccer ball often—ten or more times a game—causes mild neuropsychological damage and lowers the I.Q. (This explains a lot about some players, but what about British soccer fans?)

———————

Fact: Dance-floor dehydration syndrome can be fatal.

———————

Fact: A man is far more likely to help a good-looking woman who is bleeding than an unattractive woman who is injured.

———————

Fact: Unattractive criminals get 50% longer prison sentences than good-looking criminals.

———————

Fact: Very good-looking people earn 5% or more per hour than average-looking people. Plain women earn 5% less than average-looking women, and plain men earn 10% less than average-looking men. A majority of employers pay overweight women 20% less an hour than average-weight women, but men who are somewhat overweight earn 26% more than underweight men.

———————

Fact: If two men have identical resumés, the taller one will get hired 72% of the time. Men 6'2" or taller receive beginning salaries 12% bigger than men under six feet.

———————

Fact: Women are more than twice as likely to achieve orgasm if their male partner has extremely symmetrical features. However, such men tend to be less attentive to their partners and more apt to cheat on them. (They make studies of these things?)

Fact: One out of six adults has agreed to have sex because they were too embarrassed to just say no.

———————

Fact: Women hire private investigators more frequently than men, in order to find out if the person they're dating is marriage material.

———————

Fact: It's much harder to lie convincingly to somebody to whom you're physically attracted. P.S. Adults are more likely to lie in bed—that is, to prevaricate—than anywhere else.

———————

"An actor can be happiest if he likes his wife and loves his director. You need to like someone for it to last... and if you hate your director, every working moment is hell."
—Vic Morrow (*The Blackboard Jungle*), who died in an accident while filming *The Twilight Zone*.

★ ★ ★

"Being nominated for an Oscar is like being pregnant with a child someone else may have for all your labor pains."
— actress turned Labour M.P. Glenda Jackson.

★ ★ ★

"Politicians pretend they're virgins, ethically. They may rant and rave for a cause, while themselves pregnant with evil. A fellow [Hollywood Ten] victim, Ring Lardner, Jr., was essentially put in jail for not being conservative enough for our inquisitorial witch-hunters. One of the chief inquisitors, [congressman] J. Parnell Thomas, was in jail with Lardner. The real threat to our democratic way of life was of course not Lardner [a screenwriter], but that fat-cat politician caught padding his office payroll. Nor was Parnell the only politician in jail with his victims at that shameful time of our history."—screenwriter Dalton Trumbo (*Spartacus*).

★ ★ ★

"Politics have no relations to morals."
— Niccolo Machiavelli, in *The Prince*.

★ ★ ★

"We don't lie. We put our own interpretation on what the truth is."—Reagan National Security Advisor Robert McFarlane, quoted in *Propaganda Review*.

★ ★ ★

"Mussolini...a gift of Providence, a man free from the prejudices of the liberal school."—Pope Pius XI, 1929.

★ ★ ★

"If I had been an Italian, I am sure I would have been with you from the beginning to the end....Your movement [fascism] has abroad rendered a service to the whole world."—Winston Churchill, in a letter to Italian dictator Mussolini (pre-WW II).

"Don't forget, there are 200 million of us in a world of three billion. They want what we've got, and we're not going to give it to them."
—President Lyndon B. Johnson, 1966 (now six billion).

"That's a part of American greatness: discrimination. Yes, sir. Inequality, I think, breeds freedom and gives a man opportunity."
— Georgia governor Lester Maddox, speaking of the "man" who is male, white, heterosexual and Christian (preferably Protestant).

"Our one desire, our one determination, is that the people of Southeast Asia be left in peace to work out their own destinies in their own way."—President Lyndon Johnson, in 1964.

"In the Orient, life is cheap."
— General William Westmoreland, chief of U.S. troops in Vietnam, employing an occidental cliché and excuse.

"Victory for the Viet Cong would mean ultimately the destruction of freedom of speech for all men for all time, not only in Asia, but in the United States as well."—attorney and alarmist Richard Nixon, in 1965.

"If we quit Vietnam, tomorrow we'll be fighting in Hawaii, and next week we'll have to fight in San Francisco."
— ditto, ditto and president Lyndon Johnson, in 1967.

★   ★   ★

"If you're important enough, and say it loud enough, most people will believe anything they're told."
— Oscar-winning actor José Ferrer.

★   ★   ★

"If something is repeated often enough, it takes on familiarity, and then even a persuasive ring of truth."
— screenwriter Garson Kanin.

★   ★   ★

"The Creeds are believed not because they are rational, but because they are repeated."—Oscar Wilde.

★   ★   ★

"I got the courage to leave [wife-beater] Ike and become a big success on my own by chanting...repeating a kind of self-help mantra...a deliberate prayer or meditation."
— Baptist turned Buddhist Tina Turner.

★   ★   ★

"If your dreams repeatedly don't come true, get yourself some more realistic ones....Your dreams shouldn't be too easy to achieve, but neither should they be too difficult— no use being a masochist about it!"—would-be opera star but TV quiz show host Gene Rayburn (*The Match Game*).

★   ★   ★

"I know Clint's dream for a while was having two famous acting offspring, like Henry Fonda....He wanted to direct *The Karate Kid* for Columbia, but only if his son, Kyle, could star in it. They said no, and was he steaming. I remember for years after that, he banned Coca Cola from his presence—

he didn't drink it, and he did not want you to drink it. For some time there, it was an obsession with him...you know, like Joan Crawford and her no-wire-hangers-ever!"
— anonymous former employee for Eastwood's Malpaso production company; Columbia used to be owned by Coca Cola (now it's owned by Sony).

★　★　★

"Dr. Laura Schlessinger is not an expert in the field her listeners believe. She is no psychologist or psychiatrist— she trained in a physical field...her lack of expertise and, even more so, her religious zealotry, bigotry, homophobia, self-righteousness, etc., make her dangerous to listen to, and a bad influence on young or vulnerable people....Some of her statements are vicious or laughable, her hypocrisy with the adultery and X-rated photos she tried to sweep under the carpet,...the woman's an overpaid disaster area whose dreams and goals interfere with decency, kindness and sound, unbiased advice."—tap and ballet dancer Paul Draper.

★　★　★

"Everyone does it."—Sophia Loren, in 1999, accused of accepting $50,000 each time for gracing the front row of designer fashion shows to attract publicity; whether everyone does it or not, the Italian Fashion Academy threatened to divest the star of her honorary presidency unless she apologized for the statement.

★　★　★

"If we could just get Donald Trump to shut up, the thing might disappear altogether: NASA scientists say the ozone hole over Antarctica is smaller [in 1999] than it was this time last year. It's 9.8 million square miles, down from a record of 10.5 million square miles."—*Beverly Hills (213)* columnist Jack Martin.

★　★　★

"Hear no evil, speak no evil, and you'll never be invited to a party."—attributed to Oscar Wilde.

"I don't give a shit about the Italian lira."—Pres. Richard Nixon's reply to H.R. Haldeman as to whether he wanted to hear a report on the decline of the Italian currency.

_____

"Selena? Her music is awful. I don't know what Mexicans are into. If you're going to sing about what's going on in Mexico, what can you say? You can grow crops, you got a cardboard house, your eleven-year-old daughter is a prostitute. This is music to perform abortions to!"—Howard Stern, on the air, hours before Selena was buried on April 3, 1995.

_____

"He's a lousy comic. He thinks he's so funny. He's not, he's not! You know, they call him Deep Throat because he blows so many jokes."—alleged comic Sam Kinison on Paul Reubens, aka Pee-Wee Herman.

_____

"His father was a murderer…he loved to dance. Fact, he died dancing—on the end of a rope!"—Sam Kinison on Woody (*Cheers*) Harrelson's (still alive) father, in jail for an alleged murder (Woody maintains his father is innocent).

"I'm so sorry. I misunderstood. With a face like yours, I just assumed you were a character actress."—unnamed British journalist (who never got to work in Hollywood after that) on the set of *Dinner At Eight* (1933), meeting its star, Marie Dressler (though older, portly and plain, the beloved comedienne was the #1 box office movie star in the world).

_____

"Thank you, Mr. Falk, but for the same money I can get an actor with two eyes."—Columbia chief Harry Cohn to aspiring actor Peter Falk, who'd done a screen test to disprove Cohn's assertion that Falk's "off-center vision" (he'd lost his right eye at age three) would show on screen.

_____

"It takes more than flowers to shut me up. I'd rather have cold cash. Flowers are for funerals. If my kid ever gave me flowers for Mother's Day, I'd think he wanted me dead."—Jacqueline Stallone, mother of Sylvester and Frank (remember Frank?) (remember Sly?).

_____

"…a bloated scuzzball who claims to be what's left of John Travolta."—critic Rex Reed (Ava Gardner once said that Reed was always either at your feet or at your throat).

————————————

"Damon Wayans has the grace of a clubfoot….His talent is a lot less than his ambition, and he's not funny, which for a comedian is kind of crucial. Like, Dudley Moore also has a clubfoot, but he's funny—sometimes."—Michael Peters, who choreographed Michael Jackson's *Thriller* video.

On the other hand, Wayans is insensitively homophobic. In 1998 while performing at the Laugh Factory in L.A., the former *In Living Color* star stated, "I don't think there's no faggots in the room now," after a male couple got up and left due to his anti-gay "humor."

————————————

"Why the fuck does this have to happen to me? This is gonna ruin my tour!"—author Jacqueline Susann, whose first book tour was due to begin November 22, 1963, the day JFK was assassinated.

————————————

"My plump little hunchback."—what MGM honcho Louis B. Mayer (in a good mood!) called his teenaged star Judy Garland (she later told one columnist that "even when he complimented her performance, he grabbed a breast to accent the compliment.").

————————————

"The insane plucking and starving and discipline-greedy self-abnegation that she represents. I think that most people would rather be processed through the digestive tract of an anaconda than be Celine Dion for a day."—author Cintra Wilson (maybe someone called Celine "plump" when she was very young.…)

————————————

"Well, the bitch died today."—Bette Davis to Burt Reynolds at a party, hours after the death of Joan Crawford (Reynolds immediately introduced the gentleman of the press standing next to him, whereupon Bette immediately added, sweetly, "But she was always on time.").

————————————

"The earless wonder."— how J. Paul Getty II allegedly referred to his eldest son, J. Paul Getty III, who'd been kidnapped in 1973 and had his ear cut off before billionaire grandfather J. Paul Getty would pay the ransom.

At first the oil billionaire had refused to pay a penny in ransom, reasoning that he had fourteen other grandchildren who might then be kidnapped. He did publicly note that "I see my grandson infrequently and I am not particularly close to him." Not publicized at the time was the fact that Getty only agreed to pay the $1 million ransom as a loan to II, repayable at 4% interest.

(Later, III's mother sued II to try and force him to pay their son's mounting medical bills after he fell into a coma—temporary— after "a night of swallowing liquor and methadone and Valium." In 1983 II finally agreed to pay the bills, which he'd thought too high.)

———————

Gay people "deserve" AIDS.—so opined Michael "son of Ronald" Reagan on a 1997 *Politically Incorrect* episode.

———————

Openly gay actor/playwright Harvey Fierstein replied to the former First Adopted Son, "Fuck you, and fuck your father!" The latter comment, less obscene than Reagan's, was censored from the program.

———————

"I can't shake hands with any-body from San Francisco."— paranoid Pres. Richard Nixon on a (pre-AIDS) White House tape released in 1999, during an anti-gay diatribe to White House staffers.

———————

"They control Hollywood, they've got it all sewn up. No wonder I haven't got a chance."—Paul Lynde to fellow comedian Skip E. Lowe, blaming his career slump on Jews rather than luck, age, weight, alco-holism or his stereotypical gay image (Lynde dropped Lowe when he found out—"I can spot 'em a mile away"—he was half-Jewish).

Hollywood's "Jewish agenda" is why there have been so few Jewish-themed films over the years, why Christmas is mentioned and/or depicted in a disproportionate number of movies, why nearly all screen weddings take place in a church rather than a city hall, synagogue, etc., and why virtually the only religious symbol worn on screen is a crucifix.

"I think of women as a producing machine that brings babies into the world."—comedian Jerry Lewis (born Joseph Levitch)

explaining in 2000 why he dislikes female comedians. No need to ask his views on overpopulation.

"To me, capital punishment boils down to another potential parking space."—comedian Sam Kinison.

"Don't worry, my psychic told me I would never die in a plane crash."—Goldie Hawn "comforting" Diane Keaton during takeoff.

"An actor is not going to go on *Oprah* and say, 'I've called gossip columnists for protection,' but they all do it. Whenever you see somebody in the *Star* showing pictures of their new baby, believe me it's because *Star* had a scandal on him. They'll say, 'We're going to print this scandal,' and he'll say, 'What if I let you into the hospital for the baby's first pictures?' No celebrity wants the *Star* in the hospital after his wife's given birth. But you've got to protect yourself. When they know they're guilty, they'll pick up the phone and come to us for help. They've come to me and I've helped them."
— columnist turned E! Channel host A.J. Benza.

"Do you know about Carol Channing's famous silver plate? She once asked me if I had seen her 'plate,' and I stared at her teeth, then said no. She said, 'My silver plate, diddums, from David Merrick.' So she dragged out this famous plate that everyone had seen but me, and it was impressive, and engraved: 'Congratulations, Carol, on the $8 million gross for *Hello, Dolly!* David Merrick.' Years later, I'm talking with the producer himself, and I mention his gift to Carol, and he snorted, 'Gift, my eye! I sent her the message, but it was Charles Lowe—her PR man and her husband—who got the silver plate and had my message engraved onto it.' Whatever that plate cost Lowe, he's gotten over a million dollars in publicity out of it. Maybe $8 million."—columnist Jim Bacon.

"Privately, I called him Deep Throat, because he blew so many musical notes before we got it all recorded and per-fect."—producer Allan Carr, on his *Grease* male lead, John Travolta.

"The poor thing looks so frail, an ejaculation would blow him sky-high!"—Irene Ryan ("Granny"), on *Beverly Hillbillies* guest star Wally Cox, hired to play beau to Miss Hathaway (openly gay

Nancy Kulp); Cox, Marlon Brando's roommate, was said to be at least as strong as Brando.

★　★　★

"Caucasian? It was my army draft card. I thought it meant circumcized."—Elvis Presley.

★　★　★

"What's the matter with him now?"
— baseball celeb Yogi Berra, to his wife, after she'd informed him she'd taken their son to see *Dr. Zhivago* for the third time.

★　★　★

"Arnold Schwarzenegger had elective surgery to correct a valve problem in his heart, proving he had one."
— *Movieline* magazine, on the Austrian-American who'd invited former Nazi leader Kurt Waldheim to his wedding.

★　★　★

"Well, a feud is this way. A man has a quarrel with another man, and kills him; then that other man's brother kills him; then the other brothers, on both sides, goes [sic] for one another; then the cousins chip in—and by-and-by everybody's killed off, and there ain't no more feud. But it's kind of slow, and takes a long time."—Mark Twain's 1884 definition of a feud.

★　★　★

"Basically, you kill each other to see who has the better imaginary friend."
— humorist Victor Lownes, on going to war over religion.

★　★　★

"Religion is necessary because it keeps the poor people from killing the rich people."—Napoleon.

★　★　★

"Organized religion is a sham and a crutch for weak-minded people."—Minnesota Governor Jesse Ventura.

"You never see animals going through the absurd and often horrible fooleries of magic and religion. Only man behaves with such gratuitous folly. It is the price he has to pay for being intelligent but not, as yet, intelligent enough."
— writer Aldous Huxley.

*　*　*

"If I die before him, I want a little of my ashes put in his food so I can live inside him."—Drew Barrymore, on her pet cat.

*　*　*

"I don't have a television because I think it's the devil!"
— Cameron Diaz, who had a clause in her contract that her producers must employ a cat-sitter for her pet while Cameron was filming.

*　*　*

"I get excited about something, but it never lasts more than seven minutes. Seven minutes exactly. That's my limit. I never know why I get up in the morning."
— Marlon Brando, in the 1950s.

*　*　*

"You read what Disraeli had to say—I don't remember what he said. He said something. He's no longer with us."
— Bob Dole, at a 1999 book signing for "his" anthology, *Great Wit of the 20th Century* (Disraeli died in 1881...).

*　*　*

"Eighty percent of married men cheat in America. The rest cheat in Europe."—Jackie Mason.

*　*　*

"I believe in large families. Every woman should have at least three husbands."—Zsa Zsa Gabor. (Sister Eva agreed: "Marriage is too interesting an experiment to be tried once or twice.")

*　*　*

"Women are predators. They age and still look great. Like, I just saw both my ex-wives. They're getting younger and younger, while I'm looking so damned old that I'm falling apart. Women take your money, suck your blood, and thrive on the whole thing."
— actor Richard Harris (no, he never married a Gabor).

★　★　★

"My face has been my misfortune. It has attracted six unsuccessful marriage partners. It has attracted all the wrong people into my boudoir and brought me tragedy and heartache for five decades. My face is a mask I cannot remove."
— screen queen Hedy Lamarr, in her memoirs *Ecstasy and Me*.

★　★　★

"...we are endlessly fascinated by our betters, especially our beautiful betters. If [Princess] Diana had looked like Queen Elizabeth, we wouldn't still be reading about her death in the tabloids. And if John-John [Kennedy] and Caroline Bessette had resembled one of Bobby's toothy sons and, say, Chelsea Clinton, we wouldn't be having this discussion."
— columnist Rick Barrs, in the *New Times*.

★　★　★

"Age is a high price to pay for maturity."
— playwright Tom Stoppard.

★　★　★

"Do not resist growing older—many are denied the privilege."—Confucius.

★　★　★

Hollywood Myths

Hollywood is the movie capital of the world.
Depends how one defines that. In global influence, for better or worse, yes. In quality, extremely debatable. In quantity, no way. India makes far more movies each year than the U.S. does, and by the year 2007 will have the world's biggest national population—in a land where movies are more popular than television.

The James Bond movies are the most popular film series ever.
Only the recent death of star Kiyoshi Atsumi ended the longest-running continuing movie series in history, Japan's Tora-san series, which comprised over fifty entries in fifty years.

_E.T._ paraphernalia is popular the world over.
Not in most Muslim countries—surprised? Nor in France, where E.T. dolls are illegal because one can't sell dolls there without human faces.

Hollywood celebs love psychiatrists.
You only hear about the ones who do....Dean Martin wondered, "So who appointed him an expert? A shrink is a guy who goes to a striptease show and stares at the audience."

**Actors can coast, but directors really have to know
their stuff to survive in show biz.**
Actor/director Orson Welles revealed, "The director is the most over-rated artist in the world. He is the only artist who, with no talent what-

soever, can be a success for fifty years without his lack of talent ever being discovered."

Studio heads have to be great communicators.
Terry Semel, company-CEO of Warner Bros., avowed that "A sign of a good executive is someone who doesn't return phone calls."

Jews "took over" movies and much of show business.
No. They were there at the inception. According to mass media professor David W. Foster of Arizona State University, Jews initially "occupied emerging industries like radio, television, and the movies because old Christian money considered them to be beneath its interest and investment."

Actor are helped by watching dailies
(the previous day's filmed footage).
Some are. However, a young movie actress once asked stage and screen veteran Ethel Barrymore if it wouldn't help Barrymore's performance to view the dailies, which she eschewed? The star replied, "My dear, I never saw myself on the stage."

Singers love, or grow to love, the songs that helped make them rich and famous.
Not necessarily. Eddie Fisher still hates hearing his long-ago megahit *Oh, My Papa*. Why? "I hated my father when he was alive and I hate him now that he's dead."

P.S. Sometimes the sound of a musical hit reminds a star of her or his bad judgment. Barbra Streisand initially refused to record *The Way We Were* and asked composer Marvin Hamlisch to come up with a better song.

As artists and athletes, dancers are respected performers.

More than before, but as award-winning dancer Gwen Verdon said, "'Dancer' on your passport used to mean 'prostitute.' In fact Jean Coyn, married to Gene Kelly, had 'dancer' on her passport and was arrested in Iran as a hooker." Despite the fact that "It takes as long to learn to be proficient at dancing as to become a doctor."

Acting is an emotionally fulfilling career.

Canadian actress Kate Nelligan (*The Prince of Tides, Eye of the Needle*) puts it succinctly, "It's not about acting, technique or art. It's about effects (she left England for Hollywood). I wouldn't become an actor again if I could change. I'm too bright for a career that runs out. I thought I'd spend my life telling good stories to an intelligent public. I must have been out of my fucking mind."

Doing a same-sex love scene must be frightening or embarrassing.

Those who would be most frightened or embarrassed (or say they would) don't do them, including most gay or lesbian stars. The consensus is that most love scenes, period, are awkward. Said Ewan McGregor of his nude same-sex love scenes in *Velvet Goldmine*, "It's actually much more exciting being in a sex scene with a man. It's something outside of my normal experience."

Hollywood sexual shenanigans take place behind closed doors.

There too. But at a 1998 Oscar party hosted by a William Morris executive, New Line Cinema president Mike De Luca was fellated by a woman in full view of several guests, until the offending pair were asked to leave.

Once a star, always a star.

Stage legend Mrs. Patrick Campbell (is that sexist, or what?) lamented, "Once I was a tour de force. Now I am forced to tour."

Fans are loyal to big stars.

As Marilyn Monroe said, "When my looks start to go, so will most of my fans."

Myth: Hollywood stars are basically people like everyone else.

They may be people, but despite the average-guy image they often try to project, they lead completely different lives. They're multi-millionaires, usually with enormous egos and the sort of adulation royalty is used to. Hollywood moms may speak of trying to balance career and mother-hood, but unlike the average working woman, Demi Moore, say, has two nannies in attendance for her kids. And the cooking is done by hired help. Ann-Margret admits that for her a kitchen is "like science-fiction." Author Penny Stallings wrote that despite her cookie-baking image, Harriet Nelson "is said never to have been inside a kitchen, which would make sense given that she was a busy TV star (*Ozzie & Harriet*), wife and mother," and a successful band singer before turning to Ozzie and acting.

Myth: Stars are all narcissists, dwelling on their good looks.

It's surprising how many good-looking performers don't consider them-selves that good-looking. Elizabeth Taylor then said that her idea of a beautiful actress was Ava Gardner, who once said she felt herself far from a classic beauty and would much rather have the talent of her screen idol Bette Davis. Sex siren Rita Hayworth confessed she was ter-ribly insecure about her looks—and about losing them. French super-star Catherine Deneuve, at the time labeled "the most beautiful woman in the world," was, according to companion and director Roger Vadim (father of her son), "jealous whenever I looked at or spoke to another woman who was one-fifth as attractive as she."

And attractive actors like Henry Fonda, Ursula Andress and Kim Novak even in their primes hated to watch themselves on screen, whether during the daily rushes or in the completed picture. Director Sydney Pollack has said, "The only star I know who enjoys watching daily rushes is Barbra Streisand," whom he helmed in *The Way We Were* with rushes non-fan and then-hunk Robert Redford.

★   ★   ★

It seems as if Hollywood celebs don't lose as much hair as ordinary men. Why? Because they can afford the most discreet toupees. And because writers have traditionally revealed less about actors' secrets than actresses' plastic surgeries—since most actresses are far from bald, excepting such as Ida Lupino and Marx Brothers foil Margaret Dumont; Joan Collins' pal Zsa Zsa Gabor has stated Joan is bald, but there's no proof. The book *Forbidden Channels* offered a partial list of be-rugged actors:

Jack Benny, George Burns, Fred MacMurray, Macdonald Carey, Bing Crosby, E.G. Marshall, Don Porter, Lloyd Nolan, Andy Williams, Jack Paar, Carl Betz, Jack Edwards, Ralph Edwards, Jack Bailey, Gale Gordon, Steve Allen, Don Knotts, Lorne Greene, George Maharis, William Shatner, Martin Landau, Darren McGavin, Jack Klugman, Michael Ansara, Ricardo Montalban, Edward Woodward, Gil Gerard, Willard Scott, Burt Reynolds, Stacy Keach, Harry Anderson, Robert Mandan, Steve Martin and Tony Randall. That's not including a whole slew of movie actors and singers of varying ages.

★   ★   ★

"I don't mind….I lost it to the natural aging process that besets most men."
— movie star Ray Milland, on how he lost his hair.

Indeed he may not have minded, for unlike a Burt Reynolds or a Charlton Heston, who have yet to appear on screen sans rug, Milland was one of few then or now (Sean Connery's another) to act in the bald. But his explanation was false: many actresses and actors had their hair damaged and/or diminished via primitive equipment—like early electric hair rollers—used by studio hairdressers, who had to make do with available technology. Milland's hair suffered major losses during grooming for *Reap the Wild Wind* (1942). An outspoken homo-

LAST WORDS

"Bourbon."
— Tallulah Bankhead.

———————

"It's a long time since I drank champagne." — Chekhov.

———————

"I've never felt better!"
— Douglas Fairbanks.

———————

"Don't pull down the blinds! I feel fine. I want the sunlight to greet me."
— Rudolph Valentino.

———————

"More light!" — Goethe.

———————

"Mamma…Mamma."
— Casanova.

———————

"I have long been partial to the river view, Doctor."
— George Washington.

———————

"I am dying, but otherwise quite well."
— Dame Edith Sitwell, on being asked how she felt.

———————

"Go away! I'm all right."
— H.G. Wells.

———————

"Go on, get out! Last words are for fools who haven't said enough." — Karl Marx.

———————

"It is nothing." — Archduke Franz Ferdinand of Austria, fatally wounded by an assassin; his death sparked World War I.

———————

"Strike the tent!"
— Robert E. Lee.

———————

"So little done, so much to do."
— Sir Cecil Rhodes, after whom the African nation of Rhodesia, now Zimbabwe, was named.

———————

"Well, folks, you are about to see a baked Appell." —
Chicago murderer George Appell, while being strapped into the electric chair.

———————

"Dying is easy. Comedy is difficult." — actor Edmund Gwenn (*Miracle on 34th Street*).

———————

"You will find my last words in the blue folder." — Sir Max Beerbohm, to his secretary.

phobe—he bristled at comparisons to Cary Grant, whom he at first resembled—he privately blamed his baldness on Hollywood hairdressers but publicly gave a more "natural" explanation.

★　★　★

"My hair's kind of thinning…."— singer/actor Bobby Darin, **who however didn't admit that he'd been wearing a toupee since his early twenties, the better to match his hip, youthful image (he died at thirty-nine following heart surgery).**

Because he was "illegitimate," Darin unwittingly lived a lie. Not until he was thirty did his real mother tell him she wasn't his sister (he'd believed his grandmother was his mother). Posthumously, his mother rather lamely explained that she waited so long because "I wanted to spare him being illegitimate. He was thinking about going into politics and I didn't want it to get out that way." The revelation was semi-traumatic for Darin (ne Walden Cassotto), who later took a year off to ponder his life.

P.S. Oddly enough, before Bobby wed film star Sandra Dee, he'd been romantically involved with her mother, Mary.

★　★　★

"You know, at my age I'm not really combing my hair in the morning. I'm arranging it."— Bing Crosby, alluding to his **sparsity of hair; but in fact he too wore a toupee.**

★　★　★

Myth: Most show biz stars who have had nose-jobs are Jewish.
Many Jewish celebs have had nose-jobs. (It's a myth that most Jews have "Semitic" noses, or are even Semites, which most Jews were back when the Bible was written.) A majority of celebs who've had their noses redone, though, aren't Jewish. Hollywood historian Penny Stallings published the following mixed list of stars of yore:

Dean Martin, the Gabor sisters, Dana Wynter, Carolyn Jones, Peter O'Toole, Stefanie Powers, Suzanne Pleshette, Rita Moreno, George Hamilton, Joel Grey, Sissy Spacek, Carole Landis, Marie Wilson, Nanette Fabray, Joan Hackett, Jill St. John, Raquel Welch, Talia Shire, Marlo Thomas, Annette Funicello, and Barbara Eden.

After they became famous: Dinah Shore, Lee Grant, Vera-Ellen, Al Jolson, Cameron Mitchell, Bobby Van, Alan King, Mitzi Gaynor, Rhonda Fleming, Juliette Greco, Jan Sterling, Fanny Brice, and Milton Berle.

★　　★　　★

Myth: A rhinoplasty (nose-job) always helps a career.
It helps if you do it before anyone knows you've done it. There can sometimes be a backlash. After Jewish comedic star Fanny Brice redid hers, some critics said she wasn't as funny anymore, and a detractor said she "cut off her nose to spite her race." Which is what non-fans said about Michael Jackson's evolving nose, though in fact several of the Jacksons have had work done. And many Hispanics took umbrage when Raquel Welch denied she'd had any plastic surgery other than correcting her "Latin nose" (she's half-Bolivian). What is a "Latin nose"?

But with her original Lebanese nose—via father Danny—Marlo Thomas would not have become *That Girl*. Nor would Dino Crocetti, renamed Dean Martin, have become a crooner and matinee idol. Lou Costello of Abbott & Costello paid for Dino's operation. According to comedian Alan King, "Dean's original nose, it looked like he was eating a banana."

★　　★　　★

"Well, you know, when you think about it, fatherhood's no less important than a man's career, and that's in or out of Hollywood."—Bing Crosby.
The crooner/movie star was not his affable, easygoing image, as myriad coworkers have attested. (And despite his somewhat asexual image, he had more affairs with actresses than most of the reputed screen romeos.) Though he long extolled traditional "family values," he was a harsh, controlling and frequently belittling father. He informed Barbara Walters on national TV that he would cut his only daughter out of his life like that if she lived with a man minus marriage.

He was particularly hard on his four sons by his first wife, later all but abandoning them after remarrying and having three more kids. Bing resented the middling success of actor son Gary, who later penned a male "Mommie Dearest" tell-all titled *Going My Own Way* (Bing had won an Oscar for *Going My Way*, 1944) about his late father. Two of the

LITERATES

"As good almost to kill a man as kill a good book…who kills a man kills a reasonable creature…but he who destroys a good book kills reason itself…slays an immortality rather than a life."
— John Milton, 1644 (books cost more then).

"We all know that books burn—yet we have the greater knowledge that books cannot be killed by fire. People die, but books never die."— President Franklin Roosevelt, 1942 (to the American Booksellers Association).

"The human race, to which so many of my readers belong."
— G.K. Chesterton, 1904.

"Camarado, this is no book; who touches this touches a man."
— gay poet Walt Whitman, in 1881, from *Leaves of Grass*.

"Reviewers…are interested in writers, not writing. When they like something of mine, I grow suspicious and wonder."
— gay writer Gore Vidal.

"Beat him to death, the dog! He's a reviewer!" — Goethe.

"No man can be criticized but by a man greater than he. Do not, then, read the reviews." — Ralph Waldo Emerson, 1842.

"A bad review is like baking a cake with all the best ingredients and having someone sit on it."
— novelist Danielle Steele.

"Screenplays are to novels what board games are to chess."
— novelist Truman Capote.

"Science fiction, like Brazil, is where the nuts come from."
— Thomas M. Disch
(in *The Observer*, 1987).

"One man is as good as another until he has written a book."
— Benjamin Jowett, 1899.

"Beware the man of one book."
— Isaac D'Israeli (1791-1834).

"I thought about writing only one book…then people might think it was a fluke or someone helped me write it. Besides, if I hadn't done the novels, my dog would have been impossible to live with." — best-seller Jacqueline Susann, whose first book was about her poodle, Josephine.

"Even cynics say that novels are a thing of the past. Novels are for the few, the curious, and those with lots of nighttime hours to spare….Screenplays are high-tech, concise, and must please the whole world, from the producers to the peons." — screenwriter Stirling Silliphant.

"Writing a screenplay is making magic….A screenplay writer can and did take a mediocre novel like *Father of Frankenstein* that no one would have heard of, and transform it into a quality movie and Oscar-winning script like *Gods & Monsters*. — screenwriter and instructor Claire Feingertz.

"Doing my autobiography was no harder for me than writing a novel. I happen to be gifted with perfect recall." — stripper turned memoirist Gypsy Rose Lee.

"There's biography, and there's biomythography, which is what they want. So when they ask me, I say I've forgotten too much." — closeted gay actor Cesar Romero, who never wrote his memoirs.

"The palest ink is better than the best memory." — Chinese proverb.

other three original sons committed suicide: Dennis Crosby had confessed, "I haven't written a book....I just carry my bad memories of my father around with me—I don't dwell on them, I did not create them, but they are there," and Lindsay Crosby, who killed himself on Christmas Eve in 1989 after watching his dad sing *White Christmas* in the movie *Holiday Inn*.

* * *

"I don't talk about my old man in my interviews. This is my interview, man!"— Tupac Shakur, not revealing his estrangement from his biological father; though he left an estate in the millions, he left not a dollar to the man who didn't stick around and help raise him.

* * *

"He had quite a reputation...[but] I'm proud of him anyway."— Sean Flynn, son of movie star Errol Flynn.
Later, when asked if he might become an actor, Sean said maybe. "To carry on your father's name?" asked the Australian reporter. "No, to clear it," said Sean, perhaps referring to Errol's rape trials, chemical dependencies and notorious promiscuity. But Sean became a photographer and died in Southeast Asia during the Vietnam war. His grave wasn't located until 1991.

* * *

"...and what is more important than our children?" — Ronald Reagan, in a presidential speech.
Of course he was referring to children in general, but reports since the time he became California governor sometimes inferred that Ronald and Nancy tended to ignore the two children from his prior marriage to actor Jane Wyman. After publishing his book *On the Outside Looking In*, first son Michael Reagan told the *Washington Post* he had three wishes he hoped could come true while his dad was still president: attending a State dinner, having his kids turn on the White House Christmas tree, and flying in Air Force One. He added, "But I'm not mad about it anymore," that his wishes hadn't so far come true. In 1988, toward the end of his two presidential terms, Ronald Reagan granted one, flying with Michael on Air Force One.

Myth: Celebs in default of the law are invariably forced to perform community service or do public service ads.

Not always, but increasingly so, as certain more imaginative solutions didn't always work out well. For instance Marvin Gaye (later shot to death by his father, who was acquitted), owed back alimony and child support to his ex-wife of fourteen years, Anna Gordy Gaye (sister of Motown founder Berry Gordy). He was ordered to record an album and hand over $600,000 of its profits to her. Gaye had left his wife for a younger woman who left him three months after their marriage. He grudgingly did the recording, sarcastically titled *Here, My Dear*. It was too specialized and negative to interest much of the public, and its pot-shots at his former spouse caused her to threaten him with a $5 million invasion-of-privacy lawsuit. She considered the album just a musical revenge: "I think he did it deliberately to see how hurt I could become."

Myth: Hollywood parents are always ready to hire their own kids.

Some. Others are willing but wary. Some would rather hire anyone but. Among the latter, glamorous mothers Joan Crawford and Loretta Young, who did anything but cheer on their daughters when they became actresses. Henry Fonda was not anywhere as estranged from daughter Jane as the media made out, but did admit he felt lucky to ever be offered another role and wouldn't presume to ask that Jane be offered one too. He also allowed, "I'm in awe of what Jane does. I cannot do it." Perhaps he hesitated to act opposite her. In any event, they didn't team until Jane, as producer and star, got him into *On Golden Pond*, for which he finally won an Academy Award.

Producer, star and director Barbra Streisand hesitated to hire her real son to play her son in *The Prince of Tides* because she felt he was too old. He eventually convinced her otherwise.

Myth: Mothers are always proud of their celebrity sons.

There may be less potential friction or competition than with moms and celebrity daughters, but it depends on the mother. Minnie Malden,

DO AS I SAY, NOT AS I DO

"All this profanity is appalling. Disgusting! And needless too." — Katharine Hepburn, on what movies have come to.
Hepburn was the first person to sing the word "shit" on a Broadway stage (in *Coco*).

———————

"Everything I've gotten, I earned. I didn't marry my way up." — Nicole Kidman.
Both sentences are debatable. At any rate, according to *Esquire*, when young Nicole's mother wouldn't buy her a Barbie doll, the future thespian went out and stole one.

———————

"I taught my son to cherish and respect his [Jewish] heritage." — Sadie Berle, mother of TV star Milton Berle (ne Berlinger). But when "Uncle Miltie" became a star in the 1950s, Sadie changed her name to Sandra.

———————

"We need more honesty in politics." — Ronald Reagan.
At the 1992 Republican National Convention, Reagan attributed words to Abraham Lincoln which Lincoln never said.

"What does an actor know about politics?" — Ronald Reagan criticizing Ed Asner (then president of the Screen Actors Guild, which Reagan had headed) for opposing Reagan's contra ("against") policy in Central America.
Or maybe he just forgot? Like he forgot that he wore makeup as an actor….

———————

"Being a performer means caring about your audience. Really caring." — singer Rod Stewart.
Of course, audiences pay. Music publicist Keith Altham revealed in his book *No More Mr. Nice Guy* that "There's only one thing Rod cares about and that's Rod….Despite constant requests from charities, I never saw him dip into his pocket once." Altham nicknamed his former client "the Tartan Tightwad" and disclosed that another ex-client, Mick Jagger, never tips cab drivers more than a quarter.

———————

Charles Spencer, aka Lord Spencer, Princess Diana's brother, asked that tabloid editors be banned from his sister's funeral. Understandably.

But: he turned against the tabs primarily because they disclosed his marital infidelities, he did work as a "royal commentator" for Britain's *Today* on TV, he sold photos of his newborn son to a British tabloid, *and* he has cashed in mightily on Diana's posthumous cult by turning her burial site into "the new Graceland."

"I have seen the Princess described as manipulative, cynical, unbalanced, inconsistent, self-indulgent. I have to say I don't recognize any of this."
— ex-courtier Patrick Jephson, a week after Princess Diana's death.
A few years later Jephson wrote a book about his former employer, describing her as "capricious, cruel, paranoid, spiteful, a hysteric, vengeful, and a liar." And a liar….

"HRH Prince Charles has moved out of Kensington Palace…and taken personal, irreplaceable items with him. Diana's jewelry is her own…." — spokesman for Charles Windsor upon his separation from Diana in 1992. "His Royal Highness'" staff was so thorough in removing his effects from the palace that they ripped out the lavatory from his bathroom. Apparently it was all cisterns go.

People magazine described Mel Gibson as "a family values man." (Whose? And who do they exclude?) But Gibson's films are often exceptionally violent, from *Braveheart*, in which a gay man is fatally tossed out a window in a scene meant for laughs, to *The Patriot*, which included the impaling of a horse.
Said Gibson of *The Patriot*, "Fred Astaire made dancing look easy. Hopefully we can do the same for hatchet fights." Explaining why he was filming *Hamlet*, he said, "It's got some great stuff in it," then specified: nine violent deaths.

British character actor Harry Andrews offered, "And who can forget Mel Gibson in *Hamlet*? Though many have tried."

Bruce Willis declared that he wouldn't allow his daughters to watch his new movie *The Jackal* until they were teens, due to its violence. Novelist Harold Robbins noted, "I favor sex over violence any day. Or night," adding, "Bruce Willis is a hypocrite….What about everyone else's kids? For them it's okay, because he gets millions for making such stomach-turning movies in the first place?"

———————

"I make only family movies." — MGM chief Louis B. Mayer, who often stated that his executives were all "God-fearing family men."
But MGM was rife with double standards. It had "more than its quota of lecherous older men," according to Shirley Temple (a Fox star), who decades later revealed that Mayer tried to seduce her thirty-seven-year-old mother Gertrude while in an adjoining office. *Wizard of Oz* producer Arthur Freed exposed his genitals to eleven-year-old Shirley.

———————

"It's one of the most democratic businesses….We're all in it on one level, pulling together for the success of our latest picture." — producer Ross Hunter on moviemaking.
Hollywood used to be more egalitarian. Character actors could chum around—on the set anyway—with a picture's stars. But the difference between star and supporting cast or technical crew is as between royalty and serfs. And where once stars ate in studio commissaries with everyone else, by the '80s and '90s they no longer cared to break bread with studio employees. Now, most any star demands and gets a personal trailer with a personal chef.

———————

"In America, my girls were wealthy, famous and unhappy. They were most dissatisfied with their men and with each other." — Jolie Gabor, mother of Zsa Zsa, Magda and Eva (notice none of them returned to Hungary to get happy again).

———————

"My wife and I can hardly bear to be apart, except when I have to work." — gay actor Anthony Perkins.
Though contractually married, Perkins continued seeing men, despite his new public image as a husband and family man. In 1976, after the birth of second son Elvis (his godfather was Halston), Perkins took a "bachelor" vacation to Morocco, where he indulged in drugs and under-aged males.

———————

"I don't shy away from violence, but all my pictures should have a high moral tone. It's a line I myself try to follow." — director Howard Hawks.

Norma Shearer revealed to friends how Hawks moved his sixteen-year-old girfriend into the house while his wife Athole, Norma's sister, was ill and confined to bed. The affair continued while Athole's mental health declined. Hawks (by the way racist, homophobic and anti-Semitic) eventually married the girl.

————————

"You gotta go fight for your country. I don't care how far away Vietnam is, or if you think we're in the right or wrong, we're right, and you gotta go fight and even die if you have to."
— John Wayne.

It's well known Wayne didn't fight in WW II, when he applied for and got a 3-A status deferment due to family dependency. Friend and director John Ford invited Wayne to join the Navy, but the actor then applied for and received a 2-A classification, a deferment in the "national interest." Later, when the Duke was reclassified as 1-A, he turned to his studio for help in getting reclassified as 2-A.

Nice work if you can get it.

On the pro side, John Wayne contributed to the country's war-time morale (his anti-"Indian" and similar movies excepted). On the con side, all his fighting occurred risk-free, before the cameras, and with a predetermined outcome.

————————

Karl's mother, who lived to 104, was feisty even toward the end. When the actor once asked her how she felt, she cracked, "With my hands, stupid."

Director William Wellman threw a party for his mother in 1945. Known for getting long-winded when he'd had too much to drink, he proposed a toast, "To my mother, who bore me." She replied, "Yes, son, and now you bore me."

And out of show business, when Lillian Carter was told her son Jimmy had plans to run for president, she asked, "President of what?"

★　★　★

Myth: Most celebrities enjoy the chance to do interviews and thus air their opinions, show off their wit, or explain their roles and why they did them.

Most celebs tend to look on interviews as a necessary evil. The bigger the star, the fewer they have to do. Streisand prefers to give, say, a press interview and a TV interview per movie. Jack Nicholson tries to do none, if possible (some stars actually try to get payment for being interviewed!). Bruce Willis hates interviews because he gets asked the same questions over and over (however, sometimes a star only permits the same questions…). Then too, celebs are often misquoted or their words taken out of context, and a subsequent, corrective interview is required. Says Robert De Niro:

"After I gave an interview, I spent all my time trying to explain what I meant. I do what I have to do and I don't waste my energy by talking. People should go to the cinema, watch my movies and make up their own minds."

Finally, not every star is blessed with wit—or that much intelligence—and an interview requires the celeb's own words…unlike playing a pre-scripted role or singing a song. Nor is every star that fascinating away from the camera or mike.

★　★　★

Myth: You have to be very self-confident to go on the stage and become an actor.

In the past, most actors began on the stage. Today, thanks to TV, that's often not the case, and where stage actors would "ascend" to the movies, today nearly every TV actor wants to be a movie actor, preferably a movie star (not all stage performers think highly of Hollywood). Stand-up comics and musical performers may have to be rather extroverted, but many actors say they began acting to get self-confidence. Or to explore other aspects of their personalities. Writer/director Anthony Minghella (*The English Patient, The Talented Mr. Ripley*):

"…actors are in the business of constantly reinventing themselves or feeling somehow that who they are intrinsically is maybe not as worthy as who they can pretend to be." Many or most actors begin insecure and stay insecure. Money doesn't usually buy security or confidence.

Myth: The Oscar-winning Best Picture *The English Patient* was based on a true story.

It was a sweeping love story, so far as it went. But not complete. The protagonist was real-life Hungarian Count Laszlo d'Almasy. Not included nor referred to in the film were almost a hundred love letters written by the count to a young German soldier. But for a change, the information wasn't suppressed—it was unknown to the filmmakers until after the movie came out (no pun). By contrast, in his next film, writer/director Anthony Minghella expanded a gay character from the 1955 novel *The Talented Mr. Ripley* by Patricia Highsmith.

Myth: Actresses almost never praise other actresses, except perhaps on their professionalism, (as with Bette Davis: "Joan Crawford was a real pro, but….").

When one actress praises another, she's usually more effusive than a male actor on another actor. Example: Madeleine Stowe (who is half-Latina but allegedly eschews Hispanic roles so not to become trapped in an ethnic image) told *Movieline* magazine, "I loved *True Romance*, it's one of my favorite films…I've seen it about twenty times. Patricia Arquette, to me, is one of the sexiest women on film….I just love her. It's like you look at her and you just want to touch her."

Imagine an actor, even a gay one, saying that about another actor.

Wear a crucifix—pendant or earrings—
and people assume you are a Christian.

Jackie Collins wears crucifixes and Leopard print; it's her Look. But like big sister Joan, she is half Jewish: "My mother was Church of England and my father was Jewish. So Joan and I—all of us—didn't practice anything. I've brought up my own children the same way....I went to church once and fainted and thought, Well, I've done that."

★　★　★

Envy the golden-age movie stars with their killer wardrobes.

A wardrobe can be a stereotype. Thirties star Kay Francis became frustrated—and retired in her early forties—with being known as a clotheshorse rather than a fine performer. And Mexican beauty Dolores Del Rio found, "When they give you wonderful clothes, they give you bad parts." So she quit Hollywood and did more dramatic parts back home.

★　★　★

"I told him, 'Why would you make up a name like Tommy Tune? If you want more movie work, change that name.'"
— Gene Kelly, director of *Hello, Dolly!*

Like many, Kelly had believed the multi-Tony-winning Texan actor/choreographer/director made up his name. But he was born with it. And despite his relentlessly sunny personality, his early life wasn't a bed of roses. His memoirs begin thus: "I never had a grandfather; one was crushed in a coal mine collapse when Mom was four, and the other, after 'another hopeless day on the farm,' killed all his hired hands, shot Grandma, and then himself. She lived, he died. So I was left with two grandmothers—one was a witch and one was a bitch. I loved the witch."

Tune belatedly came out in his memoirs, but promoting his book he claimed the reason he'd never declared his sexual orientation was that, through hundreds of interviews, no one ever asked. Wrong.

★　★　★

Myth: Show biz success depends on the "right" name.

Fortunately, star quality counts for more than a name that's not too exotic and not too bland. Barbra (originally Barbara) Streisand was apprised her name was too "foreign," and Sal Mineo battled studio execs who wanted to anglicize his image to Sal Maynard. His Sicilian parents said no, and because Sal was a teen and shortish, rather than a potential Rock Hudson (ne Roy Scherer), the studio gave in. "I don't think I'd have had any more or less success with a WASP name. Who knows?"

When a singing trio went from the Gumm Sisters to the Garland Sisters, they became no more successful. Eventually baby Frances, renamed Judy Garland by comic George Jessel, became a superstar. Decades after, on Ed Sullivan, Jessel asserted that even if he'd renamed the singer/actor Hiawatha Titanic, she still would have become a star, on the strength of her talent.

P.S. One British celebrity noted, "The stupidest question I've ever been asked is whether Hermione Gingold is my real name."

★ ★ ★

Thirteen Women.

The 1932 thriller movie by that title featured ten women, but employed a "scarier" number. It starred Myrna Loy, née Myrna Williams, who in 1932 also appeared in *The Woman in Room 13*—but notice many American skyscrapers still omit a thirteenth floor….Loy's Hollywood surname was in keeping with her image, and occasional publicity, as "Oriental." For instance, she played the sensuous and thus at the time evil daughter of Fu Manchu (Boris Karloff). In those days, Asian was equated with villainous, and in *Thirteen Women* she was a villainess for being half-Oriental and for seeking revenge against the former girls' school classmates who'd discriminated against her.

P.S. In *Her Twelve Men* (1954), Greer Garson taught thirteen boys, but twelve, or a dozen, is a "positive" number, and Hollywood's positive about everything it does.

★ ★ ★

Carrington (1995) was the platonic love story, based on
a true story, about artist Dora Carrington (1893-1932), who killed
herself a few weeks after the death of her gay pal and love object,
writer Lytton Strachey.

True so far as it went. But the movie left out Dora's (played by Emma Thompson, who like Rosie O'Donnell publicly admitted her attraction to Michelle Pfeiffer) bisexuality. She was hetero on screen. Only. Even more "tolerant" moviemakers don't like to mix homosexuality with lesbianism or bisexuality, regardless of the source.

Mel Gibson's *Braveheart* (1995), purportedly historical, includes a viciously homophobic scene that never happened: The lover of Edward II is thrown through a window to his death, and the scene is played for laughs. In his movie of the novel *The Man Without a Face*, Gibson changed the gay character to hetero—and refused to sanction the original novel for a movie tie-in edition. As a producer, he helped present the possibly gay or bisexual Beethoven as strictly heterosexual, in *Immortal Beloved*.

Krakatoa, East of Java.
The movie title (1969) was a deliberate falsehood, as Krakatoa is west of Java. But the word east is exotic, non-western, and tested better with potential moviegoers….After the movie flopped, the videocassette was retitled *Volcano*.

P.S. The explosion of Krakatoa in 1883 was the loudest noise in recorded history.

In the dramatic ending of the jingoistic John Wayne vehicle *The Green Berets* (1968), the star walks into the sunset on a beach with a Vietnamese boy. But the sun is setting on the ocean behind him, with the "Vietnamese" beach facing west— like the movie's perspective. In fact, Vietnam's beaches face east.

Myth: Hollywood stars live high on the hog.
Depends. Being multi-millionaires doesn't seem to suppress the pinchpenny tendencies of some superstars. Tom Cruise and Jodie Foster— separately, of course—have been spotted in Westwood, Los Angeles, trying to get into other people's movies free or on a discount, and Sean Connery, Streisand, Clint Eastwood, Eddie Murphy and others are

known to leave bare-bones tips at restaurants, while John Travolta often gifts movie coworkers not with cash or fancy gifts but autographed photos of himself.

Cary Grant was notoriously stingy. Wife Dyan Cannon told Joan Collins, "That sonofabitch. You have no idea what a tightwad he was. I used to buy baby food for Jennifer in bulk because it was cheaper, and he still used to complain to me about the price—his own daughter, can you imagine?" Grant recycled his shirt buttons and was known for his frayed shirt collars. Friend Roddy McDowall gifted Grant with designer towels after noticing the threadbare towels in his bathroom. Some time later, visiting Grant, McDowall asked, "Why haven't you used the new ones I sent you?"

"Oh, there's plenty of life left in the old ones yet," replied the suave movie icon.

Myth: Howard Hughes had a Midas touch.

Hughes was born rich but became much richer. Yet when he turned to movie producing, his golden touch turned to tin. Partly because Hughes' taste was mostly in his mouth and he insisted on tinkering with the films he financed. Such films as *Jet Pilot*, *Underwater* and *The Outlaw* were given massive publicity campaigns that didn't turn them into profit-making hits. Hughes bought RKO studios for a tax deduction and proceeded to run it into the ground via film bombs and bad management (Lucille Ball and Desi Arnaz eventually bought what was left of RKO).

Nor was Hughes' Midas touch a sure thing outside of Tinseltown—remember the Spruce Goose?

Myth: Female movie stars are invariably classical beauties.

Talent and/or personality-plus can elevate an actress to the box office heights, as was especially evident in the 1930s, when Marie Dressler—in her sixties and stout—was briefly #1 among all film stars, and child star Shirley Temple was #1 for several years. Another box office giant was Mae West, who began her screen career at an age—fortyish—when many actresses were ending theirs. In the early '40s talented and histrionic Bette Davis dominated all other actresses, and in the '60s

Barbra Streisand broke through on talent and chutzpah, even while using her own surname (unlike such thespians from silent star Theda Bara—née Theodosia Goodman—to Wynona Ryder—née Horowitz).

★　★　★

Myth: Hollywood may not always get the historical details right, but the finished product is seamless and convincing.

Just one example to the contrary: C.B. DeMille's *The Crusades* (1935) has the king toss back his cape and look at his wristwatch. Quite apart from the fact that Richard the Lion-Hearted was gay in reality, as he was in the British-made *The Lion in Winter* (1968, played by Anthony Hopkins). Plus many other temporal and geographic inaccuracies.

★　★　★

Myth: Hollywood film censorship began in 1934.

Religious extremists, offically approved by the Democratic president, Franklin Roosevelt (shades of Bill Clinton…), forced through heightened censorship that forbade interracial couples, gay characters, non-state-sanctioned relationships, or for the most part women working outside the home. This extremism lasted, with few exceptions, until the early 1960s.

But there was movie censorship since at least the early 1920s, much of it now seemingly ludicrous. In 1932 producer Sam Goldwyn made a film of the Broadway hit *The Greeks Had a Word For It*, a play on the forbidden list of head censor Will Hays (a former Republican Postmaster General accused of bribe-taking). So it couldn't be filmed under that title. To make it seem less "dirty," the movie title was amended to *The Greeks Had a Word For Them*. (After all, "It" had a sexual connotation, as in sex symbol Clara Bow, the It Girl.)

★　★　★

Myth: The X rating is only for extremely sexual pictures.

The X rating is for what the censors most disapprove of. Which is rarely murder, mayhem and other violence. Nor rape, torture or serial-killing. A 1972 British documentary about the human body titled *The Body* was a G-rated equivalent in the UK but got slapped with an X in the USA, despite its educational intent. Reportedly, the first two movies to get an X were the lesbian-themed *The Killing of Sister George* (whose sole nudity was one breast) and *Midnight Cowboy*, which had gay-male content (and which featured Jon Voight nude from behind only).

After *MC* became a hit and earned the Best Picture Oscar and an Academy Award for—now openly gay—director John Schlesinger, its rating was revised to R. After all, money and the prestige that promises yet more profits are the bottom line in Hollywood.

Myth: There is no more film censorship in Hollywood.

"It's worse here," said visiting Spanish director Pedro Almodóvar, "because they pretend the censorship isn't censorship." The Classification and Rating Administration inhibits supposedly controversial films from being made via the threat of an X or even R rating. Most cinemas won't exhibit X-rated movies, and an R means fewer potential moviegoers. So the studios, which need mass audiences to recoup their inflated film budgets, either don't make a given picture or cave in to CARA's demands in trimming certain scenes: full female nudity can earn a mere PG, but a penis is usually an instant X. A heterosexual kiss is G, a homosexual kiss is R. Nudity of black African natives might earn a PG or R, but white Americans or Europeans earns an R or, if male, an X. Et cetera.

Director/producer Stanley Kubrick, among others, has charged that the ratings board tend to be "a bunch of behind-the-times parents from the [San Fernando] Valley." Whose biases shape and limit the movies we all watch—and don't watch.

The general and media perception is that women are more liberal about censorship issues than men. But it depends. In 1921 the General Federation of Women's Clubs took a judgmental look at 1,765 motion pictures and found that 59% were "not morally worthwhile" and 21% were downright "bad," leaving only 20% which they deemed viewable. In 1949 several Catholic groups, headed by men but mostly comprised of women, helped ensure that the film *The Prince of Foxes*, about Cesare Borgia (played by Orson Welles),

Movie reviewers are free
to say whatever they want
about a movie.

They are, at least once. But if
they slam a given studio film too
hard, they run the risk of being
barred from press screenings,
which are often crucial to
meeting a deadline and getting
your review out in time to
"compete" with those of other
periodicals. Rex Reed, who has
been (temporarily) banned
from some studios' screenings
and press junkets, notes,
"The bigwigs love constructive
criticism, so long as it's
100% positive."

———————————

Movie reviews are—of course—
always written by movie
reviewers.

Usually. But not necessarily
during Hollywood's "golden"
age, when audiences were more
naïve and shady practices were
more tolerated. For decades, a
typical press book on a new
movie ran between twenty to
thirty pages. It would begin with
illustrations of ads and posters
available to exhibitors to place in
the cinema window or lobby and
in local papers. Then came

suggested tie-ins, and toward
the end, various "pre-written"
movie reviews for newspapers
and radio stations that couldn't
afford their own critics.

———————————

A movie reviewer is a movie
reviewer (what else?).

Sometimes he or she is a studio
publicist. In June, 2001,
Columbia Pictures promised the
government it would monitor
its publicity and advertising
departments more closely after it
was revealed that print ads for *A
Knight's Tale* and *The Animal*
included glowing praise from a
non-existent movie critic named
"David Manning" from a real
weekly paper, *The Ridgefield
Press*, in Connecticut. Two ad
execs were suspended for thirty
days without pay for creating the
empty praise.

———————————

Those movie fans in movie
commercials on TV are real fans.

Usually. But just as Columbia
was found to use a fake critic, it
also, for the Mel Gibson movie
The Patriot, used fake fans.
The "couple" employed to
promote the violent film via

person-on-the-street testimonials were employees of Sony Pictures Entertainment, Columbia's parent company. For the ad, Tamaya Petteway called *The Patriot* a "perfect date movie" while Anthony Jefferson stood close beside her and smiled his agreement. Petteway is an assistant to marketing executive Dana Precious, who oversaw the promotional campaign; Jefferson is another employee.

Movie tie-ins are a recent development.
They're bigger than ever now, but go way back. For *Captain Blood* (1935), Warner Bros. pushed such tie-ins as pirate costumes for boys, bags of sand with fake gold pieces on top, spyglasses, model pirate ships, the Raphael Sabatini novel (with Errol Flynn on the cover), dashing men's ties and jackets and pipes and suspenders and even suits, and for women brush-and-comb sets, skin lotions, perfume and a (too) unique "buccaneer" dress modeled by costar Olivia De Havilland. Crass commercialism has been around a long time.

R-rated movies, which require someone under seventeen to attend with an adult, are not marketed to under-seventeen-year-olds. Internal documents from Paramount, MGM/UA and Disney's Miramax division prove that Hollywood has recently been marketing R-rated movies specifically to under-seventeens. Particularly, violent movies, for example MGM's 1998 product *Disturbing Behavior*, which includes a scene in which a high school jock murders a girl by snapping her neck, as well as a scene in which a policeman is killed. "In promoting *Disturbing Behavior*, our goal is to find the elusive teen target audience and make sure everyone between the ages of twelve to eighteen is exposed to the film," wrote MGM publicist Lamya Souryal in a memo appropriated by the Federal Trade Commission. Marketing tactics include distributing movie posters to Girl Scout troops and hiring youths to pass out stickers and bracelets at underage hangouts like shopping malls, dance clubs and even schools.

TV talk show audiences are the real thing.

There has been controversy over whether all talk show guests are real, but until recently it was assumed the folks sitting in the audience were the genuine article. Not on controversial *Dr. Laura*'s now-defunct TV show, which bowed in late 2000. *TV Guide* noted that the Gay & Lesbian Alliance Against Defamation (GLAAD) found that one Schlessinger audience member was interviewed in two separate episodes under two different capacities. She turned out to be a show staffer.

A columnist for the *L.A. Weekly* wrote that he was paid $6.75 an hour by a temp agency to join "the horrid little 'doctor's' audience" in Canoga Park, a white-bread community outside more diverse Los Angeles.

Audience members were informed that "When we agree with Dr. Laura, nod your head in agreement or break into spontaneous applause." The only negative response allowed: "A slow shake of our heads when someone—not Dr. Laura, but a guest—says something immoral or unethical."

Nature documentaries are the real thing.

Even supposedly factual material is subject to bias. Shows about nature often assign to animals human attributes they don't possess. Most animals are not monogamous, and many are omnisexual. Author and animal rights activist Cleveland Amory recalled "a friend who used to work at Disney in the 1960s and '70s said that those nature 'documentaries' which focused exclusively on animals mating and breeding were often using footage of animal homosexuality but relabeling it as 'normal.' Who, then, are we to judge nature?"

———————————

Movie biographies take liberties but stick pretty closely to the facts.

That's much truer of book biographies, which can only cover up so much. Movie and TV bios have "poetic license" to, for instance, always depict subjects like James Dean or Howard Hughes as heterosexual, when in fact both were bisexual and perhaps primarily homosexual. Books have a smaller, more literate audience, and books are—if not novels—supposed to be factual. Filmed material is seen as entertainment first, factual second if at all, and must appeal to far more people to turn a profit. Hence the heterosexualization of filmed subjects.

———————

Many actresses wear falsies, but men don't.
Many actors over the decades have worn corsets. French heartthrob Charles Boyer, for one ("Come wiz me to the Casbah"). A few took more drastic measures. Like British actor and Hollywood star James Mason. In his memoirs, screenwriter Arthur Laurents (*The Way We Were*) disclosed that the "likeable, quiet" Mason was "the apex of a triangle with his wife Pamela and a sexy ex-Jersey City cop who, whatever else he did for the Masons and neither bothered to explain, was always on hand to strap James into the false torso he wore beneath his shirt." The resultant visual increase in bulk visibly increased his intensity and his sexuality on-screen. "Mason was completely unself-conscious about the falsie; not a qualm about the cop strapping him in right on the set in front of all and sundry." Just part of the business of make-believe.

———————

Speaking of a male "falsie," the famous Art Deco dildo that Rudolph Valentino supposedly gave to fellow screen heartthrob Ramon Novarro....*Hollywood Babylon* author Kenneth Anger stated that Novarro, who was murdered by two hustler brothers—both now free—in 1968, was found choked to death with the dildo rammed down his throat. Rudy may have gifted his lover with such an object, or not. If so, it may have been stolen from the scene of the crime or suppressed by police. It wasn't mentioned in police or autopsy reports, nor in the ensuing trial, and deputy district attorney James Ideman, who prosecuted Novarro's torture-murderers, wrote, "With reference to the claim that Mr. Novarro was choked to death by means of an Art Deco dildo, I can tell you that that did not happen.
"I certainly never made any statement to the effect that such an instrument was used. I did not even know of its existence."

———————

never mentioned who Cesare's father was: the Pope. Popes with children, as well as gay popes, are a Hollywood no-no, history notwithstanding.

Women tend to be more uncomfortable with screen violence, while most heterosexual men are uncomfortable with male nudity. Thus, the 1993 trailer for *Six Degrees of Separation* was objected to because it included a 16th-century nude ("Adam") by Michelangelo! After public criticism of the puerile objection, ratings chief Jack Valenti declared that the objection had been a "mistake."

★　　★　　★

Few objective observers would nowadays credit the myths that TV executives are very liberal or ahead of their time. Though CBS was headed by William S. Paley (himself Jewish), when producers Allan Burns and James Brooks were prepping *The Mary Tyler Moore Show*, CBS brass told them, "There are four things Americans can't stand: Jews, men with mustaches, New Yorkers, and divorced women." Ergo, Mary Richards was a single woman rather than a divorcée, she lived in Minneapolis, the male characters had no facial hair, and though Mary's pal Rhoda was Jewish, her boss Lou Grant (played by Jewish Ed Asner) was not.

About a decade on, NBC chose to make Dorothy and Sophia, two of the *Golden Girls* quartet, Italian-American rather than Jewish, although the actresses playing them—Beatrice Arthur and Estelle Getty—were Jewish. "I urged them to let us be Jewish, but I guess they believed that most Americans have never met a Jewish person," revealed Getty. "They figured most Americans, if they haven't met an Italian-American, at least they've eaten spaghetti or pizza." Despite the success of shows like *Will & Grace*, TV execs and producers still tend to avoid Hispanic, Asian and gay characters too, especially as leads.

Myth: Hollywood's Jewish moguls and producers influenced film content away from the mainstream.

Au contraire, most Hollywood Jews played almost entirely to the mainstream. Jewish themes were avoided—notice how virtually all screen weddings occur in a church and how often Christmas, only, is featured or mentioned. The first major Jewish-themed film, *Gentleman's Agreement*, in 1949, was via Fox, one of two studios headed by a Gentile (the other was Disney). Anti-Semitism was an issue almost never addressed in movies. In fact, a typical MGM offering like *Balalaika*, set in a happy, fictional Russia, neutralized and even romanticized the same Cossacks who had murdered several ancestors of mogul Louis B. Mayer.

★　★　★

Myth: Actors, at least stage actors, know when to be serious and when not to be.

Ed Begley, the father of Ed Begley, Jr. and an Oscar-winner, was appearing in out-of-town tryouts of a play titled *A Shadow of My Enemy*. An important speech of his contained the word "Katmandu," the capital of Nepal. Begley did not know the word, and it struck him as funny. Always. Playwright Sol Stein wrote, "Every time Begley came to the word, he broke into a jig and sang, 'Oh, the cat woman can't, but the cat man do.' He couldn't say the unfamiliar word with a straight face." What happened?

Despite the playwright having the final word according to the Dramatists Guild, the speech itself had to go before the play reached Broadway because the star would not alter his behavior.

★　★　★

Myth: Moviemakers try to make a film the best it possibly can be.

Many do, but a director doesn't usually have the ultimate control, and in show business, money concerns take precedence over art. Playwright and editor Sol Stein recalled the time a best-selling book he'd edited was being filmed. At the director's invitation, he was aloft on an aerial perch with the cameraman, who was shooting a car and truck crash by focusing in on a steel wheel that gave like a donut. Stein found it "more moving than watching a car-truck crash from a distance, but the director was immediately surrounded by studio people saying, in effect, we can't spend this much money on a car crash and focus on a single wheel!"

The front-office men demanded the company's money's worth, and the Oscar-winning director "gave up, and a more conventional crash was used, which was a lot less moving than the cinematographer's shot."

★   ★   ★

Myth: Actors devoutly believe in the show-biz credo, "The show must go on."

Most stage actors practice it, but not all believe in it. In his memoirs, George Sanders offered, "Ours is an innocuous profession. We do not depress the economy with costly strikes. Other workers, such as those in the steel industry, should learn our motto: The show must go on; it applies more to them than to us. We work whether our employers can pay us or not. We give of ourselves more generously than any other group of people in the world."

Dick York, who played the original Darrin on *Bewitched*, said in the '80s, "Actors did not invent that 'show must go on' line. That was producers....Even if an actor's sick, his relatives are dying, he's in pain, conditions are hazardous, or there's no money to pay the cast, that show must go on! It's a brainwash, a unique low point in labor/management relations."

★   ★   ★

"All Americans born between 1890 and 1945 wanted to be movie stars."

— Gore Vidal, who in later years did cameo roles in movies.
Aside from the exaggeration, fewer people then got into acting with the express goal of becoming "rich and famous." Except for some of the prettiest young actresses, most people who got to Hollywood wanted and had some or lots of stage training. Today, aiming to become a "star," many young people don't even consider theater, but go directly into auditioning for TV, movies or at least commercials. The much-publicized sums that some actors earn act as a magnet to many young people who crave "instant" stardom but have little personality or talent to offer. The idea of learning a craft is more irrelevant than ever; lots of

youths considers themselves qualified to "act" simply because of ambition, or parents who are in the biz, etc.

Says one top casting director, "The attitude used to be, What have I got to offer show business? Now it's, What can I get out of show business?"

Myth: Large breasts are always an aid to an aspiring actress.
One of the 1950s' two or three top actresses was Audrey Hepburn (Marilyn and Liz were the others). Director Billy Wilder, who worked with Monroe and Hepburn, found Audrey's figure and her sexually non-overwhelmingness "refreshing." In the '90s, producer Aaron Spelling was asked if he was considering Geri, the former Spice Girl, for his pending film version of *Charlie's Angels*? He replied, "No one would take her seriously with boobs that big."

"Like a virgin, indeed!…She is a woman who pulled herself up by the bra straps, and who has been known to let them down occasionally."— Bette Midler, on Madonna.
Established stars often seem to forget that they once—or often!—indulged in the sort of behavior they're criticizing. Like Joan Crawford in the '50s chiding young actresses for endorsing products, or Bette in the '90s; in 1978 London fans at a Midler concert held up a sign that read "We Love Your Tits"—the Divine Miss M. laughed, then pulled down her bustier and indulged her fans. In 1979 after a concert, Bette was showering when sustained audience demand convinced her to return to the stage, in a towel. The fans screamed with delight, and she responded by undoing the towel and tossing it over her head.

P.S. In the '70s Bette joked about her friendly rival, "I donated my tits to Cher. And she was so glad to get 'em I can't even tell you." Reportedly, by 1998 the friendship was long over. Midler was quoted, "The woman's disgusting. She called me a cunt. I'll never speak to her again." (Cher also called Madonna that.)

OINKS!

"My wife's married. I'm not." — basketball player Charles Barkley.

———————

"I finally got it right." — Jack Nicholson, in 1992, on the birth of his son, after two daughters.

———————

"All men make mistakes, but those who are married find out about them sooner."
—Red Skelton.

———————

"You can't accept one [critic's opinion], particularly if it's a female and you know—God willing I hope for her sake it's not the case—but when they get a period, it's really difficult for them to function as normal human beings." — Jerry Lewis.

———————

"The big problem with dealing with older models is that they have a mind of their own."
— agent John Casablancas, who left his wife for a sixteen-year-old model.

———————

"Most [women] are fairly stupid. I don't like many of them."
— former James Bond Timothy Dalton.

"Men don't go on dates for companionship. We got guys for companionship and talking with someone….With chicks, all dates boils (sic) down to is: Let's go places and eat things!"
— Chris Farley.

———————

"Isn't she the most beautiful maid you've ever seen in your life?" — Don Johnson, on wife-at-the-time Melanie Griffith.

———————

"My notion of a wife at forty is that a man should be able to change her, like a bank note, for two twenties."
— Warren Beatty, ex beauty.

———————

"It's sinful for a woman to be in broadcasting or in some business. God made her to be a great cook, a great washer of things."
— Tiny Tim, falsetto singer.

———————

"From Colonel and Mrs. George S. Patton III—Peace On Earth."
— 1968 Xmas card message from descendant-of and wife-of, beneath a picture of Viet Cong corpses, dismembered and in a pile.

"I only beat her once."
— Glenda Jackson's former
(and only) husband.

———————

"I was so drugged out
then I hardly remember her now.
I'm told we were married a
hundred days." — Mickey
Rooney, on "wife #6."

———————

"You must never marry a
Hollywood beauty, is my sincere
advice. It's a hopeless situation.
They are worshipped and
adored….People say Ava Gardner
was beautiful. Of course she was.
What else was she?" — musician
and once-husband Artie Shaw
(Mickey Rooney was Gardner's
first husband), who also wed
Lana Turner.

———————

"I think marriage is a custom
brought about by women who
then proceed to live off men and
destroy them, completely
enveloping the man in a destruc-
tive cocoon or eating them away
like a poisonous fungus on a
tree." — Richard Harris.

———————

"The most repulsive thing you
could ever imagine is the inside
of a camel's mouth. That, and
watching a girl eat octopus or
squid." — Marlon Brando.

"…if there were nothing but old
whores and nasty old hard
women, I'd be out looking for
some young sweet little fifteen-
year-old boy." — Don Johnson.

———————

"If I had a choice of having a
woman in my arms or shooting a
bad guy on a horse, I'd take the
horse. It's a lot more fun."
— Kevin Costner,
speaking as an actor.

———————

"It's like when I buy a horse. I
don't want a thick neck and short
legs." — Mickey Rourke, on
what he seeks in a woman.

———————

"The patience of a saint, spunk,
and a head flat enough to set a
can of beer on." — Robert
Hayes, on his ideal woman.

———————

"I'm thinking about entering
politics. I'd love to do it. But I
haven't got the right wife."
— Mick Jagger.

———————

"I've chosen my wives for
their looks and preferably sweet
demeanors, and not for
anything they could do for me,
except aesthetically."
— Gig Young, who murdered his
last wife, pre-suicide.

Myth: You can believe what you see about the stars.

Special effects on big or little screens are better than ever, but the print media—particularly the tabloids—have been using one trick for decades: after she split with Sonny Bono in the '70s, Cher complained, "They had me walking down the beach at Acapulco with Jim Brown, and they pasted two photos of us together. They've done the same with me and Paul Newman, Robert Redford, and Elvis Presley, and I've never met any of them."

In the late '90s, *Esquire* jokingly ran a series of fake porn-star-poses featuring John F. Kennedy, Jr.'s head atop a nude hunk's body, strategically covered with blue dots. The spread—one photo was labeled "Cuban Missile Crisis"—was very convincing, and JFK, Jr.'s attorney sent a letter vigorously protesting the pictures on behalf of his unamused client.

P.S. Speaking of special effects, presumably the best one is still… talent!

Myth: All or most biographies of famous stars by their offspring are Mommie Dearest-style tell-alls.

Or Daddy Dearests, like Gary Crosby's. No, most such books are, on the contrary, unrevealing, highly selective—censored, even—valentines. Many regular biographers over-identify with their subjects and tend to idealize them; a few go the other way and present all the warts and little else. But relatives are the ones who feel the subject reflects directly on them, hence the frequency of familial fabrications. Especially if the dearly departed was other than heterosexual. Besides, the relative who writes is probably heir to the celebrity's estate, and may avoid telling any particular truth that might render the late star and estate less commercially viable.

Myth: Agents are a greedy, over-charging bunch.

According to the rules, an agent cannot charge more than 10% of the income that his or her acting client earns. Managers can charge anything, and do, but agents, despite their seedy, greedy image, are generally hard-working and above-board.

Myth: Playing a gay character is a risk for an actor.

For many years, this was true. Unless one were a star and thus had a hetero image—true or not. Bisexual Laurence Olivier played bisexual in *Spartacus*, gay or bi Barbara Stanwyck played a lesbian with a husband in *Walk On the Wild Side*, both in the early '60s. But the vast majority of American male actors have shunned gay roles. In recent decades, it seems as if one out of every three actors has at some point played gay. Several have won awards for so doing, including Oscars to Tom Hanks and William Hurt. The impression may now be that actors are clamoring to play gay, for the "challenge" and a pat on the, uh, back.

However, agents and managers discourage actors from a continuing gay role. Look at the careers that didn't happen for handsome young actors playing gay or bi on *Dynasty*, *Melrose Place*, etc. When the public doesn't know—or think they know—the actor, they often assume he is gay. So what? So the harm comes not from the public, but from casting directors—sometimes themselves gay—who then stereotype the actor. Eric McCormack, star of the hit sitcom *Will & Grace*, notes, "I'm more leading man as a gay man than I ever was as a straight man." The gay role made the former unknown a success, especially as it's a lead in a hit show and he's openly heterosexual.

The real risks are in real life: 25% of American teenagers who reveal they're gay are ordered by their parents to leave home.

Myth: Since *Ellen*, it's okay for TV actors to come out of the closet.

TV certainly has more gay and lesbian characters than ever. Non-lead characters, excepting *Will*. As for actors, that's something else. Virtually all who are out are supporting actors—usually not series regulars. Dan Butler of *Frasier* plays a butch hetero character; Butler is also a gay activist in real life and is a recurring, not regular, character. Another on the show is enacted by a gay actor who neither denies nor confirms it; he is a regular. A supporting but regular character on another hit sitcom is gay—again, doesn't deny it—but is not officially out. Agents, managers and network brass prefer actors to stay in the closet, especially if they're a part of a weekly show.

Least of all do TV honchos want actors to seem activist or political, even if all that means is pro-equal rights. They do not want gays being "controversial"—more to the media than to the public—and the last thing they want is a gay actor being honest about playing a gay character, as with *Ellen*. For one thing, the actress, being in a committed relationship, wanted her character to have a steady girlfriend. ABC, rather, wanted a series of casual (platonic?—as on *Will & Grace*) dates. On American TV, love, romance and commitment are still strictly for heterosexuals.

★　★　★

Myth: Unlike TV and movies, gay-themed plays have always been a hot—that is, popular—ticket.

Fact is, until the late 1960s, Broadway—thanks to New York state law—could not legally present a gay or lesbian character on the stage at all. Nor, until recent decades, could gay people legally dance together in Los Angeles, or a New York bartender serve an alcoholic beverage to "a known homosexual." Gay, not to mention pro-gay, entertainment, is a thing of very recent history.

★　★　★

Myth: The Lady in Black.

A Tinseltown invention. Hollywood's greatest Latin Lover, Rudolph Valentino, was gay or bi. As were his two wives. Rudy died prematurely in 1926 of peritonitis. "The lady in black" was a mysterious, veiled woman—supposedly a lover or super-fan of Valentino's—who visited his grave in Hollywood each year on the anniversary of his death, trailing perfume and leaving behind one single, perfect rose. In the mid-'20s, Paramount publicity had labeled Rudy "the other man in every woman's life."

Publicist Russell Birdwell, the man behind *Gone With the Wind*'s huge publicity campaign, created the first Lady in Black. Paramount wanted a gimmick to grab press attention for their reissuing of some of Valentino's films. Birdwell hired a $5-a-day extra to be the first "lady," and made sure a photographer was on hand at the crypt. The item then got planted into virtually every newspaper, and rekindled interest in the late star's movies. The original spawned several more ladies in black

over the years, some of them men in drag. And a myth was born—
motivated by money and image, in that order.

Myth: One can sleep one's way to the top.

Even to the middle is rare. The casting couch may afford an actress or
actor some initial, smaller-scale opportunities. It can also, for an actress,
seriously harm her reputation going in. Women who have been on the
couch have no recourse if the "deal" falls through; men who have gone
the couch route still retain the status of "actors," as they are far less
dependent on looks and sex appeal to get a job, and as there is much
more parity between the man on the couch and the man behind the
couch than between the producer and female starlet.

Sometimes a female star is accused of sleeping her way to the top,
often out of jealousy or spite. (Almost no man is accused of this, yet
one top male star was initially launched via his sexual contacts with a
gay mogul and other powerful execs.) Said Madonna, while playing
Evita, "I think people wanted to undermine Eva Perón's achievements
by saying she was a whore and she slept her way to the top, and I think
people do the same thing to me. I don't think it's possible to sleep your
way to the top."

Myth: Realism, in the vast majority of Hollywood's historical or ethnic depictions.

It's better than it was. But even in recent years, the impression is often
given that Germany is a nation of blonds. Hollywood still tends to cast
Jewish characters via brown-haired, brown-eyed Gentile actors—so one
isn't aware on screen of the large percentage of Jews who are blue-eyed.
Hollywood casts Italian characters as if they were all Sicilian; paler and
lighter-haired northern Italians are left out. And Italian-Americans
often got, and get, Hispanic roles. Native American roles have seldom
been played by "Indian" actors, and Indians (from India)—when
depicted at all—have been essayed by anyone but, as when black
Caribbean actor Geoffrey Holder played Punjab in the musical *Annie*.
Movies and TV still also feature a much greater proportion of blonde
women and blue-eyed people than exist in the real world.

"We are looking for a positive angle on things. For example, the health section has a 'no diseases' stricture."
— *Mademoiselle* editor-in-chief Mandi Norwood speaking of magazine changes to the *New York Observer* on May 22, 2000.

———

Just out of an alcohol rehab center, author Truman Capote was invited to a gym by *People* magazine so they could do an illustrated article on his new healthy lifestyle....
According to the book *Dish*, about behind-the-scenes media workings, "During the interview, Capote downed two glasses of vodka and kept falling over, but the *People* reporter helped prop the writer up on a Nautilus machine long enough to get pictures."
(Truman was once asked if he went in for exercise. "Oh, often," he replied. What kind? "Massage.")

———

A *Vanity Fair* photo of a very pregnant Courtney Love, scantily clad....
The article alleged that Love had used heroin while pregnant, which the singer strongly denied. Editor-in-chief Tina Brown was more concerned about smoking and reader reaction to it, so she had the cigarette the pregnant Love was holding airbrushed out of her hand.

———

"*Playgirl*: Entertainment for Women."
— on the cover of each issue....
But a huge percentage— possibly a majority—of the magazine's "readers" are gay men who buy it for the male pin-ups inside. (The magazine often changes the male nudes' names and personal stats; for instance the June, 1975, issue included an "Andrew Cooper III" whose chest bore a tattoo reading "Sam" because he was future actor Sam J. Jones, who starred in the movie *Flash Gordon*.)
Many of the nude models are gay men in reality, despite the magazine's stating otherwise. One of them, Dirk Shafer, voted Man of the Year in 1992, later

came out and starred in and directed his own movie titled *Man of the Year*.

───────────────

Variety's 1993 obituary of Raymond Burr (*Perry Mason*).... The year before, the *Globe* tabloid headlined "Raymond Burr's Got a Gay Hubby." But the supposedly respectable—and accurate—*Variety* buried Burr's true sexual and affectional orientation. The obit mentioned a brief contractual marriage Burr may have undertaken for social and professional reasons (he made up a few other "marriages," also invented a "son" who "died"), but completely left out Burr's male life partner with whom he shared over thirty years. Ironically, the obit was cowritten by an openly gay man—working for *Variety*.

───────────────

In mid-2000 *TV Guide* in its On Video section, noted the release of the cassette of the movie *Topsy-Turvy* which "beautifully reveals the truth behind the duo's love-hate relationship, the theater and Victorian England." The movie was about Gilbert & Sullivan, but hardly reveals "the truth," since it depicts both men as heterosexual, which Sir Arthur Sullivan was not. Ironically, he was played by an openly gay British actor, and in the gay American magazine *The Advocate* no mention was made in its coverage—either deliberately or ignorantly—that the film deliberately (not ignorantly) closets one of its two subjects. How Victorian can you get?

───────────────

"When he got himself arrested for brawling in a gay bar, he outed himself. Case closed." — *New York Post* columnist Richard Johnson on Oct. 4, 1998, reporting on actor and likely future star Scott Caan (son of James), who with a male companion allegedly assaulted two other males at a West Hollywood gay bar. By contrast, the *Chicago Tribune* gave no gender to Caan's "date," while Reuters News Service went so far as to claim the fight was "over a woman" (at last report, RNS was owned by anti-gay televangelist Pat Robertson).

───────────────

On February 3, 1968, the *New York Times* published a negative review of Gore Vidal's controversial novel *Myra Breckinridge*....

───────────────

But because it was a smash best-seller that the public obviously took to despite its transsexual theme, on February 18th the newspaper published a second, more positive review. (Vidal had noted that ever since the 1948 publication of his gay-themed novel *The City and the Pillar* the biased paper automatically attacked his books, when they reviewed them at all.)

———

In 1990 the *Los Angeles Times* did an obituary of Ann Warner (formerly known as Ann Page in her acting days) who married mogul Jack L. Warner and became a leading Hollywood socialite and hostess; the couple's home was said to be the most magnificent house in Los Angeles.

The *L.A. Times* obit was illustrated, in error, with another woman's photograph. (The Warner mansion later sold to David Geffen, who reportedly paid the highest price ever for a private residence in the United States.)

(During the McCarthy witch-hunt era, Harry Warner, one of the four brothers, fired a writer whose name had been put on a list of alleged communists.

The man pleaded, "This is a mistake. The plain fact is that I am an anti-communist." Harry yelled back, "I don't give a damn what kind of communist you are. Get out of here.")

———

In 1999 the *China Youth Daily* admitted that it had been falsifying its weather reports for thirty-six years.

———

In 2000 CBS-TV was found to have been producing "ambient sound" to "enhance" golf tournaments. Pre-recorded birdsongs were spliced into coverage of the events but were noticed by experts: various birdsongs were repeated without variation, which doesn't occur in nature; others were geographically impossible, such as the songs of canyon wrens during the Buick Open in Michigan (on Aug. 12th and 13th), even though canyon wrens never fly east of Texas.

———

During the Nazi era, film and newsreel clips were routinely used in fictitious and propagandist ways. For example, the movie *The Eternal Jew* included a scene of a child-murderer's panicked capture from the pre-Nazi German film *M* to represent a "typical" Jew being apprehended for his "crimes." The character in *M* was not religiously specified, but was played by Jewish actor Peter Lorre, who'd fled the German cinema for Britain, then America, after the Nazis were voted into power.

Lorre, born Laszlo Loewenstein, had changed his name to become an actor. Had he not done so, he might not have had a Hollywood career as a leading man. Jewish names were frowned on in the movie world—but were lethal in the Nazi world.

Myth: Hollywood is much more inclusive of minorities now, especially on TV.

Make that singular, and it's true. TV and movies have one minority, unofficially, while America's Hispanics, Asians, Jews and gays are under-represented, statistically. The fast-growing Hispanic community is outnumbered on TV by presumably legal aliens from outer space! Native Americans are gone with the westerns. China and India's combined populations equal over one-third of humanity, yet Americans of those backgrounds are missing from American TV. The only TV program ever to star an Asian-American, Margaret Cho, of Korean origin, lasted all of six months.

"They got me a consultant to teach me how to be more Korean," Cho explains. "Then they got nervous. My show was *All-American Girl*, and suddenly I was too different. 'Be less Asian,' they said." She was also asked to lose thirty pounds, and did—immediately, resulting in health and emotional complications. Her series was replaced by Drew Carey's, who was not asked to lose thirty pounds.

Females of every description are under-represented on TV, as are middle-aged people and senior citizens. Despite the fact that America's population is more mature than ever, the median age now being forty-four. You'd never know it from the boob tube.

Myth: Nearly all entertainment celebs have come from the U.S. and Europe.

Which leaves out Canada. Hollywood's very first star, Florence Lawrence, was Canadian. As was its biggest female star for a long time, Mary Pickford. Canada launched figures as diverse as Pamela Anderson, Robert Goulet, Lorne Green, Glenn Ford and Jim Carrey. Of course it's so easy—and often economically advantageous—for Canucks to pass as Yanks that showbiz Canadians can truly be called an invisible minority.

Myth: Film and TV violence are largely responsible for real-life shootings and other violence.

Motion Picture Association of America lobbyist Jack Valenti pointed out that violence-crazed American movies, TV programs, records and video games are marketed the world over—usually earning more money abroad than in the U.S—without the same unhappy results. In a nutshell, Europe and Asia have strict gun control laws. TV columnist Harold Fairbanks noted, "Movies made in Europe and Asia have more graphic sexual scenes and content, the kind that earn an X or NC-17 rating in the puritanical U.S. And, so far at least, there is no record of international kids arming themselves with Viagra and screwing their classmates to death." In fact, among developed nations, the U.S. has the highest rate of teen pregnancies, puritanism notwithstanding.

★　★　★

Myth: *The King & I*—and its non-musical predecessor *Anna & The King of Siam*—is a true historical story.

Anna Leonowens, who wrote the story, vastly exaggerated her importance—and any romantic undertones—in the Siamese court where she was an English tutor (not a foreign policy advisor nor feminist reformer). She especially misrepresented King Mongkut, which is why all versions of the film, including the Jodie Foster remake, *Anna & The King*, are still banned in royalty-revering Thailand. The king, who reigned from 1851-1868, was a Buddhist monk for twenty-seven years before ascending the throne. Far from speaking pidgin English, he was a scholar and spoke English and Latin as well as many Asian languages.

The *Anna & The King* press kit incorrectly claimed that the movie was shot in Malaysia—a Muslim country with people physically distinct from the Thais—for reasons of verisimilitude! Apart from the differing locals, the buildings did not match, yet the press kit stated it's hard to find the genuine architectural articles in Bangkok: false. Rather, the film was not allowed to shoot in Thailand.

P.S. The real Anna had a son and a daughter, the screen one just a son.

★　★　★

Myth: Hollywood has become more spiritually sensitive and now respects other religions on screen.

And yet virtually all screen weddings occur in a church…never mind civil or other-faith marriages. Other religions are under-represented, though when Christianity's sister faiths, Judaism and Islam, are depicted, it's usually reverentially. However, Buddhism and Hinduism, although longstanding global religions, are often portrayed as flaky, nutty, kooky and exotic. (In print and on screen, the Buddha, or Enlightened One, is frequently misrepresented as fat and Chinese.) A number of showbiz figures are Buddhists, from Harrison Ford and Richard Gere to Tina Turner, composer Philip Glass, director Oliver Stone and screenwriter (*E. T., Kundun*) Melissa Mathison. Yet the Hollywood system still panders to small-town prejudices and fears by ridiculing a safe target (they wouldn't dare treat Islam the same way—ask author Salman Rushdie…).

Myth: The Academy Award is for talent.

Big myth! It has at least as much to do with personal politics and sentiment. Umpteen talented performers have never won, not just comic geniuses like Chaplin or emotive goddesses like Garbo, but undeniable champion thesps like Richard Burton, Peter O'Toole, Glenn Close, etc., etc. And then look at the stars who did win or won too often— John Wayne won once, Jodie Foster got two, Walter Brennan got three for hamming it up in support, and Kate Hepburn four for playing it straight…. Timing is another factor: do a great job in a film that opened many months before, and you're forgotten in favor of year-end performances. Acting well in a flop is seldom rewarded. And playing a victim or cliché is too often rewarded: Jon Voight in a wheelchair or Liz Taylor as a hooker with a heart of gold. Or an actress wins because she's survived a life-threatening illness, or an actor because he died. Et cetera.

Hollywood's first great movie director, D.W. Griffith, never got an Oscar. AMPAS—the Academy of Motion Picture Arts & Sciences— was originally founded for public relations purposes. Asked his opinion of AMPAS, Griffith responded, "What art? What science?" In its early years, the Academy's voting was much more subject to the whims, dictates and prejudices of Hollywood hotshots like Louis B. Mayer and Jack L. Warner, both of whom campaigned against nominations for their own contractees if it was for a role in a picture for which they were loaned out to another studio.

Haing S. Ngor, a Cambodian Buddhist doctor, was nominated for his first Hollywood movie role, in *The Killing Fields*. His competition included John Malkovich, who ungraciously said of the supporting-actor race: "I haven't got a chance. I'm up against two Orientals, one of them an amateur, and one black guy, and Sir Ralph Richardson, who's dead." The "amateur" won; graciously, Dr. Ngor allowed, "I'm not a professional actor, but I have done this part with all of my heart, using my own similar experiences. Apparently it has touched many other hearts, which is why I think they gave me this unexpected and wonderful award."

P.S. Tragically, Dr. Ngor, who survived the killing fields of Cambodia, did not—after moving to the United States—survive the killing streets of Los Angeles, where he was shot to death by youths with guns.

★　　★　　★

Myth: The 1940s and '50s political witch-hunts were meant to root out communists.

To a large extent, the witch-hunts were a backlash against Democratic presidents Roosevelt—elected four times—and his successor Harry Truman. The newly Republican Congress took the well-timed opportunity, while eastern Europe was falling under communist control, to increase their power by hysterically creating a "red menace" in the U.S. Communism had been a more significant "threat" during the Great Depression in the '30s, and at no point has it been illegal to join that party! Rather, the witch-hunters weeded out minorities and liberals, anyone they didn't like, rather than "commies." Primarily from government jobs, although it was Hollywood that gave the red-baiters a national spotlight.

Later, when Sen. Joseph McCarthy tried to put the armed forces on trial, the whole shameful mess finally stopped. But the blacklisting of thousands of innocents did not. Anyone could become a target. However, those who escaped ruin were the rich and powerful. Lucille Ball was in fear for her career because in the '30s she'd registered as communist to please her social-activist grandfather. (In that era, with depression and fascism rampant, Marxism had seemed to many a viable alternative; it hadn't yet revealed itself as economically torpid, politically hypocritical, and a catastrophe where liberty and personal freedoms were concerned.) Of course Lucy was exempted from blacklisting—after being scared to death and earning her accusers massive publicity. A less successful actress like Marsha Hunt (*Blossoms in the Dust, Blue Denim*) did get blacklisted. Why? Hunt's "crimes" included: Signing a petition to the Supreme Court asking for a review of the convictions of two of the Hollywood Ten; supporting the Stop Censorship Committee; signing a statement issued in 1946 by the Hollywood Independent Citizens Committee of the Arts, Sciences & Professions; and so on.

Eddie (*Green Acres*) Albert's Mexican wife Margo gave money to enable orphans in Franco's fascist-ruled Spain to emigrate to Latin America. Gloria (*Titanic*) Stuart co-founded the Hollywood Anti-Nazi Committee. Others were pro-United Nations or were socialists or liberal Democrats or supporters of Roosevelt and his New Deal, which helped save the country financially but didn't favor the rich. Very few victims were communists, which wasn't even illegal. The witch-hunts were a smoke screen, and no coincidence that the majority of those whose careers and reputations were wrecked, in or out of Hollywood, belonged to either or sometimes both of two groups the reactionaries hated: homosexuals and Jews.

★ ★ ★

Myth: The blacklisting only hurt careers.

For most artists, their careers are their lives—work not necessarily done in an office, nor from nine to five. And of course actors couldn't, unlike writers, act via pseudonym. An actor's face is his or her career. Nor could directors direct under a pseudonym either. Besides blacklists, there were graylists—actors and even stars like liberal Edward G. Robinson who still got work, only less of it and of lower quality. The witch-hunts also provoked a number of suicides and premature deaths. In 1952, star John Garfield (*Body and Soul, Gentleman's Agreement*), who'd been virtually unemployed for eighteen months, died at age thirty-nine from a heart attack widely attributed to stress from his outcast condition.

Myth: That Hollywood and its movies were ever in danger of being "taken over" by the Communist Party.

Almost entirely discredited today, this rumor was once believed, despite the nature of Hollywood and its product. When movie star Gary Cooper went before the so-called House Un-American Activities Committee (HUAC), screenwriter Lillian Hellman wrote (in 1947) of "the professionally awkward stammering of Mr. Gary Cooper, who knew that Communist scripts had been submitted to him, but couldn't remember their names or their authors. And why couldn't he remember? Because he reads at night. That's sensible enough; naturally, one cannot remember what one reads in the dark." Regarding Robert Taylor and HUAC:

"…ladies screaming in elderly pleasure at the news that Mr. Robert Taylor was forced to act in a [supposedly Marxist] movie—act in a movie. Act. Act is not the correct word for what Mr. Taylor does in pictures."

The admittedly biased Hellman (a rabid Stalinist) did write reasonably about "the Congress of the United States of America being advised and lectured by a Mr. Adolphe Menjou, haberdashers' gentleman," who was so bigoted he called Katharine Hepburn "a red."

Hellman queried, "Why this particular industry, these particular people? Has it anything to do with Communism? Of course not. There has never been a single line or word of Communism in any American picture at any time. There has never or seldom been ideas of any kinds. Naturally, men scared to make pictures about the American Negro, men who have only in the last year allowed the word 'Jew' to be spoken in a picture, men who took more than ten years to make an anti-Fascist picture, those are frightened men, and you pick frightened men to frighten first. Judas goats; they'll lead the others, maybe, to the slaughter for you."

Then, as now, politicians get extra publicity and indignation by picking on Hollywood, which for the most part merely reflects society.

Myth: Actors are highly paid.

Highly unemployed is more like it. A few actors or, rather, stars earn eight figures per film, but the vast majority of thesps work seldom and earn modestly. TV actor Richard Kiley once advised, "Hollywood is like a sweepstakes…or a lottery. Your chances are much slimmer than you'd like to think….Other than fiscally, acting for the screen is not very satisfying. There's a lot of patience and drudgery involved. The test of whether you're meant to be an actor is, are you longing to get on the stage and act?"

Burgess Meredith (*Rocky*) noted, "Even an actor with a good career spends most of his time waiting for the next job, wondering if it'll come along, if it'll be good enough, and if he isn't getting too old to be in the running for anything except bitsy parts."

Puppeteer Shari Lewis (Lambchop's "mom") advised, "If you want to earn well and steadily, don't opt for show business. Be a doctor or something….You'll also get more of a chance to use your acting skills as a lawyer than the average actor does."

Myth: Stardom is worth the price.

The wages of stardom, when it happens, are huge. But there's no free lunch. Everything has a price. Part of the stellar price is having to watch your back all the time, being asked for things all the time, not knowing who's sincerely friendly, becoming more and more wary and suspicious, growing used to yes-men, growing older publicly, growing frustrated with the natural arc of a star's career, critics, legal worries, worries about looks, weight and image, possible betrayals by friends, relatives, lovers and exes, stereotyping, bad press, hate mail, box office flops, series cancellations, getting jaded, carnal and chemical temptations, spoiled offspring, trusting the servants, being routinely overcharged, tax worries, plastic surgery, ego, envy, etc., etc. (Still, nice work if you can get it!)

Myth: Some stars keep from aging without recourse to the knife.

Aging well is good genes, attitude, and maintenance. But past a certain age, nature, gravity, and wear and tear take their toll, and surgery, injections, or liposuction is required to keep a face and neck looking younger. Eyebags and jowls come to everybody. Most of the older celebs who deny having had plastic surgery or who publicly inveigh against it have had—if not facelifts—at least eye jobs and/or lipo below the jawline. Some performers don't consider this plastic surgery, in the same way that President Clinton—who co-existed with his non-show-biz eyebags—didn't consider fellatio sex.

Several stars of both genders have gone the whole hog yet publicly deny it, eager to be thought magically, preternaturally young-seeming. "We tend to enoble those who are born beautiful or who effortlessly remain good-looking," observes cosmetics tycoon Elizabeth Arden. Except that there's no such thing as staying attractive decade after decade without effort…great effort."

One seventy-ish Latin actress, a former superstar, looks wonderful for her age but insists she's never had any work done. Years ago she credited her ongoing looks to pasta; today to DNA, tomorrow…. Like her British, Hungarian, American and other counterparts, she has consistently had cosmetic surgery over the years (in the U.S., Brazil, and perhaps Europe). But the media play along; it would appear ungallant to call her on the lie, even though she assumes a mask of moral superiority by denying a truth which any doctor or surgeon would privately confirm.

Beauty is only skin deep. (Imagine the extra effort if it all went deeper!) However, ego and a desire to seem exceptional go all the way to the core. When it comes to plastic surgery you can't have your cake and eat it too. One either makes (anesthetized) contact with the knife, needle or scapula and looks younger, or one doesn't and looks more or less one's age. The choice is simple, but the truth, as Oscar Wilde said, "is rarely pure and never simple."

Celebrity Myths

Elvis Presley was a "born again" Christian.
Perhaps, but he explained, "I don't want to miss out on heaven due to a technicality," when asked why he wore a crucifix and a Star of David.

Lengthy celebrity marriages are usually the least eventful.
Ask Lynn Redgrave. In 1999 she was nominated for an Oscar for the first time since the 1960s. She also filed to divorce her husband of thirty-two years after finding out that he'd fathered a child with a woman who later married the couple's son.

Jackie Gleason was a comic original.
Early on, he brazenly stole from Milton Berle. Not just jokes, but his whole act. "What I performed at the best places in Manhattan, Gleason would soon after perform in low dives in New Jersey," recalled Berle. "I went to see him…it made me very angry, because he did my routines very well. But I warned him…and he still kept stealing from me. Until he got on television, where he didn't dare." The two became TV rivals, Gleason eventually eclipsing Uncle Miltie via *The Honeymooners*.

Jody on *Soap*, played by heterosexual Billy Crystal, was TV's first recurring gay character, in the late 1970s.
But back in the 1960s there was Dr. Smith on *Lost in Space*.…And in the '50s there was Zelda, even if the writers had her forever chasing a reluctant *Dobie Gillis*. A sweet butch, Zelda was enacted by Sheila James, now Sheila James Kuehl, California's first openly lesbian Assemblyperson.

P.S. Another "different" character who later came out in real life was one of the twins who played Tabitha on *Bewitched*. Diane Murphy quit acting at thirteen, got an MBA in management and became associate executive director of Shelter Services For Women, which operates three shelters in Santa Barbara, California.

Johnny Carson's rapport with Ed McMahon was due to his never feeling threatened by him.

Never say never. In 1965 *The Tonight Show* still started at 11:15 PM, which meant that less than a fourth of NBC's audience got to hear Carson's monologue (most local news shows didn't end until 11:30). So Johnny decided to stay in his dressing room until 11:30—a nightly "15-minute virus" he called it. So NBC called on Ed to fill in for Johnny until 11:30. Instead of stalling for time, Ed gave it his best shot, and audiences grew to like him more and more.

Until Carson the star informed him, "Look, Ed, you've gotta cool it. You're not leaving me anything." McMahon reveals, "I took a stand." He explained that he wasn't out to upstage Johnny, but neither could he do an intentionally lousy job. Carson stated he'd have to modify his act or find a new job. "I lost," says Ed. "You can't take away from the star."

P.S. In 1967 NBC finally gave in to Carson and began the show— with Johnny himself—at 11:30 PM.

Madonna probably loves oral sex.

But not like you might think. "I'm a good kisser," boasts the boy-toy collector. "Everybody says so. They don't tell me I give good head, believe me, because I don't give it....Who wants to choke?...That's part of the whole humiliation thing of men with women. Women cannot choke a guy....It doesn't go down into their throats and move their epiglottis around."

"No matter what they play on the motion picture screen," said MGM chief Louis B. Mayer, "all of my actresses are ladies." The 1940s pronouncement was meant to reassure audiences—

those who cared, and far more felt entitled to, then—that even
if a star played a man-chaser or a faithless wife, the
thespian behind the character was, in Victorian terms, spotless.
But in reality, Lana Turner was known to screw like a mink and
amassed eight husbands and dozens of lovers, one of whom she alleged
was fatally stabbed by her teenage daughter. Nor was Lana unique, to
Mayer's chagrin. In the '30s he upbraided bisexually active Tallulah
Bankhead for her affairs with men (she was unmarried). She got Mayer
off her back (so to speak; he wasn't spotless himself) by threatening to
name six MGM actresses with whom she'd had affairs, among them
Barbara Stanwyck and bisexual Joan Crawford.

★　　★　　★

Zsa Zsa Gabor claims she's never had plastic surgery, let alone a face-lift.

When the professional Hungarian complained about a face-lift joke
during a guest spot, funny man Artie Stander replied, "Zsa Zsa, one
more face-lift and you'll have pubic hair on your chin." (It was her one-
time director John Huston who declared that Gabor had discovered the
secret of "perpetual middle age.")

★　　★　　★

Clark Gable was called "the king" of Hollywood. Some assume this meant he was Tinseltown's biggest star. It was simply a temporary title that stuck: one year, he was named the box office king and Myrna Loy was box office queen— which hardly anyone remembers. (As few people realize John Wayne's "Duke" nickname was actually that of his pet canine.)

In many ways, Gable didn't act like a king. He was a tightwad his whole
life, a gay-baiter who got director George Cukor fired about a third of
the way through *Gone With the Wind* because Cukor knew a thing or
two about Gable back when he was a struggling actor: that Clark,
who'd been supported by two older wives, had allowed himself a same-
sex fling with a helpful silent screen star (William Haines), and that
Clark was—perhaps the source of his insecurity—far from well-hung
(unlike, say, Rock Hudson, Charlie Chaplin or Humphrey Bogart, to
name three other box office kings).

In fact, Gable's favorite wife, star Carole Lombard, noted that the cinematic sex symbol wasn't comfortable around most women, being more of a man's man. There was a famous quote: "If Clark had one inch less, he'd be the 'queen of Hollywood' instead of 'the king.'"

Myth: Hollywood blondes are confident to the point of brazenness.

Blonde actresses may stand out visually and appear more sexual thanks to their real or not-so-real hair color, but they aren't necessarily all that secure. Marilyn Monroe and Elizabeth Taylor had a very private feud-let, with Monroe believing that Taylor got better roles—and Oscar nominations—due to her "more serious" hair color. And in Nora Ephron's romantic comedy *You've Got Mail* with Tom Hanks, Meg Ryan reportedly insisted she be the sole blonde on screen—producers were told anyone else with golden hair had better cover up so Ryan could stand out better.

Myth: Superstars cherish their uniqueness.

There's unique and then there's different, and though being a movie star is the antithesis of being "just plain folks," insecurity often prevents many stars from being true to themselves. For instance, the fabulously self-assured Mae West pretended to be right-handed, so not to seem different from the majority. She also followed her mother's advice and kept her maternal Jewish heritage a secret. And though she presented herself as a pioneer for the rights of women, blacks and gays, she mostly eschewed female company, treated blacks as lackeys, and publicly denied the homosexuality of one of her relatives. "Moral:" uniqueness does not preclude blind conformity.

Watching Lucille Ball on any of her sitcoms, it's easy to imagine she must have been fun to work with.

It's generally known that "Lucy" was no clown in real life and was, according to everyone from her kids to Phyllis Diller to Jack Lemmon, a control freak. Lemmon felt Ball crossed the line into tyranny, intimidating elderly Jack Benny and telling the comedic genius how to read a line "funnier." Tom Bosley, later of *Happy Days*, said, "I hated working with that bitch....Thank God I'll never have to work with her again!"

Burly Claude Akins guested on an episode. Lucy associate Tommy Thompson recalled, "She grabbed his arm and said, 'Stay close to me, it's a two-shot.' He walked over to me after rehearsal and said, 'Look at my arm.' She had nails about an inch long—big nail marks were all over. He said, 'When she wants you to stand close, she means stand close.'"

It was fellow comics who sometimes especially prompted Lucy's competitiveness. Associate Johny Aitchison noted, "When [Lucy and guest Danny Kaye] were rehearsing, Danny would correct Lucy. Lucy would come right back at him. And then it got hot and heavy. Danny said, 'Just who the hell do you think you are?' She says, 'You're full of shit—that's who I am.'"

But poets are sensitive....

On the page, yes. Otherwise, it depends. Gary Merrill toured with wife Bette Davis in the stage show *The World of Carl Sandburg*. Sandburg told Merrill of a girl who introduced herself at a party: "I'm very sorry, my dear, but you bore me," he soon said, "and I don't have enough time left." Then the elderly poet walked away. Wrote Merrill, Davis' only actor husband, "I've not been able to get away with using Carl's candid words...but I have managed to keep bores at a distance. The problem is, there are so damned many of them!"

Myth: Hollywood esteems its Italian-American actors.

Today, yes. But this was not always the case. Only after World War II did Tinseltown grudgingly accept Italian surnames, and for every Sinatra—who began as a singer, not an actor—there were ten who switched, like Dean Martin (Dino Crocetti), Anne Bancroft (Anna Maria Italiano), Paula Prentiss (Paula Ragusa), Tony Bennett (Tony Bennedetto), Connie Stevens (Concetta Ingolia), Connie Francis (Concetta Franconero), Bernadette Peters (Bernadette Lazzaro), Sophia Loren (Sofia Scicolone), and on and on up through the acting/directing Marshall siblings, Penny and Garry.

De Niro and Pacino have brought prestige to acting Italian surnames, and Stallone and Travolta popularity, but as one agent still advises, "Hollywood or Broadway, singing or acting, we still warn a client, specifically a potential client, that a name like that can hamper his or her mainstream marketability." Mamma mia, do you believe it?

P.S. In the not so good old days, where Hollywood ignored Italian heritage, popular novelists did include Italian characters—negatively. Just read some of the works of James M. Cain and Agatha Christie, among too many others.

★　★　★

Myth: Planet Hollywood partners Sylvester Stallone and Arnold Schwarzenegger are friends.

In Hollywood, money's the bottom line, temporarily uniting even the worst of enemies. *Star* columnist Janet Charlton disclosed, "They try to muffle it since they're both involved in Planet Hollywood. But you'll never see them together. They both keep quiet about it….Stallone really tried to damage Arnold's career, and Arnold found out about it.

"At one point Stallone was funding a woman in England to write a book about Arnold—a very unflattering biography. Nobody knew that Stallone was financing [it] until the author was dragged into court by Arnold for untrue claims she made in the book, and she had to reveal the Stallone connection. When that came out, it became clear how deep-seated Stallone's resentment was. Arnold was so angry….Imagine finding out that your competitor and business partner is financing a nasty book about you….They still don't like each other."

★　★　★

Myth: Performers who are more into causes and charities are more apt to be helpful to show biz newcomers.

In show business, #1 is #1. The Helen Lawson Syndrome means that most performers, regardless of how generous and even-minded the image, see all other performers—particularly younger ones—as competition. As an example, superstar Burt Lancaster was a courageous, principled man, a champion of everyone's equal rights who also marched with Martin Luther King, Jr., opposed the McCarthy-era communist witch-hunts and blacklist, and did an ad as "a card-carrying member of

"Like most 'good ole boys,' Elvis was unfortunately anti-Semitic and didn't like dealing with the Hollywood studio VIPs."—Dean Martin, like Presley an associate of movie producer Hal Wallis.

"Elvis never did an overseas concert or tour because at heart he was a stay-at-home hick."— British producer Derek Nimmo. Elvis wanted to work overseas, particularly in England and Japan. But his manager, "Colonel" Tom Parker—all three names were fake—wasn't really Southern. One of the secrets of Andreas Cornelius van Kujik (a Dutch name, though he may have been born in Eastern Europe) was that he'd snuck into the U.S. via Florida as an illegal alien. Thus Parker didn't dare leave the country, of which he never became a citizen, for fear of not being allowed back in. So he never allowed Presley to work abroad, even in Canada.

Elvis was a mama's boy with good manners and old-fashioned morals.
He did all but worship mother Gladys and was deeply influenced by her. He said "sir" and "ma'am" a lot and had good manners, especially early on. But, even discounting the eventual drugs, his private values were sometimes quite non-traditional. Elvis preferred girls to women and was uncomfortable with most females his age. Thirteen to sixteen was his preferred age range for dates and sexual partners. Presley's manager kept such affairs out of the public eye, but worried about Elvis' long-running relationship with Priscilla Beaulieu. Eventually the star asked her parents if she could move in with him, but they said no, as she was 15. "Colonel" Parker pressured Elvis to marry to avoid a potential scandal, and not long after, Presley had a teenage bride.

Elvis was a cool, smooth dude. Socially and intellectually, he was sometimes naive and frequently awkward. According to James L. Dickerson, author of *Colonel Tom Parker*, Presley was "backward for his age," for instance attending Saturday morning matinees at 18 and 19 when nearly all the other moviegoers were children or young teens (and a few parents). Elvis reportedly felt more comfortable and confident relating to kids than adults.

_____

Despite his greed (50% of Elvis' salary, plus lots of side deals) and being a control freak, the "Colonel" was a master showman.

Parker was pushy, energetic, and very, very lucky. He latched on to a singing, and then a singing-acting, goldmine whom he preferred to keep in mediocre musicals that yielded profitable record albums than let him try dramatic roles which might expand his artistic range and screen longevity. Parker had worked long and hard in carnivals, and one of his pre-Elvis highlights was a carnie act of his own devising billed as "Colonel Parker's Dancing Chickens." It consisted of a hotplate sprinkled with sawdust on which baby chicks "danced" when the heat was turned up.

_____

Elvis and Priscilla's wedding was one of the happiest and most romantic in show biz history. It got tremendous publicity and was wildly romanticized by the media and Elvis fans. But basically it was a "Colonel"—dominated business affair. Following the nuptial rites, Parker rushed Elvis and Priscilla to a press conference where Presley (having been coached) answered questions about his personal life. A reception ensued, its guest list comprised mostly of Parker's cronies and business associates. In her autobiography, Priscilla wrote, "I wish I'd had the strength then to say, 'Wait a minute, this is our wedding, fans or no fans, press or no press. Let us invite whomever we want, and have it wherever we want.'" She added, "It seemed that as soon as the ceremony began, it was over."

_____

the ACLU" when political campaigner George Bush tried to smear the American Civil Liberties Union. But as an actor, Burt's sole interest was Burt:

"I had been a Burt Lancaster fan," recalled Joan Rivers of her small role in a party scene in *The Swimmer* (1967). "But here he was refusing a little bit player her moment in the sun…a star who was not generous, somebody totally self-centered….In my scenes with Lancaster, he would step backward, forcing me to turn my face toward him and away from the camera. While I was speaking my lines, he was constantly in motion, shaking his drink, wiping his mouth, moving his hands. Since eyes go to motion, the attention would be on him. No actor was allowed to touch him. If I laid a hand on him, then the camera would have to show whose hand it was. This is the old movie rule for bit players—'Always touch the money.' Then they cannot cut you out of the scene."

Myth: Big male stars must be great kissers.

Romantic leads must be good, or convincing, actors, but not necessarily good kissers. Even the heterosexual ones. Gay or bi Cary Grant was known for disliking and doing few kissing scenes—even in a film as passionate and romantic as *An Affair To Remember*. Leading lady Ingrid Bergman said, "Cary is wonderful at looking and sounding romantic, but he'd rather not do it, you know."

Hollywood columnist Arlene Walsh wrote that current hetero leading man "Harrison Ford's leading ladies all seem to concur that he may be the sweetest, nicest guy you would ever want to meet—but he can't kiss. He just finds it impossible to kiss on screen, and the talk among his leading ladies is that he is probably not very good offscreen either."

Myth: Four-time Oscar-winner Katharine Hepburn has always been regarded as a great talent.

When she arrived on the scene in the 1930s, Hepburn was considered by many critics, as well as theater and filmgoers, to be too mannered and too mannish, not to mention affected. Dorothy Parker wrote that Kate ran the gamut of emotions on-stage "from A to B." Agatha Christie felt she "babbled, always holding court." And in the '90s, former director

Elia Kazan opined that "She'd committed herself to a particular tradition of acting…she was out of another world….Stars of that ilk [felt] a duty to their audiences to uphold a certain image of glamour, heroism and bravery. A star never did anything wrong. It's completely artificial. People are not like that. Essentially, it's the tradition of the 19th-century theater carried over."

P.S. Walter Brennan, a TV star after years as a supporting movie actor, won three Oscars but was not widely considered a great talent. And many an undeniable talent has never won a single Oscar.

★   ★   ★

Myth: Mel Gibson is Australian.

He was born in the U.S., and his father reportedly didn't want his sons serving in the Vietnam war, so the family emigrated to Australia, where Mel was of course seen—and heard—as an American. Many or most Aussies still consider Gibson a Yank who was partly reared Down Under. Hollywood considered him "foreign" at first, but today most traces of any acquired Australian accent are gone, the better to fit in with other American movie stars.

★   ★   ★

Myth: Angela Lansbury seems so nice, almost a pushover, at least by Hollywood standards.

By any standards, she's a survivor, and a smart one. Long an underrated supporting actor, she bloomed in middle age on Broadway (*Mame*) and finally became a superstar later, on TV (*Murder, She Wrote*, the title more than reminiscent of a '60s film starring Margaret Rutherford as Miss Marple: *Murder, She Said*). Lansbury's manners are impeccable, especially for Hollywood. But her standards are high: "I don't forgive," she informed *Modern Maturity* magazine in 1999. "Never. I cannot. You don't pick up as if nothing happened, do you? When I am betrayed, it absolutely turns me to stone.

"But you have to be able to forgive, right? Otherwise it will create bad blood for a long time. I'm the one who suffers, while the other person just blodges on. So I have to work on that."

★   ★   ★

Myth: Dr. Seuss must have been a wonderful father.

Surprising how many people assume the creator of wonderful children's books was a father. His name was Theodore Geisel, he was contractually married, and according to various reports and insiders was gay. As definitely was Hans Christian Andersen, the writer of such classics as *The Ugly Duckling* and *The Little Mermaid* (the Disney animated feature of which was produced and the lyrics written by openly gay Howard Ashman, whose Academy Award was posthumously accepted by his life partner). Much of the most popular and enduring material for children is created by gay people, most of them still hiding the fact that they are not heterosexual.

★ ★ ★

Myth: Apparently heterosexual men like Milton Berle, who are or were famous for doing drag, don't mind being thought of as gay.

Drag generally has nothing to do with sexual orientation. Studies say that most men who secretly wear women's clothing—for instance female underwear—are heterosexual and married. But stereotypes connect drag with gay men, even though what was once considered drag on women—pants and suits—is now standard women's businesswear. British drag divo Benny Hill strenuously objected to being thought of as gay—it's not certain whether he was; remember, many of the worst homophobes tend to be closet cases. And in 1999 Milton Berle, who pioneered drag on American TV in the 1950s, sued a real estate company for $6 million because they ran a print ad showing "Uncle Miltie" dressed as Carmen Miranda.

The suit alleged that younger generations who never saw his series might see the ad and jump to the conclusion that the ninety-one-year-old comic was homosexual. Ooh, ghastly. (Or they might think he's Brazilian?)

At ninety-one is *anyone* still sexual?

★ ★ ★

**Myth: Such funny celebrities as Bette Midler
or Joan Rivers must be more interesting to meet than dramatic types like Glenn Close or Anthony Hopkins, or
"shy" types like Johnny Mathis.**

That's assuming that celebs are the same in real life as when they are working—or playing a role. Rivers and Midler happen to be shy types in real life. Says Bette of her stage persona, the brash and bawdy Divine Miss M., "I love her, and audiences love her, but that's not the real me." Remember too that female celebs are necessarily more wary of strangers in public. And that British celebs usually have better manners. Someone like Johnny Mathis comes across as shy or reserved on stage but in real life is fun, outgoing and sometimes bawdy.

★   ★   ★

Myth: Katharine Hepburn is a prude, New England-style.

Like most people, she has grown somewhat more prudish with age, not that she was ever a wild 'n crazy gal. On the other hand, she was the first-ever star to utter a four-letter word on Broadway, in the musical *Coco* (1969), based loosely on designer Gabrielle Chanel's life. Kate shocked audiences nightly by exclaiming, "Shit!" And in her final movie appearance (*Love Affair*, 1994) she used the expression "fuck a duck."

★   ★   ★

**Myth: *That Girl* Marlo Thomas is an easygoing sweetheart,
like her TV character.**

Thomas played bubbly Anne Marie, and that was in the '60s. As employees and many coworkers know, Ms. Thomas is a take-charge person with quite a temper. "Forget Freddy. Forget Jason. When it comes to monsters, Marlo is unequaled." So wrote her longtime majordomo Desmond Atholl in his tell-all book *That Girl and Phil*. Thomas' husband Phil Donahue was an easygoing sweetheart, but Marlo lived and expected to be treated like royalty. One chapter dealt with the crisis of the not-white-enough white French tulips, which sent Marlo into a shrieking tizzy while Atholl kept replacing the "cream-colored" offenders with new tulips, at $250 a bunch. The right shade of white never did materialize that day.

"Two months later, I was not alarmed when Miss Thomas once again shrieked after I had just finished completing the flower arrangements." But it wasn't about getting the exact shade of tulips; the celeb's business manager "had just telephoned with the unfortunate news that in one year she had spent $98,000 on flowers and plants! Which reminds me of another story about the pink azaleas that were not the right shade of pink...."

Myth: Sixties star Jean Seberg committed suicide after it got out that she'd had a baby by a member of the Black Panthers.
Completely false, and the work of FBI chief J. Edgar Hoover, on whose hate list the blonde actress—as well as Jane Fonda, Marlon Brando and other liberals who'd donated money to the Black Panthers—found themselves. Another reason Hoover hated Seberg was because she'd gone to live in France (as had Fonda in the '60s). When she became pregnant by husband Romain Gary, a French writer and diplomat, Hoover planted the story—picked up by several major periodicals— that the American actress was expecting via a black revolutionary. At that time, such a rumor could harm a woman's career, as happened when Swedish Inger Stevens wed a black man and blonde Sue Lyon (*Lolita*) married a black convict.

Seberg's baby lived two days. To show that it was white, she had it displayed in a glass casket, and soon after began a series of suicide attempts, none of them successful until 1979 (via barbituates). The following year, Romain Gary fatally shot himself.

Myth: The great love affair between Juan Perón and Evita.
This was reinforced by the film *Evita*, in which Madonna played the Argentinian First Lady too kittenishly, omitting most of the brittle anger and desire for vengeance which haunted and fueled the once-poor love child from the sticks. Perón was twenty-five years older than Eva. His first wife was a seventeen-year-old blonde who, like Evita, died prematurely. Just before Evita, he was cohabitating with a teenage girl whom he passed off as his daughter. After he and Eva Duarte tied the knot, they had separate bedrooms and she became a full-time political maneuverer. During

the marriage, he had rent girls and mistresses, the youngest of them thirteen. After Evita's death there were minor scandals when he became involved with high school girls. The fact that the former colonel was a pedophile was an open secret which never harmed his career.

Perón met his third wife, Isabel, a cabaret entertainer, when she was very young. After his death, she succeeded him, in the 1970s, as president of Argentina.

★ ★ ★

Myth: Actors like Clint Eastwood and Sonny Bono became mayors in order to serve their local communities— or just for the publicity.

Publicity may be one of the factors, but being a mayor does take time and work, and there are easier ways to get publicity. Often, the primary motivation for running for local office is to change the rules, to get one's way. Bono, who ran a restaurant in Palm Springs, admitted, "I didn't like the stupid laws and regulations I, as an entrepreneur, had to put up with....I got damn mad about it." In Sondra Locke's tell-all book about her former longtime lover Clint Eastwood—*The Good, the Bad, and the Very Ugly*—she revealed, "I knew he wasn't the dedicated mayor he pretended to be."

She wrote that after the Carmel city council refused his plans for a new downtown building, "Clint was livid. 'They don't know who they're fuckin' with,' he raged. 'I'll build that damn building the way I want it if I have to run the fucking city council to do it.' Before I knew it he had engaged a political consulting firm and was elected mayor." His building went up, his way—he too owned a local restaurant. Carmelites were impressed that "a busy movie star like that [is] interested in serving our little community!" Locke felt, "The truth was he'd just wanted to have his way. Who he was serving was Clint."

When asked to run for a second term, he replied, "I would love to help you out, but I need to spend more time with my children in their formative years." Sondra wrote, "I would hear Clint use that excuse more than once; obviously, they were no longer in their formative years. Still, he loved the idea of being the mayor," and he privately called the California resort "my kingdom."

MATERIAL BOYS & GIRLS

— Cybill Shepherd.

"Women are living to be 92 years of age on average now."—Linda Evans, former "Dynasty" star, in a 1999 infomercial for a beauty mask. If only.

"I've been so tied up with promoting the Farrah cosmetic range that I don't feel I've had any time for world affairs."
—Farrah Fawcett in the 1970s. Alas, Farrah didn't turn to world affairs, but instead moved on to ventures like Farrah wigs, Farrah dolls and, yes, a Farrah Fawcett (faucet) plumbing fixture, not to mention Ryan O'Neal and posing and painting in the nude at 50 in *Playboy* and on TV.

"People say I'm so young, and all the success and stuff I have. But everything I have, I've earned."
—Winona Ryder, star and frequent shopper, in 1997.
No comment (one has the right to remain silent).

"People don't believe it yet, but right now I'm very underpaid."
—Jennifer Lopez, commenting on her $2 million salary for *Out of Sight*, for which George Clooney got about $10 million and for which J-Lo had asked for $5 million. Underpaid is of course a relative term.

"A certain standard of living is necessary to be taken seriously as a player in Hollywood."
—director Peter Bogdanovich, after declaring bankruptcy, when a lawyer questioned his still paying $250 to have his hair cut.

"I prefer to live simply."
—Brad Pitt.
He seems true to his word—especially sartorially—but not when it comes to Jennifer Aniston's dog Enzo. In 1999 Pitt bought Enzo a $1,000 leather bed from Gucci and cohosted a lavish party for the pooch's birthday. Enzo reportedly has a Vuitton suitcase and goes almost everywhere with his couple.

Myth: Some stars give their all to charity.
Some take quite a bit, too. In 1986, the stars of the first Comic Relief concert—Billy Crystal, Whoopi Goldberg, and Robin

Williams—stayed, separately, in $1,000-a-night suites in their New York City hotel. Comic Relief, of course, is in aid of the homeless. Another time, Goldberg (née Caryn Johnson) took a train to Washington, D.C., and bought half the seats in the club car for herself and entourage, at a cost of $2,500. She was going to D.C. to testify on the effect of budget cuts on the poor. What was she, an expert?

Myth: Big spenders, big tippers. Gossip columnists The Hollywood Kids quoted a Hollywood waitress: "Mel Gibson thinks if he smiles at you, that's your tip." Another offered, "Chuck Heston thinks the mere fact of your serving him is privilege enough," with or without a smile. In 1999 columnist Arlene Walsh wrote, "Big Spender: Wesley Snipes may be cheap about paying a 20% tip on a bottle of champagne, but he has no problem dropping $24 million for a three-story, Big Apple townhouse."

P.S. Mel Gibson believes, "Being a star is being a target. It's like having your pants down around your ankles and your hands tied behind your back. You become a good opportunity (sic) for some parasite to throw darts in your chest." Solution: Move to the Australian Outback and keep your pants up.

"Most of us (TV actors) are not greedy."—David Duchovny, "The X-Files."

In August, 1999, as the *New Times* put it, David "filed a lawsuit against Fox for cutting a sweetheart deal with the network FX to show reruns, thereby reducing his financial windfall from millions and millions and millions to merely millions and millions."

"You bet we're partners. You said it!"—Lou Costello, of Abbott & Costello, in the 1950s. By then, the comedy team's popularity had shrunk and their movies were losing money. Costello had always resented his second billing, and finally abolished their old contract and 50-50 split. Bud, less ambitious and energetic than Lou—and secretly epileptic—had no choice but to go along. The public watching their TV series had no idea that Abbott was now an employee working for Costello's company.

The portly Lou died of a heart attack in 1959. Bud, 11 years his senior, died in 1974.

———————

Myth: Laurel was the dumb one; by comparison, Hardy was the smart one.

As with Abbott & Costello, the on-screen dummy was the prime mover behind the comedic pair. Unlike Bud and Lou, Stan and Ollie got along beautifully and remained a team. Workaholic Stan Laurel was the brains behind many of their classic routines, while Oliver "Babe" Hardy preferred to spend his off-screen time golfing and socializing. As with the later duo, the slimmer Laurel was older than Hardy but outlived him.

———————

"The Bond people, the regulars, are very tightly knit, like a family."—Desmond Llewelyn, who played Q in 17 007 films, more than any other regular.

Sadly, the 85-year-old was killed in a 1999 car crash in England returning home alone after a book signing. His funeral was attended by hardly any costars and only one of the Bonds Llewelyn had worked with, Roger Moore. (Contrary to his mechanical image, Llewelyn

breezily admitted in *Computer Life* magazine, "In real life, I'm allergic to gadgets. They just don't work for me, not even those plastic cards for hotel room doors."

———————

"I made this album to make people feel good. We need that… I see nothing wrong with that."—John Wayne, on his record album *America, Why I Love Her.*

The album, recorded during the height, or depth, of Watergate, wasn't calculated to make all Americans feel good. One of its then-non-controversial non-classics was "The Hyphen," in which the Oscar-winning star tried to shame such groups as "Mexican hyphen Americans" and "Afro hyphen Americans"— but not Irish-Americans or German-Americans, etc. "The Hyphen" philosophized that neither a swastika nor hammer-and-sickle could "flame the flames of hatred faster than The Hyphen."

———————

"Clint Eastwood and I will never win an Oscar. We're too popular."—Burt Reynolds.

He was half right. Eastwood won for directing and producing *The Unforgiven.*

"I was nominated for the Academy Award for *Of Human Bondage* (1934), and I should know!"—Bette Davis in the 1970s.

But she wasn't nominated, Blanche, she wasn't. *Bondage* featured Bette's breakthrough role as Mildred the waitress. The following year she was nominated for the so-so *Dangerous* and won, mostly because her peers felt she'd deserved it for Mildred, a bitchy role declined by several image-conscious stars. Davis' confusion over the non-nomination may have resulted from a write-in campaign mounted on her behalf for *Of Human Bondage*.

———————

"Do I know books!"—literary agent to the rich and famous Irving "Swifty" Lazar.

Perhaps he should have changed the exclamation mark to a question mark, for the swift one seldom made time to read his clientele's manuscripts. This came to light when a suspicious client inserted $100 bills between the pages of his manuscript, which was eventually returned with all the cash intact. Lazar later admitted to this peculiar habit.

———————

"I just wanted to tell it like it was . . . pull no punches." —Ronald Reagan, about his memoirs, which however initially made no mention of his first marriage to Jane Wyman (due to Nancy's influence, it was speculated) until editor Michael Korda convinced the ex-prez that such an omission would diminish the book's interest and integrity.

Myth: British celebs keep their cool better than American ones.
Maybe they once did, but not today's batch of Brits, as evidenced at the
2000 Golden Globes ceremonies, attended by movie star Hugh Grant
and his girlfriend, model/actress Elizabeth Hurley. After she was accidentally touched on the shoulder by a man, she shrieked, "Get away
from me, you idiot!" then tossed her drink at him and sobbed, "You're
simply disgusting. Go away!" Meanwhile, Grant, so cool and noncha-
lant in films, was hysterically trying to summon security on his cell
phone. Stiff upper lips indeed.

★   ★   ★

**Myth: It's girls, girls, girls in the lives of celebrity
bachelors and divorced men.**
It may or may not be. And sometimes not as much as one thinks. After
Howard Stern's wife left him, he took a four-day vacation in the Bahamas,
with nary a babe in sight. He spent his time with male buddies, including
his personal trainer, a hairstylist, and a New York restaurant manager. In
1999 movie hunk Matthew McConaughey was arrested at his home in
Austin, Texas, for drug possession. He was stark naked, and his sole guest
was another man. The two were reportedly "dancing to the sound of
bongo drums." And in the early morning hours of the Northridge earthquake which devastated Los Angeles in 1994, actor George Clooney's
houseguests were a male pal, naked, and a pet pig, likewise.

★   ★   ★

**Myth: Blond-hunk-dreamboat types, from Troy Donahue to
Leonardo DiCaprio, are the most sought-after ideals.**
With few exceptions, the blond boys don't have long stellar careers.
(Where are Troy and Tab today?) The men who make and cast movies
are generally more comfortable with brunet or nondescript actors. The
"too pretty" concept still applies for males, except if they are young.
Zogby's Celebrity World, which polls the public about celebs, asked
1,206 people who would triumph if blonde ice queen Sharon Stone
and blond teen fave Leo DiCaprio went head to head in a streetfight?
Some 56.2% voted for Stone, and only 16.2% for DiCaprio.

Blond former TV star John Schneider (*The Dukes of Hazzard*) also tried a singing career. But the highest he reached was #14 in 1981 doing Elvis' hit *It's Now or Never* (an Italian song in disguise). *Dukes* costar Denver Pyle offered, "John's great for some people to look at, but he's getting frustrated 'cause that don't lead to the big stardom he's hoping for....He's getting deep-down sore about it, but I think if he's not terrific [sic] lucky, he'll have to settle for the TV now and then."

Another TV blond, David Soul of the then-hit *Starsky & Hutch*, also sang his way to notice. Enthusiastic Merv Griffin had him on his show more than twenty times, until series TV beckoned. A small-screen superstar (only) with *Hutch*, Soul's wife-beating came to national light in 1982 when third wife Patti had her husband arrested and then, unusually, followed through with a court case. She recalled that he would pin her to the wall, throw her across their yard, hit her, spit in her face, and during her third trimester of pregancy, "He sat on my stomach for twenty minutes, telling me what to say and think." It got to the point where, she informed *People* magazine, "when I'd so much as smell beer or wine, it would trigger a fear in me."

Soul was ordered to undergo rehabilitation, saying that up until then he "didn't understand the extent of Patti's fear."

Don't judge a book by its cover, blond or otherwise. Dreamboats often work best in dreams—or beds. But as Courtney Cox said, "I can't be with somebody just because it's great sex, because orgasms don't last that long."

★   ★   ★

Myth: Former TV star Tom Selleck (*Magnum, P.I.*) is a male Mary Tyler Moore, as nice as that Hawaii-based guy he played.

An image is composed of the character someone else writes and the (usually) best behavior the actor brings to the part and to his public persona. The media often exaggerates: a critic wrote that Magnum and Selleck were "one" and that he "hasn't a single unredeeming flaw"; other critics have insisted that Carroll O'Connor was the opposite of Archie Bunker, Bea Arthur was the opposite of Maude, Shannen Doherty wasn't quite Brenda, and of course all those gay characters are played by non-gay actors. Uh-huh.

Don Ameche, Selleck's father in the flop movie *Folks!* (1992) said, "Tom is a hard worker, but he's also rather hard and aloof…his sparkle is reserved for the camera." A former male model, Selleck progressed to being a Marlboro Man and had a bit part as "Stud" in *Myra Breckinridge* (1970). He went nowhere fast and reached stardom, on the small screen, late. John Huston, of *Myra*, later opined, "The ones who bloom late, in our business at any rate, often bloom bitter.…I don't know what else is behind Mr. Selleck's unusual politics." (In 1996, Selleck supported Pat Buchanan for president.) Selleck himself advised *TV Guide* of his impatience with fans and that he didn't want to be Mr. Nice Guy. People who worked with him on his very short-lived post-*Magnum* series agreed that he wasn't, and the network noted that the non-comedic actor had wanted too much control.

A woman who attended an ultra-conservative all-day seminar with him explained, "I was surprised how different he is in person…the clenched jaw, not at all easygoing.…He didn't make it in the movies, so I guess now it's just a TV film here or there." And those *Friends* guest bits as an aging hunk.

★　　★　　★

Myth: Jim Varney, the buck-toothed, rubber-faced actor behind the hilarious Ernest P. Worrell, either was his character or couldn't play anything else.

The Kentucky native, who died in 2000 at age fifty of lung cancer, wasn't bitter about it but believed he didn't get due credit as a performer. "It's not just me, of course.…How many comedy pictures, how many comedy actors, ever get up for Academy Awards? And when you're Southern, they already figure you're comedy material—you're not even having to try."

But Varney had an Emmy-winning 1989 TV series called *Hey Vern, It's Ernest* in which he played multiple characters of varying ages, accents, physicalities and genders, including Auntie Nelda, the mother-in-law from hell. In the feature *Ernest Goes to Jail* he enacted the hero and the villain, each vividly distinct without the use of makeup. And he played relatively straight in the big-screen *Beverly Hillbillies*, as Jed Clampett. Besides which, impersonating the same goofy character on

TV commercials for over six years and still keeping him fresh and funny takes more than a little talent—KnoWhutIMean?

*   *   *

**Myth: Easygoing, set-a-spell Buddy Ebsen and his cama-
raderie with fellow *Beverly Hillbillies* cast members.**

True, there were no squabbles on the hit sitcom back in the '60s. Everyone pretty much got along, and the younger actors who played Jethro and Elly Mae felt lucky to be on the show, as opposed to so many today who feel competitive and compelled to demand huge salaries. But Raymond Bailey, who enacted banker Mr. Drysdale, felt contemptuous toward Nancy Kulp, who played his secretary Miss Hathaway. "I was in virtually every episode," she said, "and Mr. Bailey resented that and my popularity, such as it was."

Ebsen went on to star as *Barnaby Jones* after his Clampett days ended, but despite its long run, he never asked any of his former *Hillbillies* colleagues to guest on his new series, which rankled the others. Then, in the 1980s, Nancy Kulp ran for Congress in Pennsylvania, and to her amazement, California Ebsen got "involved in our [PA] politics, of which he knows nothing," by making radio ads "supporting my Republican opponent and claiming I'm too liberal for Pennsylvania— a Hollywood pinko, as it were! I was speechless at such a betrayal, and something so needless and cruel, such [smear] tactics." Ebsen reportedly gloated over Kulp's defeat (Kulp did serve on the board of directors of the Screen Actors Guild), and in his memoirs barely acknowledged her existence on *The Beverly Hillbillies*.

Kulp, who was very private—and gay—did not write her memoirs. She ascribed Ebsen's "soreness and vindictiveness" to his having lost, due to an accident, the role of the Tin Man in *The Wizard of Oz*. An aspiring dancer/comedian, Ebsen might have become a star via the 1939 classic, instead of languishing professionally until his 1962 hit sitcom. As for movies, his only notable role was as Audrey Hepburn's abandoned hillbilly husband in *Breakfast at Tiffany's*.

*   *   *

Myth: The Betty Ford Clinic has cured most of Hollywood's addicts.

Quite a few, however quite a few also backslide after exiting the much publicized, even chic, clinic. A.A. has helped at least as many alcoholic celebs, with far less fanfare. In 1990, after a "drunken escapade with several women in a Modesto, California, bar," Mel Gibson was told by his doctor to stop drinking altogether or face permanent liver damage. With the aid of Alcoholics Anonymous, he has done so.

"That's a legend or—whatdoyacallit? [A myth.] Next question!"—producer Don Simpson (*Flashdance, Top Gun*), to an interviewer asking about the Hollywood casting couch.

Simpson, one of the worst perpetrators of the casting couch, also once declared, "Anybody who thinks they can fuck their way into this business is an idiot." In the industry, Simpson was known for drugs and for abusing women—prostitutes and actresses alike. He required his secretaries to read him porno aloud and referred to them with labels like "garbage brain," "stupid bitch" and "dumb shit."

Once, when an actress auditioned for him, he interrupted her and asked, "Okay, do you want to do some coke, or would you like to fuck me?" He later clarified, "We could either discuss this nicely and you could probably get a part, or you could go through the charade of reading for it."

Due to his string of hit movies, Simpson was one of Hollywood's most admired men.

"She's a refreshing mixture of talent and down-to-earth simplicity….She's uncomplicated…and rather sweet." —Tim Flack, CBS VP of Creative Affairs, in 1991, about Whitney Houston.

Time has proven that Houston is not uncomplicated, nor an all-around sweetheart. Her behavior has been diva-ish indeed and, since wedding Bobby Brown in 1992, frequently self-indulgent, not to mention confrontational. Show biz chronicler Margaret Moser wrote, "Onstage,

Whitney talked like a choir girl. Offstage, she swore like a sailor….Appearing for a group of children with AIDS, Whitney hugged them, cried, and posed for the cameras. A few minutes later, a dry-eyed Whitney reportedly hissed under her breath to her bodyguard, 'Get me the fuck out of here, away from these musty-assed, smelly kids!'"

★   ★   ★

Myth: Mary Tyler Moore is (or was) very much like her small-screen alter ego, Mary Richards.

Again, actors act. Miss Richards was a man-made TV fantasy, a plucky but usually passive feminine ideal. MTM was a star, had her own company, and when she sold it made approximately $103 million. TV historian Jeff Rovin called her "cool and aloof….When she leaves a TV set, the values of NutraSweet crank shut and her smile disappears." Though now involved with animal rights, MTM has stated that she wouldn't "give up my weekends to espouse a cause." She has described TV viewers as people who "don't want to have to think," yet admitted to using pot: "I find it no more dangerous than the martini…I have every night before dinner."

During the run of *The Mary Tyler Moore Show*, guest star Barbara Colby was shot to death in L.A. MTM allowed that she was sorry, but wasn't going to "lose sleep over…the desperate aspects of our lives and society." Ironically, Mary's only child, Richard Meeker, died via a gun—accidentally, at twenty-four. MTM acknowledged, "I was kind of a perfectionist mother, and I demanded a lot of him. I think I was responsible for a lot of alienation." An aspiring actor, Meeker had landed a few bit parts on TV—without Mary's help. When he died, MTM was promoting her feature film *Ordinary People* (directed by Robert Redford), in which she played a demanding, perfectionist mother who has just lost a son. She received an Oscar nomination for it, although some insiders said the character was closer to MTM than the bubbly, girlish and never-married Mary Richards.

Though not flamboyant, MTM technically qualified as a diva, and was used to having her say and getting her way. One of her short-lived post-Richards series costarred a young David Letterman, who half-joked, "Sure she has the right to do what she wants. Though I'll tell you

ANTI-OINKS!

"My mother gave me this advice: Trust your husband, adore your husband, and get as much as you can in your own name."
— Joan Rivers.

_____

"Men are six feet, women are five feet, twelve inches."
— Margaux Hemingway, tall model, actress and suicide.

_____

"Men decide it all. What clothes we wear, what is 'feminine,' what to call us—not just the derogatory names, but a man is a 'man,' a woman is a 'girl,' which is a child, or a 'lady,' which is a duty. It's astounding how we still defer....What I cringe at is at the movies. In the past, there was more equality—both had their clothes on. Now, it's sex scenes. The man has everything on, even his shoes, but the actress, well, we all have to get a load of her, naked and degraded, thanks to these vulgar, one-sided men who make what pass for movies these days."—Peggy Cass (_Auntie Mame_).

_____

"[Sean Connery] is a big Easter Island statue, he's so damned old! At least make him pollinate with someone like Meryl Streep. She's still young enough to be his daughter, but no! They have to have someone who's his great granddaughter! Big fat fossil fuel—you're doing love scenes! Just let him pump gas!"—Judy Tenuta, comedian, accordionist and actress (_Butch Camp_).

_____

"The difference is, men are threatened by women because they think we'll laugh at them. Women are threatened by men because they think men will attack or kill them. Size and aggression...women learned to give men a wide berth out of a sense of self-preservation."
— pioneering female TV talk show host Virginia Graham.

_____

"Okay, now we're included. But now it's 'men and women.' Always men and women, always in that order. 'The men and women who serve their country.' It couldn't be 'The people who serve'? No, then we'd be people, not a separate species, and we wouldn't be in second place. But I'll tell you something: the moment you divide people into categories, there's always going to be one particular category that comes first, that is judged better...."—Cybill Shepherd.

"I can understand liberated men writing 'he or she,' but why a woman would use the same...baffles me. A female, writing, should use 'she or he.' We all overuse 'he,' whether it's for the deity or an animal, for the standard human being—never mind we're a good 50% of the race....My pet peeve is calling a city 'she,' or a car or boat—anything that a man rules or gets inside and drives. Is that archaic?"—Sylvia Sidney, 1930s film star and ongoing actress.

"Penis envy is greatly exaggerated....There's also Venus envy, you just don't hear about that so much."—lesbian novelist Rita Mae Brown.

"Males are taught nearly from birth to deprecate females and anything feminine. If an action is graceful or unaggressive, it's like sister, so it's sissy, and that's as bad as can be, right? Anything 'like a girl,' or a woman, my goodness, what bigger insult? Even though we all have mothers and sisters....And even women,

as mothers, practice this mindless, aggressively oriented nonsense....Wake up, women! Time to stop putting down half of humanity to try and build up the other half."
— Congresswoman Bella Abzug.

"It's like the France syndrome. You know, the French people love their country but hate each other. With a huge, even maybe majority, section of women, they love or anyway pay lip service—lipstick service, of course—to the concept of femininity, but dislike each other."
— scenarist/novelist Anita Loos (*Gentlemen Prefer Blondes*).

"I tell the ladies how simple it is: Just value your daughters as much as you do your sons...and don't set them against each other. There's an old saying goes: A good beginning makes for a good ending."—Butterfly McQueen (*Gone With the Wind*).

"If the school bully or wiseass said to my daughter, or for that matter my son, that she throws or plays like a girl, I would hope she'd have the presence of mind to answer back, 'Yeah—Martina Navratilova!'"

something. I'm getting a little tired of going out to the house on weekends and mowing the lawn."

Myth: Sal Mineo's murder has never been solved.

Because he was openly gay, Mineo's murder-by-stabbing in the carport of his West Hollywood apartment building was misreported in a sensationalistic and homphobic way. Stories were fabricated of a "lovers' quarrel," and there were reports that Swedish actor Björn Andresen (*Death in Venice*) was the last to see Sal alive. Andresen later explained that he'd never even been to the United States. Because Mineo, like many celebrities, occasionally did drugs, there were rumors of fatal vengeance by some drug dealer. Also S&M rumors. Et cetera.

The truth was sordidly simple, but not generally reported once it was known. Sal Mineo (1939-1976), Oscar-nominated for *Rebel Without a Cause* and *Exodus*, was in the wrong place at the wrong time. He became the victim of a young, black heterosexual robber named Lionel Ray Williams, who thrust his hunting knife up to the hilt into Sal's chest. The next year, Williams was arrested in the poor L.A. suburb of Inglewood, for outstanding traffic tickets. He was then extradited to Michigan on charges of forgery; while there, he admitted to a cellmate—as he had to his girlfriend in L.A.—that he had indeed killed Sal Mineo. Though he denied the admission during his trial, he was found guilty and sentenced to "a minimum of fifty years" for the "second-degree murder," nine counts of first-degree robbery, and one of second-degree robbery.

Eleven years later, he was out on parole. A 1999 E!-channel episode of *Mysteries & Scandals* had Williams confessing callously on camera, "Man, I killed Sal Mineo—that's a hassle."

Myth: Bill Clinton only likes them younger.

Perhaps chesty is the correct adjective. Actor turned Tinseltown gossip Charlene Tilton (of *Dallas*) reported that during a White House gala during the president's last year in office, he was seated next to Elizabeth Taylor and Sophia Loren (two years Liz's junior, but also sixty-plus). The Italian beauty had on a gown with a plunging-neckline. Wrote

Tilton, "The prez couldn't help devouring her with his eyes. Finally, tell-it-like-it-is Liz Taylor, seated on Bill's other side, asked if he was going to be a boob and gawk at Sophia's cleavage all night."

Myth: Some superstars, like Garbo, are completely anti-publicity. Others, like Liz Taylor or Sharon Stone, shun it, but not as firmly.

Remember that without publicity, there is no stardom. Most stars, having achieved their goal, want publicity when it suits them. Even Garbo didn't completely shun publicity until quite late in life. She knew that two celebs together (male and female, that is) generate more than twice the publicity one celeb gets alone. Had she been so allergic to attention, she wouldn't have painted the town with male celebs like conductor Leopold Stokowski (Disney's *Fantasia*) or nutritionist Gayelord Hauser; or designer Valentina or Spanish aristocrat Mercedes de Acosta.

While filming *Cleopatra* (1963) in Rome, a friend took Elizabeth Taylor out of town, thinking she would enjoy the quiet and anonymity. Rather, Liz missed being recognized and was indignant that she could walk the streets without creating a commotion.

Sharon Stone is typical of many divas. Eating at the Polo Lounge in the Beverly Hills Hotel, she complained to her husband that two businessmen were staring at her. He got up, went to their table and threatened, "I'll punch out both of you!" A waiter got the men to move—celebs nearly always get their way, right or wrong—in return for the restaurant picking up their tab. But not many years before that, Stone attended the premiere of the movie *Forrest Gump* (1994). When she departed, the paparazzi didn't take any note. So she went back in the cinema and made her exit again. Still nothing.

She repeated the routine. Third time lucky: reporters and photogs started "pestering" poor Sharon.

"Another thing I'm grateful [for]—I got the most popular last name in the whole country."
— Grateful Dead guitarist Jerry Garcia, in 1993.

He spoke a bit too soon. Garcia is the most popular, or common,

Hispanic surname, and Hispanics are the fastest-growing minority in the U.S. It's projected that Garcia will become the most common last name in the country by 2010, as it's more widespread in Spanish than Smith or Jones are in English.

**"*The Blue Angel* was my first film. It is a classic…
it has never been remade.…She must be out of her mind!"**
— **Marlene Dietrich, on the press rumors that Madonna would star
in a remake of her 1930 starring vehicle.**

Perhaps the eighty-plus legend was out of her memory when she forgot there had been a 1959 remake of *The Blue Angel*. But for decades she'd insisted it was her screen bow, though Dietrich had made almost twenty movies, over almost a decade, by then. When Madonna began copying the German's Look, Marlene demanded, "Who is this Miss Madonna?…She's no angel—on the contrary!" The Material Girl had been attracted to the story of a sultry singer who lures an older man, a dignified professor, to humiliation and ruin. She also admitted her attraction to the young version of Dietrich, saying she wouldn't have minded having an affair with her: "Like, who wouldn't?"

"I'm just an ordinary Italian-American working girl."
— **Madonna, before she had muscles or shuttled between hair colors.**
How many girls, working or otherwise, would have had the chutzpah to chase after John F. Kennedy, Jr.? An FBI dossier on the late heir has revealed that the ambitious blonde made several plays for him. Mother Jackie warned him to stop seeing the "crass social-climber" whom she also called a "tramp" (never mind that Jacqueline Bouvier social-climbed herself, when she married into the Kennedy clan).

More recently, Madonna has been going British. Literally. She's bought a home in London and plans to rear her children there. Increasingly, she has an (on-again, off-again) English accent, and when it was pointed out, she exclaimed, "Who cares? I can say what I want." Like she hasn't always?

"Kamu Kamu Gokkun is my favorite Japanese fruit bar."
— **Whoopi Goldberg, in a Japanese ad that earned her $800,000.**
Maybe it is. But can she name any other Japanese fruit bar?

Americans who don't travel overseas may not be aware that top stars who wouldn't be caught dead pitching products in the U.S. often do commercials for foreign products, in return for big bucks—one theory being, Who cares what other countries think about you, so long as you don't live there? Jodie Foster recently picked up $1.3 million for hawking Caffe Latte abroad, and even Woody Allen, who was too elite—or something—to attend the Academy Awards in Hollywood, has done ads for a Japanese department store. Such commercials are typically beautifully done, and are sometimes very entertaining or amusing, but of course their "foreign" stars do them for one reason alone (especially since they virtually never use, or even know, the product): mucho dinero.

Myth: Hollywood esteems and respects its older actors and legends.

Orson Welles: "So many of the younger new directors make flattering comments about my past movies. But none of them seem to get around to making me an offer…the young moguls don't offer to help finance something new so I can direct another film."

Bette Davis: "Well, getting another award is always nice, and life-achievement honors are nice too. But what I'd really relish would be a juicy new part."

Marlene Dietrich: "When your skin isn't as moist as it used to be, when you look to those bankers and lawyers as if they've squeezed every last cent out of you they could, they drop you.…Hard come, easy go."

George C. Scott: The Hollywood movie crowd don't respect you when you're old, they respect you when you're dead."

Myth: TV shows only get canceled because of low ratings.

Controversy, as interpreted by the guys at the top, can end a series—and some are kept on despite low or middling ratings for demographic reasons or in the hopes they'll improve. Back in the '70s the highly rated

Bridget Loves Bernie—starring Meredith Baxter and now-ex-husband David Birney—was axed because of ethnic/religious protests; it featured a newlywed couple, one Jewish, one Irish. *Lou Grant*, a dramatic series spin-off from *The Mary Tyler Moore Show*, was later canceled despite good ratings, although CBS called them "declining." Why? Series star Ed Asner had publicly opposed the Reagan administration's military involvement in Central America. Charlton Heston and others had noisily taken him to task, and Asner stood by his beliefs. Bye-bye stardom....

★　★　★

"My delight and my joy is to help talented young actors—and what could be more fulfilling?"
— super-columnist Hedda Hopper.

For decades, Hedda—whose only child was secretly gay William Hopper of *Perry Mason*—tried to "out" Cary Grant (before there was such a word), whom she detested. When Liz Taylor was engaged to hubby #2, Englishman Michael Wilding—Hedda had no use for Brits—she wrote that she'd warned Liz that Wilding had had an affair with fellow limey Stewart Granger (real name: James Stewart). Wilding sued—but Granger didn't—and won. (Both men were in fact bisexual.)

Any young actress who crossed Hedda was said to have her career chances chopped in two. Unless she befriended Hopper's foe Louella Parsons, who was a super-columnist first. Hedda had failed as an aging character actor, only then turning to writing—hence the bitterness. Anyone who hadn't been nice to Hedda on the set of their movies was automatically on her hate-list.

A typical vendetta was her crusade against Larry Parks, who became a star in *The Jolson Story* (the 1946 hit had a 1949 sequel). Hopper campaigned to have him barred from every studio. During the latest HUAC hearings, in 1951, he was browbeaten into naming names. The witch-hunters had implied if he "cooperated," he could save his career. But even after informing, he was blacklisted and put out of work, finally seeking employment in Europe. Parks' loyal wife until his death (1914-1975) was Betty Garrett, best known for *Laverne & Shirley*.

★　★　★

Myth: Writer/director Billy Wilder's assertion that the Hollywood Ten, among other victims of political witch-hunting and blacklisting, weren't very talented anyway.

As the Ten were all writers and/or directors, Wilder's callous comment may have had more than a hint of rivalry to it. Ring Lardner, Jr. worked on classics like *A Star is Born* and *Nothing Sacred*, and won an Oscar for the Tracy-Hepburn vehicle *Woman of the Year*. In 1950 he too was sentenced to a year's imprisonment for "contempt" of HUAC; he then had to write via pseudonyms in order to make a living, and his own name wasn't back on the screen until 1965.

John Howard Lawson, a founder of the Screen Writers Guild and thus "suspect" just for union activity, scripted DeMille's first talkie—C.B. was one of the red-baiters—and several anti-fascist films, another strike against him. After his year in jail he went into exile in Mexico.

In the '40s, Dalton Trumbo was earning $75,000 a screenplay. After serving his sentence—and bearing in mind that it was never illegal to be a member of the Communist party—he wrote several quality scripts, and as "Robert Rich" won an Oscar in 1959 that of course he could not claim. His comeback was in 1960; Kirk Douglas (ne Issur Danielovitch) used his box office muscle to give Trumbo screen credit for *Spartacus*. He also wrote *Exodus*, about the re-establishment of modern Israel. Trumbo later wrote an anti-war novel, *Johnny Got His Gun*, which he later also directed when it became a film.

Billy Wilder also dissed golden-age director Mitchell Leisen, for whom he wrote scripts, injecting homophobia into his condemnation. He also turned on many of his stars, once he himself became a director: "I get along very, very well with actors, except when I work with sons of bitches like Mr. Humphrey Bogart."

"I've got to don my breast plate once more to play opposite Miss Tits."—Richard Burton, on his *Cleopatra* costar Elizabeth Taylor, of whom he also said, "I don't even see her acting…she does nothing—I'm going to wipe her off the screen!"

But when the Welsh stage actor saw the movie's rushes, he conceded that Taylor, a screen actor since childhood, stole all their scenes via her

MORE CELEBRITY MYTHS

Baby Bob, the spokesbaby for freeinternet.com
"He" is a girl named Hunter (the voice via actor Ken Campbell). In show biz the "average" person is still a male, regardless of who plays "him"—think back to Toto, Dorothy's male terrier, played by a female dog named Terry. According to the Screen Actors Guild, some 70% of all film, TV and commercials roles go to male actors.

———————

"Barbie, the all-American doll" —as she is often described. Yes, she is "all-American" and (not *but*) she's really Jewish! Barbie was created by a Jewish couple and named for another Jewish girl, Mattel cofounder Ruth Handler's daughter Barbara.

———————

Likewise, Superman was created by two young Jewish men, and the big S on his chest doesn't stand for Superman but for the duo's surnames, which both begin with S.

———————

"The Queen of Nice." — as Rosie O'Donnell is often described.
Her well-chronicled on-set tantrums seem to have diminished since her TV talk show slipped into a comfortable groove. But it's still not a good idea to lock horns with the big O. Success and maturity have mellowed her, but a former Los Angeles neighbor named Carlos retains some hairy memories of the gal next door: "When she was a semi-nobody, she slept by day and stayed up all night watching MTV—at full blast, to the discomfort of other folks in the building trying to sleep. Being from the East Coast, she was blissfully unaware that L.A. walls in 'deluxe' apartment buildings are paper-thin and that the sounds of Valkyrian wrestling matches, showers à deux, squeaky mattresses [and] screaming arguments over the phone carried through loud and clear. She was also door slammer invictus: Rambo kicking a door shut was no match for her, take my word for it. The entire building shook to its foundations, cowering before such awesome, Amazonic brute force."

"Howard Hughes was actress Terry Moore's first husband."
— statement in Marci Wiener's *Hollywood Beat* column, September 24, 2001.

Years ago, Moore said, "I don't think Howard slept with a lot of girls. He liked to collect girls." The bisexual Hughes (one lover was Cary Grant) was known to date and put actresses under contract, most later admitting the relationships were platonic.

Years after, in her book on Hughes, Moore claimed he was "100% straight." Coauthor Jerry Rivers, Terry's fifth husband, later admitted, "You gotta bend your [biographical] subject to mainstream tastes, for big success."

In fact, Howard Hughes had one wife, actress Jean Peters. Terry Moore has not produced a marriage certificate or other legal evidence, but according to author Tony Thomas' *Howard Hughes in Hollywood*, her claim was "persistent enough for the Hughes estate to make a 1983 settlement with her for an unstated amount. Says Moore, 'I can live off the interest for the rest of my life.'"

An unproven rumor is that a condition of the settlement may have been to depict Hughes as heterosexual.

———————

"No one has done more for our boys in Vietnam than Bob Hope."—"toastmaster general" George Jessel.

"As with Mother Teresa, so with Mr. Hope," said talk show host Virginia Graham. "Some have done as much or more, but they didn't get the same publicity or unquestioning veneration."

Comedian Skip E. Lowe notes in his memoirs, "Everyone thinks Bob Hope sweated it out in the killing fields. Sadly, not true. Bob was concerned with one thing—giving NBC good footage so they'd buy up his shows. Once the cameras were off, so was Bob. Spend a night in Saigon? Are you kidding? He was a show-boy soldier, though he let the world believe otherwise. He did his shows, then flew off to his luxury hotel accommodations in Bangkok."

Lowe recalls a night in Danang when "tens of thousands of sopping wet soldiers" waited for Hope to make his appearance. "I happened to be backstage and overheard Bob. 'We'll never get decent footage in all this rain. Put on some go-go girls so we can get outta here.' Those guys didn't care about the rain. This was their once-in-a-lifetime chance to see their hero." But "Bob waited a few minutes, and when the rain didn't let up, 'Let's pull out of here!'" To avert a riot, the go-go girls went on, "and that was that. The great Bob Hope no-show! Thanks for the rainy-day memories, soldier Bob!"

———————————

By contrast, Martha Raye entertained in Vietnam for seven years, also doing nursing and anything she could to help. Lowe wrote, "Although Bob Hope wouldn't dream of doing Special Service shows, many of the performers on his USO shows (like Raye) got down and dirty with us," going into the fields to mingle with, befriend and aid the boys. Without the benefit of cameras.

———————————

The friendly, chummy relationships between Elizabeth Taylor and Malcolm Forbes and Michael Jackson.... Chen Sam, Taylor's long-time publicist, was the mastermind behind the very public, mutually profitable ersatz friendships. She arranged the "romance" between Liz and gay tycoon Forbes. "Chen came to me and asked if I knew of any rich men who'd be willing to donate money to Elizabeth's charity," says an ex-editor for *Forbes* magazine, quoted in the book *Dish*. "I knew that Malcolm was looking for a beard. Chen hooked them up."

Forbes knew how to get his money's worth, and on an AIDS fund-raising junket in Japan in 1988, he invited Liz aboard his yacht The Highlander. She was greeted by bagpipers and, to her surprised disgust, the crew of Robin Leach's TV show *Lifestyles of the Rich and Famous* (and closeted, in this case). Liz also knows how to get her money's worth, and has a policy of not appearing on TV for free. She refused to step aboard Forbes' yacht to be filmed until Malcolm agreed to present her with an Erté painting.

The relationship with Michael Jackson is not dissimilar....

———————————

"John Ford, a great director and a meticulous perfectionist."
— biographical description of the great director.

A meticulous perfectionist? Not quite. He was sometimes known to rip out pages from a script to shorten the working day. Known as One-Take Ford, on the set of *Cheyenne Autumn* (1964) he was asked by Sal Mineo if they could do a second take. Ford replied, sure, but there'd be no film in the camera. Sal, whom Ford kept calling "Saul," wore an "Indian" wig but had asked his director if he should grow his hair long. Ford had testily answered, "No, it's only a movie. No one will notice." Several critics and spectators did, and do.

"Everybody's favorite uncle, Uncle Walt."
— Disney, that is.
Not everybody's. Once TV came along, Walt Disney sought to become—and did—as famous as any of his stars, live or animated. His image was carefully tailored, though he eventually let slip, "I love Mickey Mouse more than any woman I've ever known," including his wife. Posthumous biographies, among them *Hollywood's Dark Prince* by Marc Eliot, have revealed that Disney was: fiercely anti-union, alcoholic, anti-Semitic, impotent, insecure and vengeful, a cheapskate, a communist witch-

hunter, a secret FBI informer for twenty-six years, and greedy—often taking full credit for what his employees cocreated or created entirely on their own. Supposedly illegitimate, he lied about his adoption, but big deal. He lived in a society too puritanical to realize that no children are "illegitimate." Still, kindly "Uncle Walt" was not.

American accents....
Increasingly, they're necessary to work in Hollywood. When Australian Judy Davis and British Tracey Ullman appear in Woody Allen movies they play Americans. Hollywood used to be far more inclusive of foreign characters and foreign performers. Tinseltown immigrants who in years past would have retained their own vocal patterns or accents now erase them, so that English actor Cary Elwes and Scottish singer Sheena Easton—even when not performing—now sound like average Americans. Australia's *Women's Day* magazine calls it "a spreading intolerance of cultural and national difference, a virtual verbal imperialism....It's a lowering of standards and diversity prompted by money and conformity."

Al Jolson, star of the first "talkie," *The Jazz Singer*, in 1927.

It wasn't the first. Jolson sang in it but had no dialogue. His few spoken words were ad-libs—the famous and prophetic "You ain't heard nothin' yet!" But sound on film had already happened. In 1901 a German physics professor named Reuhmer first recorded sound waves on film. Five years later a French inventor, Eugene Lauste, patented a system for recording sound using an arc and vibrating wires. By 1907 a Paris firm was already producing talking "movies" for Pathé by having actors mime action in synchronization with a pre-recorded disk which was then amplified to fill an auditorium. But it was the combined impact of the hugely popular Jolson in a hit movie from a commercially astute American studio—founded by four Polish Jews renamed Warner—that pushed talkies to the forefront. What we would consider the first Hollywood talkie, *Lights of New York*, followed the next year but is nearly forgotten today, much of the reason being its lack of a tour-de-force superstar performance.

––––––––––––––

compelling stillness, charisma and camera technique. The movie star love story of the '60s didn't commence with love at first sight, but with rivalry and a stage Brit's contempt for a Hollywood star and her disdain for the blustering Shakespearean soliloquies into which he often burst. Once they'd become lovers, she would interrupt his performance with a sigh and a rolling of the violet eyes; after they were married, she would say, "Would you shut the fuck up?"

★　★　★

Myth: European stars are more laid-back than their litigious Tinseltown counterparts.

Again, it depends. The most publicized French director of the '60s was Roger Vadim, as much for the women in his life as for his films. When he penned his autobiography, *Memoirs of the Devil*, he revealed a lot about wife Brigitte Bardot (with whom he had no children), wife Jane Fonda (with whom he had a daughter), and paramour Catherine Deneuve (with whom he had a son). Bardot and Deneuve sued, Fonda did not.

In her memoirs, Bardot described her son and only child as a "tumor feeding off me." Ex-husband Jacques Charrier she called "a vulgar, dictatorial and uncontrolled macho, a gigolo, alcoholic and despicable." He sued her and won. Then when he wrote a book and put Bardot down, she sued him and won. So voilà.

★　★　★

"A tattoo really expresses your feelings sincerely. Like, permanently."

— Johnny Depp, after engraving his arm with "Winona Forever."

But after he broke up with Winona Ryder, he changed the tattoo to Wino Forever. He moved on to lucky Kate Moss, and when somebody made the irrelevant remark that Depp was "fixated" on white women, he responded, "I ain't no fucking white, that's for sure. Kate is definitely not. She's about the furthest thing from white there is. She's got that high-water booty."

This is the same star who reportedly cuts himself on the arm to mark major events in his life: "In a way, your body is a journal, and the scars are sort of entries in it." And they say actors are superficial.

★　★　★

"An actor sometimes has to struggle to hang on to his dignity."—Warren Beatty.

According to film historian Margaret Moser, Beatty once "fell to the ground in front of Jack L. Warner, grabbed the mogul's knees, and told the [producer] that he would kiss his shoes, even lick them, if Warner gave him money" to make *Bonnie & Clyde* (1967). The deeply embarrassed mogul gave him $1.6 million to make the huge hit, after which Warren never again had to compromise his dignity.

He may have had, however, to struggle with his arrogant streak, which had manifested itself in the early '60s, when Beatty was up for the role of John F. Kennedy in the screen version of the autobiographical book *PT 109*. Jack Warner recommended that Warren go to Washington to visit the president and soak up the atmosphere. The budding star replied, "If the president wants me to play him, tell him to come here and soak up some of my atmosphere." The film was later made with another actor.

P.S. Beatty's very first job was scaring away rats in the alley behind the National Theater in Washington, D.C. (a good place to find rats).

★   ★   ★

"They say doing drugs is bad on your skin. I don't do as much as they say I do. Anyway, we're about the same age, and I think my skin looks better than yours."
— John Belushi, to costar and fellow Blues Brother Dan Akroyd.

The then-slim Akroyd reportedly answered, "Yeah, man, but you got so much more of it." Eventually the formerly Canadian star got heavy himself, so now the donut's on the other foot. As for Belushi, a star on TV's *Saturday Night Live* before turning to movies, his biographies—and his death at thirty-three—attest to the fact that he did a mind- and body-boggling amount of drugs. At Belushi's Manhattan funeral, Akroyd surprised the crowd by playing a tape of a song instead of delivering a eulogy for his late friend and costar. The song: the Ventures' *The 2,000 Pound Bee*.

But Belushi's legacy continued, cinematically speaking. As one critic put it, "John's younger brother, James, also became an actor and carried on the Belushi tradition of portraying overweight louts on-camera."

Some persistent TV rumors, only one of them true:

Mick Jagger's real father is *Andy Griffith* star Don Knotts.

Dick Clark actually hates rock 'n roll.

The theme song of *Mr. Ed* played backwards includes a message from "Satan."

Mr. Ed "talking" was due to the horse trying to remove peanut butter from the roof of his mouth.

Walt Disney's cryogenically preserved body lies frozen in a secret vault somewhere underneath Disneyland.

In the last years of her life, *Andy Griffith's* Frances Bavier dwelled under the delusion that she really was Aunt Bee.

Depressed from the sudden lack of attention after his series was canceled, Flipper the dolphin committed suicide.

Like many Hispanic actors, *I Love Lucy's* Desi Arnaz had no accent speaking English, and only used it as a gimmick.

Lucille Ball and Vivian Vance were "more than friends."

Many or most of the "real life" guests on shows like Jerry Springer's are actors, acting.

The Untouchables finally went off the air not because of low ratings, but pressure from the Mafia.

Jerry "the Beaver" Mathers was killed in the Vietnam War.

Ken Osmond, who played Eddy Haskell on *Leave It to Beaver*, grew up to be a porn star.

Ken Osmond grew up to be a cop. (True!)

Finally, some celebrity puns from Dr. Clifford Scheiner, via Lyle Stuart:

"What is Kevin Bacon?" "A cake he'll have Robert Frost."

"Son, what did you do to make Lucille Ball?' "I hit her with my Yo Yo Ma."

"Is Glenn Close?" "Yes, I think Sid Caesar."

"Did you get to the ball game in time to see Winslow Homer?" "No, but I saw Danielle Steel and found out how well W.C. Fields."

"Did Norman Lear?" "No, he just gave Fred Astaire."

"He who laughs last laughs best."—traditional

"She who laughs, lasts."— Gloria Steinem

"He who laughs last thinks slowest."— Jerry Seinfeld

Index

313